Study Guide

for use with

Introduction to Accounting
An Integrated Approach

Third Edition

Penne Ainsworth
University of Wyoming

Dan Deines
Kansas State University

Prepared by
Debra Kerby
Truman State University
Division of Business and Accounting

Scott Fouch
Truman State University
Division of Business and Accounting

 Irwin

Boston   Burr Ridge, IL   Dubuque, IA   Madison, WI   New York   San Francisco   St. Louis
Bangkok   Bogotá   Caracas   Kuala Lumpur   Lisbon   London   Madrid   Mexico City
Milan   Montreal   New Delhi   Santiago   Seoul   Singapore   Sydney   Taipei   Toronto

Study Guide for use with
INTRODUCTION TO ACCOUNTING: AN INTEGRATED APPROACH
Penne Ainsworth and Dan Deines

Published by McGraw-Hill/Irwin, an imprint of The McGraw-Hill Companies, Inc., 1221 Avenue of the
Americas, New York, NY 10020. Copyright © 2004, 2000, 1997 by The McGraw-Hill Companies, Inc. All
rights reserved.

1 2 3 4 5 6 7 8 9 0 CUS/CUS 0 9 8 7 6 5 4 3

ISBN 0-07-247395-9

www.mhhe.com

The McGraw Hill Companies

Study Guide Table of Contents:

Chapter 1
Accounting and Business

Chapter Overview

This chapter defines accounting and discusses the usefulness of accounting in business. It highlights the evolution of accounting through history and presents the basic concepts of accounting and how income is measured. The chapter also presents the different types of businesses and business organizational structures. The chapter concludes with a discussion of the relationship among the primary financial statements.

If you have not worked in a business setting, you will not be familiar with many of the terms and concepts discussed in this or following chapters. You will need to memorize unfamiliar terms and be able to classify items as assets, liabilities, or owners' equity. Memorize the fundamental accounting equation. It forms the framework for analyzing economic events and recording them in an accounting system. Familiarize yourself with the basic accounting principles and concepts and learn to apply them to decision making. Learn the characteristics, advantages, and disadvantages of the various types of business ownership. This knowledge will help you assess the implications of many business decisions you may need to make.

Read and Recall Questions

Learning Objective:
LO.1 Describe the development of business and accounting.

What is business? Why do people engage in business?

Employees perform five basic functions for businesses. Describe each of the functions and explain how each uses accounting information.

- Marketing function

- Human resources function

- Production and operations function

- Finance function

- Accounting function

Briefly describe the four recent changes in business operations.

- Customer-focused operations

- Global markets

- Manufacturing and communication advances

- e-business

Learning Objective:
LO.2 Explain the elements of accounting (assets, liabilities, owners' equity, revenue, expenses, and net income).

Define accounting in your own words.

Briefly trace the history of accounting from ancient Babylonia to the stock market crash of October 1929. Who described the method of bookkeeping known as the Method of Venice?

What is the fundamental accounting equation? Why must it always balance?

Define the following elements of accounting:

- assets

- liabilities

- owners' equity

- revenue

- expense

- net income

Describe the business entity concept and explain its importance to accounting.

Why is the going concern concept important to accounting?

Briefly describe the monetary unit concept and the periodicity concept.

Distinguish between cash-basis and accrual-basis accounting.

What are generally accepted accounting principles (GAAP)? Who is responsible for determining GAAP in the United States?

Learning Objective:
LO. 3 Identify the differences among the basic types of businesses and business organization structures.

Describe the characteristics of the following types of businesses:

- a merchandising company

- a service company

- a manufacturing company

Describe the characteristics of each of the following types of business organization structure:

- sole proprietorship

- partnership

- corporation

What is the purpose of the income statement?

What is the purpose of the statement of cash flows? Why doesn't a company's net income equal its net cash flows?

What is the purpose of the balance sheet (statement of financial position)?

What is the purpose of the statement of owners' (stockholders') equity?

What relationships do the following ratios measure?

- Current ratio

- Return on sales ratio

- Debt to equity ratio

Why must publicly held companies be audited by an independent accountant (auditor)?

Outline of Key Concepts

I. Accounting responds to the users' needs for information.
    A. Business is the exchange of goods or services on an arm's-length basis resulting in mutual benefit for both parties involved.
    B. Employees perform five basic functions for a business.
        1. Marketing function
        2. Human resources function
        3. Production and operations function
        4. Finance function
        5. Accounting and information systems function
    C. Business operations have changed recently to adapt to the future.
        1. Customer-focused operations
        2. Global markets
        3. Manufacturing and communication advances
        4. e-business

II. Accounting has evolved through the centuries.
    A. Ancient Babylonia—the Code of Hammurabi.
    B. Old Italy—merchant trading
        1. Luca Pacioli—described double-entry bookkeeping
    C. Industrial revolution and the advent of the corporation
    D. Stock market crash of 1929
        1. Securities Act of 1933
        2. Securities Exchange Act of 1934

III. Accounting is the information infrastructure of the firm/economy that permits it to achieve its objectives.
    A. Assets = Liabilities + Owners' Equity
        1. Assets—rights to use resources that have expected future economic benefits.
        2. Liability—obligation to transfer economic resources to suppliers of money, goods and services at some point in the future.
        3. Owners' equity—the claims on the business to transfer the residual interest (net assets of the business) to the owners.
    B. Four accounting concepts
        1. Business entity concept—the business records should be separate and distinct from the personal records of the business owners.
        2. Going concern concept—absent any information to the contrary, the business entity will continue into the foreseeable future.
        3. Monetary unit concept—money is the common measurement unit of economic activity.
        4. Periodicity concept—the success or failure of the business must be determined at regular intervals.

C. Cash basis accounting—income is the difference between the cash received from customers and the cash paid to employees and other suppliers of goods and services.

D. Accrual basis accounting—income is the difference between the sales (revenues) earned and the expenses incurred during the period, regardless of when cash is received or paid.

1. Revenue—amount earned from providing services or transferring resources to customers.

2. Expense—amount incurred from using resources or services in an effort to generate revenue.

3. Net income—the company's total revenues less its total expenses for a period of time.

E. Generally Accepted Accounting Principles (GAAP)—the set of reporting standards applicable to all companies that issue financial reports for external users.

1. Financial Accounting Standards Board (FASB) is responsible for determining GAAP in the United States.

IV. Three basic types of business organizational structures.

A. Sole proprietorship—a business owned by one person whose personal wealth is at risk if the business fails.

1. Unlimited liability—once the business's assets are used up, the personal assets of the owner can be used to satisfy liabilities of the business.

B. Partnership—business owned by two or more individuals whose personal wealth is at risk if the business fails.

1. Each partner has unlimited liability.

2. Mutual agency—each partner has the power to act for, and legally obligate, all other partners.

C. Corporation—a business entity that is legally separate and distinct from its owners.

1. Limited liability—assets invested in the corporation are at risk but investors' personal possessions are not at risk if the business fails.

2. Double taxation—profits earned by the corporation are taxed twice—once at the business level and again at the owner level if the profits are distributed as dividends.

V. Three basic types of businesses.

A. Merchandising company—a business that obtains and distributes goods to customers.

B. Service firm—a business that provides services to customers (clients).

C. Manufacturing firm—a business that converts raw materials into finished goods.

VI. Financial statements and the independent auditor's report provide information to external users.

A. Income statement—shows the net income (total revenues less total expenses) of the company for a period of time (typically one year).

9

B. Statement of cash flows—shows the cash inflows and outflows of the company for the same period of time as the income statement.
   1. Cash flows are classified as operating, investing, or financing.
C. Balance Sheet (Statement of Financial Position)—shows the amounts of the company's assets, liabilities, and owners' equity at the end of the fiscal year.
D. Statement of Owners' (Stockholders') Equity—shows the changes that occurred in owners' equity during the period of time covered by the income statement.
E. Report of the Independent Accountant (Auditor)—an audit determines whether the company followed GAAP when preparing the financial statements and whether the assertions made by management are reliable.
F. Ratios measure relationships between financial statement items.
   1. Current ratio—is a measure of company liquidity.
   2. Return on sales ratio—is a measure of company profitability.
   3. Debt to equity ratio—a measure of a company's solvency and its ability to meet its long-term obligations.

Problem I

Indicate whether the following statements are either true (T) or false (F).

_____1. Accounting systems have remained relatively unchanged in the last 100 years.
_____2. A merchandising company produces products from raw materials for sale to consumers.
_____3. The Financial Accounting Standards Board is responsible for developing accounting standards for external reporting.
_____4. A business operated as a corporation will be subject to double taxation.
_____5. Money has always been considered the common measurement unit of an economic activity.
_____6. The marketing function is responsible for planning and controlling the operations of a business.
_____7. A share of stock is the certificate that represents ownership in a corporation.
_____8. A limited partner's personal possessions are at risk if the business should fail.
_____9. An asset is an obligation to transfer economic resources to suppliers of goods and services at some point in the future.
_____10. E-business is less expensive than paper transactions.

Study Guide, Introduction to Accounting, An Integrated Approach

Problem II

Indicate the correct answer by circling the appropriate letter.

1. Which of the following is considered a separate legal entity?
   a. partnership
   b. corporation
   c. sole proprietorship
   d. all of the above are separate legal entities

2. Which functional area within a company has the responsibility for determining the wants and needs of its customers?
   a. finance function
   b. marketing function
   c. accounting and information systems function
   d. human resource function
   e. production and operation function

3. Wal-mart would be considered a _____ firm.
   a. service
   b. merchandising
   c. manufacturing
   d. none of the above

4. Which functional area would have the responsibility for preparing financial statements used by the owners of a business?
   a. finance function
   b. marketing function
   c. accounting and information systems function
   d. human resource function
   e. production and operation function

5. At the end of its first year of operations, Acme Corporation had total assets of $432,000 and total liabilities of $212,000. What is Acme's owners equity at the end of the year?
   a. $644,000
   b. $220,000
   c. $432,000
   d. $212,000
   e. none of the above

11

6. Which of the following statements is designed to show the difference between total revenues and total expenses for the year?
   a. balance sheet
   b. statement of cash flows
   c. income statement
   d. statement of owners' equity

7. Which of the following is not an advantage of a corporation over a partnership?
   a. unlimited life
   b. limited liability
   c. no entity level tax imposed
   d. all of the above are advantages of a corporation

8. Which of the following would be considered a liability of the company?
   a. The owners contributed $20,000 to the company.
   b. The company owns land to be used for a production facility.
   c. The company owes $5,000 to a supplier for merchandise purchased last month.
   d. The company's customers owe it $12,000 for services provided.

9. Which of the following is considered a benefit of E-business?
   a. increased sales opportunities
   b. improved communication
   c. lower costs
   d. all of the above are benefits of E-business.

Problem III

The following is a list of important ideas and key concepts from the chapter. To test your knowledge of these terms, match the term with the definition by placing the number in the space provided.

_____ Accounting
_____ Accounting equation
_____ Assets
_____ Business entity concept
_____ Corporation
_____ Double taxation
_____ Expense
_____ Financial Accounting Standards Board (FASB)
_____ Financial statements
_____ Going concern concept

_____ Limited liability
_____ Monetary unit concept
_____ Partnership
_____ Periodicity concept
_____ Product life cycle
_____ Revenue
_____ Sole proprietorship
_____ Stakeholders
_____ Unlimited liability

Study Guide, Introduction to Accounting, An Integrated Approach

1. The concept that requires that an accounting system reflect only information about economic events that pertain to a particular entity

2. A business entity that is legally separate and distinct from its owners

3. A situation in which the money invested in a corporation is at risk but investors' personal possessions are not at risk if the business fails

4. Assets equal liabilities plus owners' equity

5. The group the SEC holds responsible for determining accounting standards in the United States

6. The rights to use resources that have expected future economic benefits

7. An amount earned from rendering services or transferring resources to customers

8. A situation in which the profits earned by the corporation are taxed twice--once at the business level and again at the owner level if the profits are distributed as dividends

9. The concept that asserts that money is the common measurement unit of economic activity

10. Statements prepared to communicate the results of business activities to interested users

11. A situation in which owners are personally responsible for the debts of the business

12. An amount incurred from using resources or services in the effort to generate revenue

13. The concept that requires that the success or failure of the business be determined at regular intervals

14. Those people and entities (both internal and external to the company) that have a stake, or interest, in the outcomes of the company

15. The time span from the conception of the product until it is no longer demanded by consumers

16. The information infrastructure of the firm/economy that permits it to achieve its objectives

17. A business owned by one person whose personal possessions are at risk if the business fails

18. The concept that assumes that, absent information to the contrary, the business will continue into the foreseeable future

19. A business owned by two or more individuals whose respective personal possessions are at risk if the business fails

Problem IV

Referring to the Dreyer's consolidated financial statements (Appendix), calculate the following ratios for 1999:

Current Ratio

Return on Sales Ratio

Debt to Equity Ratio

Problem V

Complete the following sentences by filling in the correct response.

1. The _____ and _____ _____ function is responsible for providing useful information to the other functional areas and external parties.

2. The _____ _____ concept requires that the accounting system keep a business's economic events separate from other economic events of the owners.

3. A _____ _____ is an asset that is likely to be used or consumed within one year.

Study Guide, Introduction to Accounting, An Integrated Approach

4. Under the _____ basis of accounting, income is measured as the difference between the sales earned and expenses incurred during the period.

5. The _____ function is responsible for managing the financial resources of a company.

6. When the SEC requires companies to prepare annual financial statements, it is applying the _____ concept.

7. A company that produces microcomputers would be considered a _____ firm.

8. _____ _____ represents the claims on the business to transfer the residual interest to the owners.

9. _____ auditors have responsibility for ensuring the integrity of the accounting system.

10. _____ _____ is a situation in which each partner has the power to act for all other partners.

11. Absent information to the contrary, the _____ _____ concept assumes that a business entity will continue in existence into the foreseeable future.

12. By using _____ _____, a company can test its products before they are actually produced.

Solutions for Chapter 1

Problem 1

1. F	6. F
2. F	7. T
3. T	8. F
4. T	9. F
5. F	10. T

Problem II

1. b
2. b
3. b
4. c
5. b
6. c
7. c
8. c
9. d

Problem III

16	Accounting	3	Limited liability
4	Accounting equation	9	Monetary unit concept
6	Assets	19	Partnership
1	Business entity concept	13	Periodicity concept
2	Corporation	15	Product life cycle
8	Double taxation	7	Revenue
12	Expense	17	Sole proprietorship
5	Financial Accounting Standards Board (FASB)	14	Stakeholder
10	Financial statements	11	Unlimited liability
18	Going concern concept		

Problem IV

$$\text{Current Ratio} = \frac{168,813}{139,300} = 1.21:1$$

$$\text{Return on Sales Ratio} = \frac{9,872}{1,099,817} = .00897$$

$$\text{Debt to Equity Ratio} = \frac{267,293}{73,694} = 3.63:1$$

Problem V

1. accounting, information system
2. business entity
3. current asset
4. accrual
5. finance
6. periodicity
7. manufacturing
8. Owners' equity
9. internal
10. Mutual agency
11. going concern
12. computer-assisted design

Chapter 2
Business Processes and Accounting Information

Chapter Overview

Chapter 2 describes the management cycle and the four basic business processes. The chapter describes the balanced scorecard approach to performance measurement and management. In addition, the chapter explores the role of internal control and discusses the application of internal control principles to cash receipts and payments.

This chapter extends the introduction to business and accounting presented in Chapter 1. When studying the section on internal controls, relate these policies and procedures to your work experiences and experiences as a consumer. Even if you have not worked as a cashier, you have observed internal control procedures at a cash register checkout, such as the printing of cash register receipts, independent cash counts, and monitoring by video cameras. Think about the incentives to steal and/or manipulate cash receipts or cash payments. This process will help you identify procedures useful for controlling cash receipt and disbursement activities. Use your own experiences with balancing your checkbook against the monthly bank statement as a frame of reference for performing a bank reconciliation.

Read and Recall Questions

Learning Objective:
LO. 1 Explain the management cycle and the four basic business processes.

Businesses make and implement decisions in three phases. The first is the planning phase. Why is planning important for a business?

Describe strategic plans and operating plans. What is the relationship between these two types of planning?

Explain the performance phase of the management cycle. How is the accounting system used in the performance phase?

What is the purpose of the evaluating phase of the management cycle?

Define business process.

Briefly describe the following four business processes:

- Business organization and strategy

- Operating

- Capital resources

- Performance measurement and management

Study Guide: Introduction to Accounting, An Integrated Approach

Define organizational strategy.

What are the characteristics of a mechanistic organizational structure?

Describe the characteristics of an organic organizational structure.

Describe the three subprocesses of the operating process.

What are investing activities? What are financing activities?

<table>
<tr><td>Learning Objective:
LO. 2 Describe the balanced scorecard approach and its four perspectives.</td></tr>
</table>

Describe the balanced scorecard approach to performance measurement and management.

What is the financial perspective? Why is it important?

Explain the following financial ratios:

- Return on investment

- Quick ratio

- Return on owners' equity ratio

- Gross margin ratio

Describe the internal perspective of the balanced scorecard approach.

Distinguish between valued-added and nonvalue-added time.

What is customer response time? Identify the five components of the customer response time.

Identify and describe the four types of quality costs.

Explain the customer perspective of the balanced scorecard approach. Identify common measurements associated with the customer perspective.

What is the purpose of the learning and growth perspective of the balanced scorecard approach? How is this perspective measured?

Define internal control system.

Identify the three objectives of an internal control system.

Describe the following internal control procedures:

- Requiring proper authorization

- Separation of duties

- Maintaining adequate documentation

- Physically controlling assets and information

- Providing independent checks on performance

Explain why controls over cash receipts and disbursements are so critical to a business.

Describe the lockbox collection system. Why is it used?

Learning Objective:
LO. 4 Perform a two-column bank reconciliation.

Describe the information contained in a bank statement.

Explain the importance of the bank reconciliation process as an internal control procedure.

Define the following terms associated with the bank reconciliation process:

- Outstanding checks

- Deposits in transit

25

- Nonsufficient funds (NSF) checks

- Service charges

Outline of Key Concepts

I.   The management cycle is divided into three phases.
     A. Planning phase—management determines its objectives and the means of achieving those objectives.
         1. Strategic plan—sets the broad course for the business and covers a relatively long period.
         2. Operating plan—guides shorter-term decisions, including day-to-day functioning of the business.
     B. Performing phase—business actually completes its planned business operations.
         1. The accounting system is used to record the impact of events on the company.
     C. Evaluating phase—provides information to internal and external users about the company's performance.
         1. Involves comparing actual operating results with planned results. Differences can be the result of:
             a. The plan was good but the activities were not performed well.
             b. The plan was not very good and the activities were done well.

II. A business process is a collection of activities that takes one or more kinds of input and creates an output that is of value to the customer.
     A. Business organization and strategy process—determines the plans of action for the company.
         1. Organizational strategy—a company's long-term plan for using its resources.
             a. Mechanistic organizational structure—activities and employees are arranged by function; control is maintained at the top; decision-making is centralized; adopt an efficiency strategy.

       b. Organic organizational structure—activities and employees are arranged in cross-functional teams; decision-making is decentralized; adopt a flexible strategy.

  B. Operating process—profit-making activities of the business.

    1. Divided into two or three subprocesses:

       a. Marketing/sales/collection/customer service

       b. Purchasing/human resources/payment

       c. Conversion (if the company is a manufacturer)

  C. Capital resources process—involves the investing and financing activities of the business.

    1. Investing activities—involve the purchase and sale of long-term assets and other major items used to achieve the business's strategy.

    2. Financing activities—involve obtaining the cash or other resources to pay for investments in long-term assets, to repay monies borrowed from creditors, and to provide a return to owners.

  D. Performance measurement and management process—involves evaluating performance and using the information to plan for the future.

III.   Balanced scorecard approach—translates a company's strategy into measurable objectives.

  A. Financial perspective—used to control activities and measure results of the operating and capital resources processes.

    1. Return on investment—the return generated per dollar of total investment.

       a. Net income/Average total assets

    2. Quick ratio—a measure of a company's ability to meet its current obligations as they come due.

       a. (Cash + Temporary investments + Receivables)/Current Liabilities

    3. Return on owners' equity ratio—measures the return generated per dollar of owners' equity.

       a. Used to assess whether the company is generating a sufficient return for its owners.

       b. Net income/Average owners' equity

    4. Gross margin ratio—examines the relationship between sales and cost of goods sold.

       a. Represents the amount available to cover the rest of the company's operating expenses.

       b. Gross margin/Sales

  B. Internal Perspective—seeks to find measures of improvement in both the way work is done and the manner in which people are utilized.

    1. Time is frequently monitored.

a. Value-added time—time spent on activities that add value to the company's products/services or processes.

b. Nonvalue-added time—time spend on activities that do not add value to the company's products/services or processes.

2. Customer response time—amount of time that elapses between a customer placing and receiving an order.

   a. Order response time

   b. Processing time

   c. Queue time

   d. Storing time

   e. Shipping time

3. Quality and costs of quality are monitored.

   a. Prevention cost—the cost incurred to prevent mistakes from occurring.

   b. Appraisal cost—the cost incurred to detect mistakes as early as possible.

   c. Internal failure cost—the cost incurred to fix mistakes before the mistakes become known to the customer.

   d. External failure cost—the cost incurred to fix mistakes after the mistakes become known to the customer.

4. Employee satisfaction, retention, and productivity are monitored.

C. Customer Perspective—relates to monitoring the company's customer base.

1. Companies attempt to increase the value of their customer base by increasing market share, acquiring more or larger customers, and increasing customer satisfaction and loyalty.

2. Companies monitor the following:

   a. Number of new customers acquired

   b. Profit generated by new customers

   c. Growth in market share

   d. Customer satisfaction

   e. Customer complaints

   f. Customers lost

   g. Customer loyalty

   h. Changes in buying habits

D. Learning and growth perspective—concerns the company's ability to take actions now to ensure its future.

1. The company's future, in part, depends on its current expenditures for:

   a. Research and development

   b. Employee growth

   c. Information systems

Study Guide: Introduction to Accounting, An Integrated Approach

IV. Internal control systems meet the objectives of promoting operational efficiency, ensuring the accuracy of accounting information, and encouraging compliance with applicable laws and regulations.
   A. Requiring proper authorization—ensure that the persons responsible for certain activities have the authority to enforce the policies associated with those activities.
   B. Separation of duties—dividing duties that have the potential for one person to violate company policies among two or more employees.
      1. Prevent employees from performing more than one phase of any business transaction.
         a. Approval
         b. Execution
         c. Custody
         d. Recording
   C. Maintaining adequate documentation—documents capture all the necessary information about a transaction in an efficient and effective manner.
      1. Allows managers to trace responsibility for transactions and to maintain employee accountability.
   D. Physically controlling assets and information—limiting access to assets and accounting records by unauthorized personnel.
   E. Providing independent checks on performance—includes having another employee who was not involved in the original activity check the work.
      1. Guards against theft, fraud, and errors.

V. Security over cash is critical because possession implies ownership.
   A. Procedures for safeguarding cash receipts include:
      1. Physically safeguarding the cash
      2. Separating the duties of those with custody of cash from those who keep the accounting records
      3. Deposit cash receipts quickly and record receipts as soon as possible
      4. Independently check cash balances and cash handling procedures
      5. Lockbox collection system
   B. Procedures for controlling cash disbursements include:
      1. Separating responsibilities for check writing, check signing, check mailing, and keeping accounting records
      2. Ensuring that payments are properly authorized
   C. Bank reconciliation—control procedure to adjust the recorded cash amount and to reflect any differences between its cash balance and the cash balance according to the bank.
      1. Bank statements are sent by banks to businesses and individuals who have accounts showing all transactions in each account for the period.
         a. Service charge—fee charged by the bank for services to the customer.

29

b. Nonsufficient funds (NSF) checks—checks deposited but returned for a lack of funds.
2. Highlights any differences due to the timing of withdrawals, deposits, and other account increases and decreases.
    a. Outstanding checks—checks written by the business and deducted from the business's cash account, but the bank has not processed them yet.
    b. Deposits in transit—deposits recorded in the business's cash records and sent to the bank, but the bank has not received and recorded the amount of the deposit before the bank statement was sent.
    c. Company must deduct any service charges and nonsufficient funds checks.
    d. Company must add any collections recorded by the bank but not yet recorded in the business's records.
    e. Company must add or deduct errors made by the business.
    f. Company must notify the bank of any errors made by the bank.

Problem I

Indicate whether the following statements are either true (T) or false (F).

_____1. A good system of internal controls prevents an employee from performing more than one phase of a business transaction.
_____2. The bank reconciliation should be performed by the person responsible for depositing the cash in the bank.
_____3. Companies operating in an uncertain environment usually have a mechanistic organizational structure.
_____4. Business processes involve more than one functional area within the business.
_____5. An adjusting entry will be made to the cash account in the general ledger to account for any outstanding checks on the bank reconciliation.
_____6. Routine transactions involving relatively small amounts of cash should not need authorization by upper-level management.
_____7. A lock-box system improves a company's internal control procedures.
_____8. Capital resources processes are the profit-making activities of the business.
_____9. The financial perspective looks primarily at the internal operations of the company.
_____10. The number of information systems upgrades is a common measurement found in the internal perspective.

Study Guide: Introduction to Accounting, An Integrated Approach

Problem II

Indicate the correct answer by circling the appropriate letter.

1. Which of the following is not a characteristic of a company operating in an uncertain environment?
   a. experiences rapidly changing products and/or customers
   b. concentrates on customer satisfaction and new product development
   c. activities and people are arranged in cross-functional teams
   d. decision making is typically centralized

Use the Dreyer's consolidated financial statements (Appendix) for the next two questions:

2. What is Dreyer's quick ratio for 1999?
   a. .69:1
   b. 1.13:1
   c. .31:1
   d. .89:1

3. What is Dreyer's gross margin ratio for 1999?
   a. .297
   b. .354
   c. .762
   d. .238

4. Which of the following is a cost incurred to fix mistakes before the mistakes become known to the customer?
   a. prevention cost
   b. appraisal cost
   c. internal failure cost
   d. external failure cost

5. All of the following would be considered performance measurements in the customer perspective except _____.
   a. market share
   b. customer loyalty
   c. customer satisfaction
   d. return on owners' equity

6. Which of the following would be considered a measurement used in the internal perspective?
   a. return on sales ratio
   b. customer retention
   c. employee retention
   d. time to market

Problem III

The following activities occurred in Xectar Company, a small commercial and residential construction firm. In the space provided, indicate whether the activity occurred in the planning (PL), performing (PR) or the evaluating (E) phase of the management cycle.

_____1. Raw materials are purchased from a lumberyard.
_____2. The company decides to obtain a 10 percent market share for residential construction by the end of its third year of operations.
_____3. Advertisement is placed on a local radio station.
_____4. Due to high residential construction demands, the commercial division is closed and employees are transferred to the residential division.
_____5. Cash is collected from a customer.

Problem IV

The following is a list of important ideas and key concepts from the chapter. To test your knowledge of these terms, match the term with the definition by placing the number in the space provided.

_____ Appraisal cost	_____ Mechanistic organizational structure
_____ Balanced scorecard approach	_____ Nonvalue-added time
_____ Deposits in transit	_____ Organic organizational structure
_____ Efficiency strategy	_____ Outstanding Checks
_____ Flexibility strategy	_____ Prevention cost
_____ Internal control system	_____ Value-added time
_____ Internal failure cost	

Study Guide: Introduction to Accounting, An Integrated Approach

1. Checks written, mailed, and deducted in the business's cash records but that the bank has not processed yet

2. Bank deposits that the business has recorded in its cash records and sent to the bank or put in the night depository, but that the bank has not received and recorded before it sent the bank statement to the business

3. Time spent on activities that do not add value to the company's products/services or processes

4. A strategy that focuses primarily on the reduction or containment of costs, improvements in productivity, and penetration of products/services in the market by having the lowest cost

5. A strategy in which a company strives to adapt to changing market conditions by developing new products/services, markets, and technologies

6. Time spent on activities that add value to the company's products/services or processes

7. A cost incurred to prevent mistakes from occurring

8. The cost incurred to detect mistakes as early in the process as possible

9. The set of policies and procedures designed to promote operational efficiency, ensure the accuracy of accounting information, and encourage management and employee compliance with applicable laws and regulations

10. A process for translating a company's strategy into measurable objectives and plans organized into four perspectives

11. A cost incurred to fix mistakes before the mistakes become known to the customer

12. A structure in which activities and people are arranged by functions

13. A structure in which activities and people are arranged in cross-functional teams

Problem V

1. _____ strategy is a company's long-term plan for using its resources.

2. Companies that operate in an uncertain environment usually adopt an _____ organizational structure.

3. The balanced scorecard approach translates a company's strategy into measurable _____.

4. Two areas of analysis in the internal perspective are _____ and _____.

5. Time spent on storing and moving finished products would be considered _____ time.

6. A company's largest unrecorded asset will be its _____ _____.

7. The balanced scorecard is a _____ approach to planning and measuring company performance.

Problem VI

What are the five procedures used in an internal accounting control system?

_____
_____
_____
_____
_____
_____

Study Guide: Introduction to Accounting, An Integrated Approach

Problem VII

The following information related to the Cash account is available for the month of December:

a. The bank statement balance at December 31 is $23,967

b. The following checks were written by the company in December but have not cleared the bank:

Check Number	Amount
11,234	$1,789
12,435	$2,678
12,450	$1,500

c. The following debit memos from the bank were included in the December bank statement:

Nonsufficient Funds Check $550
Service charge $150

d. The company incorrectly recorded a deposit from a customer as $960 instead of $690.

e. There was a $4,500 deposit in transit.

f. The ending balance per books was $23,470.

Required: Prepare a bank reconciliation for the month of December.

Bank Reconciliation
December 31

Solutions for Chapter 2

Problem 1

1. T	6. T
2. F	7. T
3. F	8. F
4. T	9. F
5. F	10. F

Problem II

1. d
2. a
3. d
4. c
5. d
6. c

Problem III

1. PR
2. PL
3. PR
4. E
5. PR

Problem IV

8	Appraisal cost	12	Mechanistic organizational structure
10	Balanced scorecard approach	3	Nonvalue-added time
2	Deposits in transit	1	Organic organizational structure
4	Efficiency strategy	13	Outstanding Checks
5	Flexibility strategy	7	Prevention cost
9	Internal control system	6	Value-added time
11	Internal failure cost		

Problem V

1. Organizational
2. organic
3. objectives
4. time, quality
5. nonvalue-added
6. customer base
7. holistic

Problem VI

The five procedures used in an internal accounting control system are (a) requiring proper authorization for transactions, (b) separating incompatible duties, (c) maintaining adequate documents and records, (d) physically controlling assets and documents, and (e) providing independent checks on performance.

Problem VII

Bank Reconciliation
December 31

Balance per bank		$23,967
Add: Deposits in transit	4,500	
Deduct: Outstanding checks	<5,967>	
Adjusted balance per books		$22,500
Balance per books		$23,470
Deduct:		
NSF check	550	
Service charge	150	
Correction of error	270	
Adjusted balance per books		$22,500

Chapter 3
Operating Processes: Planning and Control

Chapter Overview

Chapter 3 begins by describing the operating processes of the business. The chapter examines the sequence of activities in the revenue, expenditure, and conversion processes. In addition, Chapter 3 explains the importance of understanding cost and revenue behavior. Cost and revenue estimation techniques such as the high-low method and linear regression analysis are illustrated.

In this chapter you will need to learn the distinctions among the revenue, expenditure, and conversion process activities. Learning these distinctions will help you analyze, record, and report economic events in the accounting information system.

Understanding cost and revenue behavior is essential for estimating costs and revenues. You must learn to determine whether costs or revenues are variable, fixed, or mixed. This knowledge will assist you in preparing useful plans and making well-reasoned business decisions. As you analyze mixed costs or revenues, relate the analysis to your knowledge of calculating the slope and intercept of a straight line. Linear regression analysis will not be familiar to most of you. Do not be concerned about the underlying statistical and mathematical assumptions with this technique right now. Focus instead on the information that is communicated from the output of linear regression analysis.

Read and Recall Questions

Learning Objective:
LO. 1 Identify the activities in the three operating subprocesses.

Describe the purpose of the revenue process.

Identify the three goals of the revenue process.

Identify the five primary activities in the revenue process.

Explain how companies determine which products and services meet customers' needs.

Identify the two activities that a company must perform when an order is received.

What is a sales discount, and why is it offered to a customer?

Distinguish between free on board (FOB) destination and free on board (FOB) shipping point.

If the terms of a sale made on December 30, 2003, are FOB destination and the goods arrive at the buyer's place of business on January 4, 2004, explain in which year the seller should record the sale and the decrease in inventory.

Define sales returns and sales allowances. Why do companies track these costs?

What is the purpose of the expenditure process?

Identify the three goals of the expenditure process.

Identify the four primary activities in the expenditure process.

Explain the purpose of a purchase requisition.

What is the purpose of the purchase order? How does it bind the purchaser and supplier?

Define purchase returns and purchase allowances.

What are purchase discounts? Why should a buyer take advantage of purchase discounts?

What is the purpose of the conversion process?

Identify the two goals of the conversion process.

Identify the four primary activities in the conversion process.

Study Guide: Introduction to Accounting, An Integrated Approach

Identify at least five factors that make scheduling production difficult for manufacturers.

Define manufacturing overhead.

Explain how demand-pull production can reduce costs.

<table>
<tr><td>Learning Objective:
LO. 2 Describe fixed, variable, and mixed costs and revenues.</td></tr>
</table>

Explain the concepts of cost and revenue behavior.

Define relevant range. Explain its significance to cost and revenue behavior.

Define activity drivers. What is their relationship to costs and revenues?

Define fixed cost and fixed revenue. How do fixed costs and fixed revenues behave when measured on a per-activity basis?

Define variable cost and variable revenue. How do variable costs and variable revenues behave when measured on a per-activity basis?

Define mixed cost and mixed revenue.

Learning Objective:
LO. 3 Use the high-low method to determine fixed and variable costs and revenues.

Briefly explain the high-low method of cost or revenue estimation.

Discuss the strength(s) and weakness(es) of the high-low method.

Learning Objective:
LO. 4 Apply linear regression analysis to determine fixed and variable costs and revenues.

Briefly explain linear regression.

Discuss the benefits of using linear regression to estimate costs or revenues.

Define the following terms:

- Y variable or dependent variable

- X variable or independent variable

- Multiple R or correlation

- R Square

Outline of Key Concepts

I. Revenue process—series of interrelated activities designed to generate revenue.
    A. Revenue process has three goals.
        1. Provide customers with the product/service they want at a price they are willing to pay.
        2. Receive payment from customers in a timely fashion.
        3. Provide customer support to ensure future sales.
    B. Revenue process has five primary activities.
        1. Determine marketing and distribution channels to generate sales.
            a. Analyze customer's buying habits and perform customer surveys.
            b. Two basic forms of sales are cash or credit.
        2. Receive and accept orders for goods and services.
            a. Determine the credit and payment policies for the customer.
                i. sales discount—company allows the customer to pay less than the full invoice price if the customer remits payment within a specified period of time.
            b. Determine if the goods are available.
        3. Deliver goods and/or services.
            a. Free on board (FOB) destination—legal title to the goods does not pass until the customer receives the goods. It implies that the seller pays the freight charges.
            b. Free on board (FOB) shipping point—legal title to the goods passes to the buyer when the goods are picked up by the common carrier. It implies that the customer pays the freight charges.
        4. Receive payment from customers.
            a. Sales invoice provides information about the quantity and type of goods, price, and terms of the sale agreement.
        5. Provide customer support.
            a. Keep record of sales returns and sales allowances.
                i. Sales allowance—reduction from selling price as compensation to an unhappy customer.

Study Guide: Introduction to Accounting, An Integrated Approach

II.   Expenditure process—series of interrelated activities designed to enable the company to generate revenues.

    A. Expenditure process has three goals.

        1. Receive the highest-quality goods/services at the lowest cost.

        2. Pay for goods/services in a timely manner.

        3. Develop good relationships with suppliers of goods/services.

    B. Expenditure has four primary activities.

        1. Determine the company's need for goods/services.

        2. Select suppliers and order goods/services.

            a. Assess service and quality as well as price.

        3. Received goods/services.

            a. Must inspect, store, and secure the assets.

            b. Purchase return—goods that do not meet the company's specifications and are returned to the supplier.

            c. Purchase allowance—a reduction in the purchase cost when the company accepts the goods but is unhappy with the goods.

        4. Pay suppliers for goods/services.

            a. Purchase discount—discount offered by the supplier to encourage timely payment.

III.   Conversion process—series of interrelated activities designed to produce the goods the company sells.

    A. Conversion process has two goals.

        1. Manufacture the highest-quality products.

        2. Utilize labor and other manufacturing resources in an efficient and effective manner.

    B. Conversion process has four primary activities.

        1. Schedule production.

            a. Machine setups—adjustments made to machines to get them ready to manufacture the next type of product.

            b. Cells—machines related to the production of certain products or types of products are close to each other to reduce travel time between machines.

            c. Demand for the product is the overriding factor in scheduling production.

            d. Other factors are the complexity of the product and production process.

        2. Obtain raw materials.

            a. Raw materials are obtained through the expenditure process.

            b. Material requisition is used to obtain needed material for the production process.

        3. Use labor and other manufacturing resources to make products.

            a. Manufacturing overhead—cost of all manufacturing resources used to make products that are not directly associated with production.

4. Store finished goods until sold.

IV. Cost and revenue behavior—how a cost or revenue reacts to a change in the level of operating activity.
   A. Relevant range—the span of operating activity that is considered normal for the company.
      1. Given this assumption, costs and revenues can be defined linearly.
   B. Activity driver—base that reflects the consumption or provision of resources.
      1. Activities, as measured by activity drivers, provide or consume resources, as measured by costs and/or revenues, changes in the amount of the activity driver ultimately cause, or drive, changes in costs and/or revenues.
   C. Fixed costs or fixed revenues—do not change in total as the amount of the activity driver changes throughout the relevant range.
      1. On a per-activity basis, the amount of fixed cost or revenue varies inversely with the activity level.
   D. Variable costs or variable revenues—change in direct proportion to the change in the amount of activity driver throughout the relevant range.
      1. On a per-activity basis, the amount of variable cost or revenue does not change.
   E. Mixed costs or mixed revenues—vary, but not proportionately, to a change in activity throughout the relevant range.
      1. Changes both in total and per unit of activity throughout the relevant range.

V. Cost/revenue estimation methods determine the relationship between total costs/revenues and a particular activity driver to estimate future costs/revenues.
   A. High/low method—a cost or revenue estimation that uses only two data points to determine the cost/revenue formula.
      1. Uses the highest and lowest levels of activity driver to define the relevant range and determine the total cost or revenue line.
      2. Variable rate per unit of activity driver = (Highest cost – Lowest cost)/(Highest activity – Lowest activity)
      3. Fixed cost = Total cost – (Variable rate x Activity level)
      4. One significant weakness of the method is that it ignores most of the data available.
   B. Linear regression analysis—a statistical technique that uses multiple data points to determine the total cost or revenue formula.
      1. Two significant strengths of linear regression include:
         a. Uses all available data points.
         b. Has indicators that measure the strength of the cost/revenue and activity relationship.
      2. Y variable or dependent variable—the amount of this variable depends on some other variable.
         a. Total cost data

3. X variable or independent variable—the amount of this variable does not depend on any other variable.
    a. Activity driver data
4. Standard error—measure of variability around the mean.
5. T Statistic—a statistical measure of the significance of the slope of the regression line.
6. Multiple R—a measure of correlation. It ranges from –1 to +1.
    a. A positive correlation means that as the amount of the X variable increases, the amount of the Y variable increases.
    b. A negative correlation means that as the amount of the X variable increases, the amount of the Y variable decreases.
7. R Square—indicates the strength of the relationship between the independent and dependent variable.
    a. It ranges from 0 to 1, and the larger the number the stronger the relationship.

Problem I

Indicate whether the following statements are either true (T) or false (F).

_____1. A mixed cost will increase in total but decreases per activity as the cost driver increases.

_____2. The higher the R-squared, the stronger is the relationship between the cost driver and the cost.

_____3. The expenditure process only occurs in manufacturing type firms.

_____4. The conversion process is a sequence of events conducted within a business rather than between a company and an external party.

_____5. A weakness of the linear regression method of estimating costs is that it only uses two data points in its analysis.

_____6. In linear regression, the cost driver will be considered the independent variable.

_____7. When a customer uses an outside credit card, the transaction is treated as a cash sale.

_____8. When products are shipped FOB destination, title of the goods passes when the goods are picked up by the common carrier.

_____9. When products are shipped FOB shipping point, the seller must pay any shipping charges.

_____10. The overriding factor in scheduling production is demand for the company's product.

_____11. The person who takes the sales order should not be the person who approves the customer for credit.

_____12. As companies become more automated, the amount of manufacturing overhead relative to materials and labor decreases.

Problem II

Indicate the correct answer by circling the appropriate letter.

1. The sale of goods to a customer occurs in the _____ process.
   a. expenditure
   b. revenue
   c. conversion
   d. none of the above

2. Which of the following is not a primary activity associated with the expenditure process?
   a. determining the business needs for goods and services
   b. generating customer orders
   c. selecting suppliers and ordering goods and services
   d. receiving, securing, and storing the goods

3. The document that provides the supplier with a list of what required items are needed and their quantities, in addition to other terms, like shipping dates is the _____.
   a. purchase requisition
   b. purchase order
   c. receiving report
   d. vendor's invoice

4. The purchase of inventory that will be sold to customers occurs in the _____ process.
   a. expenditure
   b. revenue
   c. conversion
   d. none of the above

Use the following cost data for the next two questions:

Xene Company has provided the following quarterly data for the past two years on its maintenance costs:

	Activity Driver Machine Hours	Total Costs Maintenance Costs
1	3,500	$4,800
2	2,600	$3,700
3	4,500	$5,800
4	2,900	$4,200
5	5,400	$6,500
6	3,400	$4,200
7	4,700	$5,700
8	3,900	$5,300

Study Guide: Introduction to Accounting, An Integrated Approach

5. Using the high/low method, Xene's estimated fixed maintenance cost is _____ per quarter.
   a. $1,100
   b. $1,675
   c. $2,600
   d. $3,900

6. Xene estimates that 5,000 machine hours will be needed in the next quarter to meet customer demands for its product. Using the high/low method, what will be the total estimated maintenance cost for the quarter?
   a. $4,500
   b. $5,200
   c. $6,100
   d. $6,150

7. Which of the following would not be captured in a company's information system as the result of a personal sales call?
   a. product or services promoted
   b. date and location of sales call
   c. customer characteristics such as business size or number of employees
   d. all of the above information would be retained

8. Adding a memory chip to a laptop computer will occur in the _____ process of a computer manufacturing company.
   a. expenditure
   b. revenue
   c. conversion
   d. none of the above

9. Which of the following is not considered a primary activity in the revenue cycle?
   a. providing customer support
   b. receiving and accepting orders for goods and services
   c. selecting a supplier and paying the order
   d. receiving payment from customers

10. All of the following are primary activities of the conversion process except
   _____.
   a. scheduling production
   b. obtaining raw materials
   c. using labor and other manufacturing resources to make products
   d. collecting cash from customers

Use the following information for the next two questions:

11. Onyx shipped $200,000 of merchandise to LTD by common carrier on December 27th. The terms of the sale were 2/10, n/60, FOB destination. The product arrived at LTD on January 3rd. In determining accounting net income, the sale will be reported _____.

    a. on December 27th
    b. on January 3rd
    c. when payment is received
    d. when the order was received

12. What is the amount of the sales/purchase discount?
    a. $200,000
    b. $20,000
    c. $8,000
    d. $4,000

Study Guide: Introduction to Accounting, An Integrated Approach

Problem III

The following is a list of important ideas and key concepts from the chapter. To test your knowledge of these terms, match the term with the definition by placing the number in the space provided.

_____	Bill of lading	_____	Manufacturing overhead
_____	Conversion process	_____	Mixed cost
_____	Expenditure process	_____	Mixed revenue
_____	Fixed cost	_____	Relevant range
_____	Fixed revenue	_____	Revenue behavior
_____	Free on board destination	_____	Revenue process
_____	Free on board shipping point	_____	Variable cost
_____	Machine setups	_____	Variable revenue

1. A cost that does not change in total as the amount of the activity driver changes throughout the relevant range

2. A revenue that changes in direct proportion to the change in the amount of activity driver throughout the relevant range

3. A cost that varies, but not proportionately, to a change in activity throughout the relevant range

4. A series of inter-related activities designed to enable the company to generate revenue

5. A situation where legal title to goods passes to the customer when the goods are received

6. A cost that changes in direct proportion to the change in the amount of activity driver throughout the relevant range

7. A series of inter-related activities designed to generate revenue

8. A shipping agreement between the business and the common carrier

9. How a revenue reacts to change in the level of operating activity

10. A series of inter-related activities designed to produce the goods a company sells

11. Adjustments made to machines to get them ready to manufacture the next type of product

12. The cost of all manufacturing resources used to make products that are not directly associated with production

13. A situation where legal title to goods passes to the customer when the goods are picked up by the common carrier

14. A revenue that varies, but not proportionately, to a change in activity throughout the relevant range

15. A revenue that does not change in total as the amount of the activity driver changes throughout the relevant range

16. The span of operating activity that is considered normal for the company

Problem IV

1. Two important sources used to determine customers' product needs are the _____ analysis of customer buying habits and a _____ of customer preferences.

2. The advantage of the bidding process for a customer is that it encourages _____ among suppliers.

3. When an order is received a company must decide the _____ policy and determine if the _____ are available.

4. A good information system requires a record of _____ _____ by customers as well as any _____ _____ given to unhappy customers.

5. The final activity in the revenue process is providing _____ support.

6. A goal of the expenditure process is to receive the highest _____ of goods or services at the lowest _____.

7. Businesses and its suppliers often work together in product _____ and _____ scheduling.

8. Demand-pull production eliminates the need for a _____ _____ inventory.

9. A mixed cost has both a _____ and a _____ cost component.

10. _____ _____ is a cost estimation method that uses multiple data points and statistical analysis to determine the total cost or revenue formula.

11. A variable cost will change in direct proportion to changes in the _____ _____.

Study Guide: Introduction to Accounting, An Integrated Approach

Problem V

The following data are available for shipping costs incurred by the Amex Company. The regression output was obtained from the data input into a regression program:

	Units Shipped	Total Shipping Costs		
January	12,000	$26,500	Regression Output:	
February	11,000	$23,500	Intercept	4110.396
March	15,000	$34,900	X Coefficient	1.805
April	10,000	$21,000	Standard error	0.238
May	7,000	$17,300	R Square	0.852
June	8,500	$20,100		
July	9,000	$19,000		
August	13,000	$24,500		
September	12,500	$25,000		
October	11,800	$24,900		
November	8,800	$21,000		
December	8,300	$20,700		

a. Using the high/low method, determine the cost estimation equation.

b. Using the regression output, determine the cost estimation equation.

c. Using the regression output, estimate the total cost if 14,000 units will be shipped next month.

Solutions for Chapter 3

Problem 1

1. T	7. T
2. T	8. F
3. F	9. F
4. T	10. T
5. F	11. T
6. T	12. F

Problem II

1. b	9. c
2. b	10. d
3. b	11. b
4. a	12. d
5. a	
6. c	
7. d	
8. c	

Problem III

8	Bill of lading	12	Manufacturing overhead
10	Conversion process	3	Mixed cost
4	Expenditure process	14	Mixed revenue
1	Fixed cost	16	Relevant range
15	Fixed revenue	9	Revenue behavior
5	Free on board destination	7	Revenue process
13	Free on board shipping point	6	Variable cost
11	Machine setups	2	Variable revenue

Problem IV

1. marketing, survey
2. competition
3. credit, goods
4. sales returns, sales allowances
5. customer
6. quality, cost
7. design, production
8. finished goods
9. fixed, variable
10. Linear regression
11. activity driver

Problem V

a.

	Units Shipped	Total Shipping Costs
High	15,000	$34,900
Low	<7,000>	<$17,300>
Difference	8,000	$17,600

$$\frac{\$17,600}{8,000} = \$2.20 \text{ per unit shipped}$$

Total shipping costs = ($2.20 x units shipped) + fixed costs

$34,900 = ($2.20 x 15,000) + fixed costs

fixed costs = $1,900

Cost Estimation Equation:
Total shipping costs = ($2.20 x units shipped) + $1,900

b. Cost Estimation Equation:

   Total shipping costs = ($1.805 x units shipped) + $4,110

c. Estimated Shipping Costs for Next Month = ($1.805 x 14,000) + $4,110 = $29,830

Chapter 4
Short-Term Decision Making

Chapter Overview

Chapter 4 extends the discussion about cost/revenue behavior by illustrating how cost behavior impacts profit planning and short-term decision making. The chapter describes how cost-volume-profit (CVP) analysis is used to understand the relationship among selling price, costs, volume, and profits. The chapter also explores short-term operating decisions such as special order, outsourcing, and product mix decisions.

At first, you might try to memorize the decisions made in this chapter. If you use this approach, you will not be successful in analyzing the myriad of profit planning and short-term operating decisions that you may encounter. You need to learn how to apply broad decision-making concepts to these types of decisions. Having a good grasp of the cost/revenue behavior patterns you studied in Chapter 3 will be helpful as you analyze the unstructured problems in this chapter. You must develop a good understanding of relevant, sunk, and opportunity costs. You should also think through the decision rules associated with each of the operating decisions presented in this chapter. Then practice applying the cost definitions and decision rules to different decision-making exercises and problems.

Read and Recall Questions

Explain how short-term operating decisions differ from recurring operating decisions.

Define sunk cost and explain why a sunk cost is never relevant in a short-term operating decision.

Define opportunity cost and explain why an opportunity cost is always relevant in a short-term operating decision.

Define incremental revenue, incremental cost, and incremental profit.

Identify the three steps in relevant variable analysis.

Learning Objective:
LO. 1 Describe the differences among product, nonproduct, unit-related, batch-related, product-sustaining, and facility-sustaining costs.

Distinguish between product and nonproduct costs.

Briefly define the following three manufacturing product costs:

- Direct materials

- Direct labor

- Manufacturing overhead

Study Guide: Introduction to Accounting, An Integrated Approach

Briefly describe the following four cost behavior levels:

- Unit-related costs

- Batch-related costs

- Product-sustaining costs

- Facility-sustaining costs

Learning Objective:
LO. 2 Explain the purpose of, and perform, cost-volume-profit (CVP) analysis.

Define cost-volume-profit (CVP) analysis.

Identify the key assumptions of CVP analysis.

What is the breakeven point? What is the significance of the breakeven point?

Define contribution margin per unit.

Indicate the formula for calculating the number of units that must be produced and sold to breakeven.

What is the formula for converting after-tax profit to before-tax profit?

Describe sensitivity analysis and explain why it is useful in CVP analysis.

If there is an increase in the tax rate, what is the effect on contribution margin, breakeven point, and desired profit?

Study Guide: Introduction to Accounting, An Integrated Approach

Explain how a short-term special order differs from recurring customer orders.

Explain the decision rule for a short-term special order.

Besides short-term profits, what other factors should be considered when making a short-term special order decision?

What are outsourcing (make-or-buy) decisions?

Explain the decision rule for outsourcing (make-or-buy) decisions.

Besides short-term profits, what other factors should be considered when making an outsourcing (make-or-buy) decision?

What is the purpose of a product mix (keep-or-drop) decision?

Explain the decision rule for making a product mix decision.

Besides short-term profits, what other factors should be considered when making a product mix decision?

Outline of Key Concepts

I.   Unplanned opportunities and threats lead to short-term operating decisions.
      A. Short-term operating decisions differ from other operating decisions.
            1. Assume that capacity is fixed.
            2. Cannot be planned in the company's normal planning process.
            3. Are unique; must be analyzed as a distinct opportunity.
      B. Model—representation of reality.
            1. Help sort and organize information.

II.   Cost-volume-profit (CVP analysis—the study of how costs, revenues, and profits change in response to changes in the volume of goods or services provided to customers.
      A. CVP analysis is based on several assumptions.
            1. The activity driver is the number of units produced and sold.
            2. Selling price remains constant per unit regardless of the volume sold.
            3. Variable cost remains constant per unit regardless of the volume produced and sold.

4. Fixed cost remains constant in total regardless of the volume produced and sold throughout the relevant range.
5. The number of units produced or purchased equals the number of units sold.
6. The sales mix remains constant.

B. Breakeven point is where total revenues equal total costs and profit is equal to zero.
1. Total revenue = Selling price per unit x Number of units sold
2. Total cost = (Variable cost per unit x Number of units produced) + Fixed cost
3. Profit = Total revenue – Total cost
4. Contribution margin per unit is the difference between selling price per unit and variable cost per unit.
5. Contribution margin is total sales less total variable costs at a given level of activity.
6. Breakeven units = Fixed cost/Contribution margin per unit

C. Determining the target profit level.
1. Target sales in units = (Fixed costs + target profit)/Contribution margin per unit
2. To earn a particular amount of profit after taxes, a company must earn more profit before taxes.
   a. Before-tax profit = After-tax profit/(1 – tax rate)

D. Sensitivity analysis—process of changing the key variables in CVP analysis to determine how sensitive the CVP relationships are to changes in these variables.
1. Changes in the selling price causes a change in both the contribution margin and the breakeven point.
   a. An increase in selling price increases the contribution margin and decreases the breakeven point.
   b. A decrease in selling price decreases the contribution margin and increases the breakeven point.
2. A change in the variable cost per unit causes a change in both the contribution margin and breakeven point.
   a. An increase in the variable cost per unit causes a decrease in the contribution margin and increases the breakeven point.
   b. A decrease in the variable cost per unit causes an increase in the contribution margin and a decrease in the breakeven point.
3. A change in fixed cost causes a change in the breakeven point but not in the contribution margin.
   a. An increase in fixed costs causes an increase in the breakeven point.
   b. A decrease in fixed costs causes a decrease in the breakeven point.
4. A change in the tax rate affects only the number of units that must be sold to obtain a desired profit after taxes.
   a. Does not change the contribution margin or breakeven point.

III. Relevant variable analysis helps companies make short-term operating decisions.
    A. Companies classify costs as product or nonproduct costs.
        1. Nonproduct costs—related to selling the product and services or administering the company.
        2. Product costs—costs related to obtaining or manufacturing the product.
            a. Direct materials—cost of materials that are directly traceable to the product and are costly enough to warrant tracing.
                i. Indirect materials—cannot be traced to the product or are not costly enough to warrant tracing.

            b. Direct labor—cost of employees who manufacture the product.
                i. Indirect labor—cost of production employees who do not physically manufacture the product.
            c. Manufacturing overhead—all costs incurred to manufacture products other than direct materials and direct labor.
    B. Costs are typically analyzed at four levels.
        1. Unit-related costs—costs that vary with the number of units.
        2. Batch-related costs—costs that vary with the number of batches.
        3. Product-sustaining costs—costs that vary with the number of product lines.
        4. Facility-sustaining costs—costs incurred to maintain the company's capacity to operate.
    C. Relevant variable—a cost or revenue that will occur in the future and differs among the alternatives considered.
        1. Sunk cost—a past cost that arises from past decisions.
            a. Never relevant in a short-term operating decision.
        2. Opportunity cost—the benefit foregone when choosing one alternative over another.
            a. Is the benefit provided by the next best alternative.
            b. Always relevant to a decision.
        3. Incremental revenues and costs are relevant when they differ between alternatives.
            a. Incremental revenue—additional revenue expected from the alternative.
            b. Incremental cost—additional cost associated with an alternative.
            c. Incremental profit—difference between incremental revenue and incremental cost of a particular alternative.
    D. There are three steps in relevant variable analysis.
        1. Identify the possible alternative actions.
        2. Determine the relevant revenues, costs, and/or profits of each alternative.
        3. Choose the best alternative.

Study Guide: Introduction to Accounting, An Integrated Approach

IV. Special order (Accept-or-reject) decisions--initiated by a customer who requests a lower price or asks the producer to prepare a bid.
   A. Operating decision rule:
      1. Accept a special order if the relevant profit is positive.
      2. Reject a special order if the relevant profit is negative.
   B. There are other factors to consider.
      1. How does the decision impact long-term profitability?
      2. How does the decision affect other customers?

V. Outsourcing (Make-or-buy) decision—company must determine whether it should do something internally or outsource the activity to another company.
   A. Operating decision rule:
      1. Make a product internally if the relevant cost of making the item is less than the relevant cost of buying the item externally.
      2. Buy an item externally if the relevant cost of buying the item is less than the relevant cost of making the item.
   B. Other factors to consider.
      1. Quality of the supplier's product and processes.
      2. How does the decision impact the long term?

VI. Product mix (Keep-or-drop) decision—company must determine whether it should keep selling a product line or discontinue offering it in the short term. The product may be reintroduced later.
   A. Operating decision rule:
      1. Keep a product line if the relevant revenues lost exceed the relevant costs saved from discontinuing the product line.
      2. Drop a product line if the relevant revenues lost are less than the relevant costs saved from discontinuing the product line.
   B. Other factors to consider.
      1. The impact on sales of other products.
      2. How does the decision impact the long term?
      3. The image of the company.

Problem I

Indicate whether the following statements are either true (T) or false (F).

_____1. Short-term decisions are based on the assumption that business cannot change its plant capacity in the time affected by the decision.

_____2. Short-term decisions are planned as a part of the normal management process.

_____3. Sunk costs will be considered relevant in most short-term operating decisions.

_____4. Opportunity costs are irrelevant in the decision-making process.

_____5. Rent on a warehouse would be considered a facility-sustaining cost.

_____6. Qualitative factors should not be considered in the short-term decision-making process.

_____7. Depreciation of long-term assets is not a relevant cost in short-term decision making.

_____8. Cost-volume-profit analysis assumes a linear relationship between cost and the number of units produced.

_____9. As fixed costs decrease, the breakeven point in sales dollars will increase.

_____10. An increase in the effective tax rate will cause a company's breakeven point in sales dollars to increase.

Problem II

Indicate the correct answer by circling the appropriate letter.

1. Airwest provides a company plane for executives to visit various plants around the world. The company is considering having executives fly commercial rather than use the company plane. Which of the following would be considered a sunk cost in the decision process?
    a. Each flight uses $15,000 in fuel.
    b. Commercial tickets would average $1,500 per flight.
    c. The company plane originally cost 1.5 million.
    d. None of the above are sunk costs.

2. Which of the following costs would not be considered relevant variables in short-term decision-making?
    a. the benefit provided by the next best alternative to the decision being considered
    b. incremental revenues that differ between the two alternatives
    c. incremental costs that differ between the two alternatives
    d. the amount of money spent last year on the project

Study Guide: Introduction to Accounting, An Integrated Approach

3. The Weststar Company manufactures and sells short-block engines. Budgeted sales and cost data for the year is as follows:

	Total
Sales price	$800,000
Direct materials	300,000
Direct labor	100,000
Unit-related overhead	50,000
Contribution margin	350,000
Product-sustaining costs	140,000
Facility-sustaining costs (allocated)	60,000
Net profit	$150,000

Budgeted data is based on projected sales of 1,000 engines. Westar has received a special order from a company in Germany for 300 engines at a sales price of $600 each. Westar has the plant capacity to accept the order. If the order is accepted, Westar will incur additional shipping costs of $50 per engine. If the order is accepted, the effect on Westar's net income will be an

_____.

    a. increase by $35,000
    b. increase by $60,000
    c. increase by $30,000
    d. increase by $105,000

4. Which of the following is not a qualitative factor that must be considered by a manufacturing firm in a make-or-buy decisions?
    a. quality of product
    b. reliability of supplier
    c. employee moral
    d. cost of product

5. Which of the following would not be considered a manufacturing overhead cost?
    a. direct labor
    b. indirect materials
    c. utilities for factory building
    d. indirect labor

6. Maritz Manufacturing makes a product that includes the component, elcon. Total budgeted costs of producing elcon for the coming year are included below:

	Total Cost	Unit Cost
Direct materials	$200,000	$10
Direct labor	240,000	12
Unit-related overhead	180,000	$ 9
Batch-related costs	70,000	
Facility-sustaining costs	$300,000	

Maritz is considering using a sub-contractor to supply elcon at a price of $40 per unit. If Maritz purchases the product from the outside supplier, facility-sustaining costs will remain unchanged. What will be the effect on net income if the product is purchased rather than produced?
    a. decrease by $180,000
    b. decrease by $110,000
    c. increase by $120,000
    d. increase by $190,000

7. Which of the following is not an assumption of cost-volume-profit analysis?
    a. In the short-run, facilities can be expanded or abandoned.
    b. Selling price remains constant per unit regardless of the volume sold.
    c. Variable cost remains constant per unit regardless of the volume produced and sold.
    d. For manufacturing firms, the number of units produced equals the number of units sold.

Use the following information for the next four problems:

Ducks Limited sells handcrafted duck decoys for $50. A supplier has agreed to sell the decoys to Ducks Limited for $24 per decoy. The company rents all of its office equipment and it's building for $3,000 per month. All salespersons work for a straight commission of $2 per decoy sold.

8. The contribution margin ratio is _____.

    a. 32%
    b. 48%
    c. 52%
    d. 54%

9. The breakeven point in terms of units sold per month is _____.
    a. 125 units
    b. 150 units
    c. 200 units
    d. 300 units

10. If the company's goal is to generate $15,000 in pre-tax profits per month, its total dollar sales must be _____.
   a. $25,500
   b. $35,000
   c. $37,500
   d. $54,000

11. Assume that the company is subject to a 30% tax rate and its goal is to generate $7,000 per month in after-tax profits. How many units must Ducks Limited sell (round up)?
   a. 512
   b. 542
   c. 612
   d. 987

12. Mirex sells a product for $50 per unit. The variable cost per unit is $20 and total fixed costs are $120,000 per year. Mirex's supplier has indicated that cost per unit will increase to $22 next year. As a result of the cost increase, Mirex's new breakeven point in terms of sales dollars will be _____.
   a. $200,000
   b. $214,286
   c. $217,680
   d. $222,567

13. ABC company currently operates two product lines. The operating results for the last period are as follows:

	Product 1	Product 2
Unit sales	20,000	30,000
Sales	$800,000	$ 600,000
Cost of sales	300,000	420,000
Contribution margin	500,000	180,000
Selling and administrative costs	230,000	270,000
Net profit/<loss>	$ 270,000	<$ 90,000>

Additional analysis reveals that $300,000 of facility-sustaining selling and administrative costs is allocated equally between the two products. The remaining costs are assumed to vary with the number of units sold. If product 2 is deleted, profits will _____.
   a. increase by $60,000
   b. increase by $30,000
   c. increase by $90,000
   d. decrease by $60,000

Problem III

The following is a list of important ideas and key concepts from the chapter. To test your knowledge of these terms, match the term with the definition by placing the number in the space provided.

_____ Direct labor   _____ Opportunity cost
_____ Direct material   _____ Product cost
_____ Incremental cost   _____ Product-sustaining cost
_____ Incremental profit   _____ Relevant variable
_____ Indirect labor   _____ Sunk cost
_____ Manufacturing overhead   _____ Unit-related cost
_____ Nonproduct cost

1. A cost or revenue that will occur in the future and that differs among the alternatives considered

2. The cost of production employees who do not physically manufacture the product

3. A past cost and, therefore, never relevant in a short-term operating decisions

4. The difference between the incremental revenues and incremental costs of a particular alternative

5. The additional cost associated with an alternative

6. A cost that varies with the number of units

7. A benefit foregone when choosing one alternative over another

8. A cost that varies with the number of product lines

9. A cost that is incurred to obtain or manufacture a product

10. A cost that is related to selling the product and services or administering the company

11. The cost of materials that are directly traceable to the product and that are costly enough to warrant tracing them

12. All costs other than direct materials and direct labor that are incurred to manufacture products

13. The cost of employees who manufacture the product

Problem IV

In the space provided, indicate whether the cost will be considered a product (P) or a nonproduct (NP) cost.

_____1. Freight-in on raw materials purchased
_____2. Cost of placing an advertisement in a local newspaper
_____3. Indirect labor
_____4. Depreciation on the manufacturing plant
_____5. Shipping costs on merchandise sold
_____6. Receptionist salary (for the President)
_____7. Direct materials
_____8. Salaries of plant workers
_____9. Utilities in the administrative headquarters
_____10. Indirect materials

Problem V

1. Fox Company currently operates two product lines, A and B. The operating results for the last period are as follows:

	A	B
Unit sales	10,000	20,000
Sales	$500,000	$400,000
Cost of sales	350,000	175,000
Contribution margin	150,000	225,000
Selling and administrative costs	175,000	150,000
Net profit/<loss>	<$ 25,000>	$ 75,000

Additional analysis reveals that $250,000 of facility-sustaining selling and administrative costs are allocated equally between the two products. The remaining costs are assumed to vary with the number of units sold. Should product line A be deleted since it does not contribute to overall profitability?

2. Ferris manufacturing, which makes transformers, is operating at full capacity of 10,000 transformers a year. Contribution margin per unit sold is $300. Ferris currently makes the casing but is considering purchasing the part from an outside supplier. Current manufacturing costs as follows:

	Total Cost of Casing	Unit Cost
Direct materials	$180,000	$18
Direct labor	150,000	15
Unit-related overhead	70,000	$ 7
Batch-related costs	20,000	
Facility-sustaining costs	$100,000	

The part will cost $105 each if purchased from an outside supplier. If the part were purchased, 3,000 additional transformers could be produced and sold. Should the company continue to make the casing or purchase it from an outside supplier?

3. Yourhat Inc. has just started a business which makes custom hats for sports teams. Hats are purchased from suppliers for $4.50 per hat. Yourhat then makes a team logo that is sewn on the hat at a total cost of $1.50 per hat. Yourhat's only other costs are annual fixed costs estimated to be $30,000. Based on a marketing study, Yourhat expects to be able to sell its hats for $10 each.

a. How many hats will have to be sold for Yourhat to break even?

b. If Yourhat wishes to reach an annual pre-tax profit of $200,000, its total dollar sales must be how much?

c. Assume that Yourhat is subject to a 35% effective tax rate. How many hats must be sold to earn after-tax profits of $175,000?

d. Congress is currently considering adopting a flat tax of 20%. If such legislation was adopted, how many hats must be sold to earn the $175,000 in profits referred to in (c) above?

Solutions for Chapter 4

Problem 1

1. T
2. F
3. F
4. F
5. T

6. F
7. T
8. T
9. F
10. T

Problem II

1. c
2. d
3. c
4. d
5. a
6. b

7. a
8. b
9. a
10. c
11. b
12. b
13. d

Problem III

13 Direct labor
11 Direct materials
 5 Incremental cost
 4 Incremental profit
 2 Indirect labor
12 Manufacturing overhead
10 Nonproduct costs

 7 Opportunity costs
 9 Product costs
 8 Product-sustaining costs
 1 Relevant variable
 3 Sunk costs
 6 Unit-related costs

Problem IV

1. P
2. NP
3. P
4. P
5. NP

6. NP
7. P
8. P
9. NP
10. P

Problem V

1.

	Alternatives		Incremental Change
	A and B	B only	
Sales	$900,000	$400,000	
Variable cost of sales	525,000	175,000	
Variable selling cost	75,000	25,000	
Contribution margin	$300,000	$200,000	<$100,000>

Note: Facility-sustaining selling and administrative costs are not included in the analysis because they do not differ between the alternatives.

Fox should keep both product lines. Eliminating product A would result in a $100,000 decrease in net profit.

2.

	Alternatives		Incremental Change
Relevant factors	Make	Buy	
Revenues	$ - 0 -	$ 705,000	$ 705,000
Costs:			
Direct materials costs	180,000		180,000
Direct labor	150,000		150,000
Unit-related overhead	70,000		70,000
Batch-related overhead	20,000		20,000
Purchase price of casings		1,050,000	<1,050,000>
Profit			$ 75,000

Note: The contribution margin on the 3,000 additional units will only be $235 (($300 - ($105 - $40)) due to the increased cost of the part if purchased. Therefore, the increase in the contribution margin is $705,000 (3,000 units x $235).

The analysis indicates that Ferris should purchase the casings from the outside supplier. The increased profits due to freed-up capacity more than offset the additional costs paid for the parts.

3. a.

$$\frac{FC}{CMPU} = Q \qquad \frac{\$30,000}{\$4.00} = 7,500 \text{ units}$$

b.

$$\frac{FC + P}{CMR} = \$ \qquad \frac{\$30,000 + \$200,000}{.40} = \$575,000$$

c.

$$\frac{FC + \dfrac{P}{(1\text{-Tax rate})}}{CMPU} = Q \qquad \frac{\$30,000 + \dfrac{\$175,000}{(1 \ - \ .35)}}{\$4.00} = 74,808$$

d.

$$\frac{FC + \dfrac{P}{(1\text{-Tax rate})}}{CMPU} = Q \qquad \frac{\$30,000 + \dfrac{\$175,000}{(1 \ - \ .20)}}{\$4.00} = 62,188$$

Study Guide: Introduction to Accounting, An Integrated Approach

Chapter 5
Strategic Planning Regarding Operating Processes

Chapter Overview

Chapter 5 discusses the process of determining selling prices and explains how various pricing strategies are used to determine selling prices. The chapter also focuses on expenditure process activities related to inventory. It concludes by describing a variety of compensation packages offered to employees.

Knowledge of pricing strategies will help you understand why companies set their introductory product prices as they do. You can use your knowledge to be a better, more-informed consumer. Although you do not have to perform calculus computations, the EOQ inventory model provides an example of the application of calculus to a business issue. Relate the discussion of employee compensation to your own work experience. The discussion of employee bonuses can be linked to the current controversy regarding CEO compensation.

Read and Recall Questions

Learning Objective:
LO. 1 Describe the process of determining selling prices and demonstrate how various strategies are used to determine selling price.

Identify the factors that may affect the selling price.

Explain how a change in the selling price affects demand for a staple item and a luxury item.

How does product quality and service affect demand for a product?

Describe the following competitive environments:

- Pure competition

- Monopolistic competition

- Monopoly

- Oligopoly

Define the following legally or socially unacceptable pricing practices:

- Price fixing

- Price gouging

What is a cost-based pricing policy?

Describe the two primary pricing strategies used by companies.

Define penetration pricing.

Why are predatory pricing and dumping illegal pricing practices?

Explain the rationale for skimming pricing.

Define life-cycle pricing. Which costs must be estimated when using life-cycle pricing?

Discuss the steps used in target pricing.

Identify the four primary reasons for maintaining inventory.

Identify the two primary reasons for not maintaining inventory.

Briefly explain the following two inventory-related costs:

- Ordering costs

- Carrying costs

Study Guide: Introduction to Accounting, An Integrated Approach

Explain the purpose of the economic order quantity (EOQ) model.

Identify the assumptions of the EOQ model.

What is the formula for the EOQ model?

Define the reorder point. What is the formula for the reorder point.

Briefly describe the just-in-time (JIT) inventory model.

83

JIT has a number of implications for a company. Discuss the implications of JIT on quality, suppliers, employees, and customers.

Identify the goals of a JIT system.

Learning Objective:
LO. 3 Discuss the process of determining the compensation package offered to employees and calculate wages and bonuses paid to employees.

Briefly describe the following pay plans:

- Piece-rate pay

- Commission pay

- Hourly pay

- Salary pay

Study Guide: Introduction to Accounting, An Integrated Approach

Distinguish between gross pay and net pay.

Why do companies pay for health and life insurance for their employees and subsidize insurance payments for the employees' families?

Why do companies offer paid leave to employees?

What is a bonus and why is a bonus offered?

Define the following bonus-related terms:

- Bonus rate

- Bonus base

Outline of Key Concepts

I. Setting the selling price has long-term consequences.
    A. Selling price may affect and be affected by the following factors and will be reflected in balanced scorecard perspectives:
       1. Quantity demanded by customers (customer perspective).
       2. Quantity supplied by competitors (learning & growth perspective).
       3. Legal, social, and political factors (learning & growth perspective).
       4. Company's costs in the long run (internal perspective).
    B. Selling prices affect a customer's willingness to purchase good and services.
       1. If the selling price of a product increases, the quantity of the product demanded decreases.
       2. If the selling price of the product decreases, the quantity of the product demanded decreases.
       3. Selling price does not affect the demand for a staple item as much as a luxury item.
       4. Product quality and service also affect demand.
    C. Competitive environment affects selling price and quantities supplied.
       1. Pure competition—environment where a large number of sellers produce and distribute virtually identical products and services.
       2. Monopolistic competition—environment where many companies produce similar, but not identical, products.
          a. Companies can influence selling prices by advertising, quality, and service.
       3. Monopoly—a company that has exclusive control over a product, service, or geographic market.
          a. Government imposes legal constraints on monopolies.
       4. Oligopoly—a few firms control the types of product and services and their distribution.
          a. Price fixing—a group of companies agree to limit supply and charge identical prices for their goods and services.
          b. Price gouging—practice of setting excessively high price with the intent of reaping short-term excessive profits.
    D. Selling prices must be high enough to cover all costs and provide a profit to owners.
       1. Markup—an additional amount added to the cost of products and services.
          a. Selling price = Cost + (Cost x Markup percentage)
    E. Generally companies determine prices based on one of two strategies.
       1. Set prices based on the market, subject to the constraint that it is necessary to cover the long-run costs of the company.
       2. Set prices based on costs, subject to the constraints of customers, competitors, and legal/social factors.
       3. There are a variety of pricing schemes used with these strategies.

Study Guide: Introduction to Accounting, An Integrated Approach

a. Penetration pricing—the company sets its selling price low in an attempt to gain market share with the intention to increase its selling price in the future.

b. Skimming pricing—the company initially sets a high price for its product with the intention of lowering its price later.

F. Life-cycle pricing—a company attempts to establish a selling price that can be maintained throughout the life of the product.

1. The price may initially be below its initial costs, but as production efficiency improves cost will decline.

2. Company must understand and estimate all the costs over the life cycle from research and development through customer service.

G. Target pricing—based on the concept of maintaining a constant price over the product's life cycle, but it is market based.

1. The company first determines the selling price based on market surveys.

2. Next it determines the markup needed to provide a sufficient return to stockholders.

3. Third, it takes the selling price less the required markup to determine the target cost.

4. The goal is to produce products in a cost-effective manner to achieve an adequate return for the owners.

II. Determining appropriate levels of inventory is a critical activity of the conversion process.

A. Companies maintain inventories for four primary reasons.

1. To meet customer demand.

2. To smooth production scheduling.

3. To take advantage of quantity discounts.

4. To hedge against price increases.

B. There are two main reasons to not maintain inventory.

1. Costs associated with holding inventory.

2. Inventories hide problems with quality.

C. Inventory planning is a process of balancing costs of ordering inventory against the costs of carrying inventory.

1. Ordering costs—costs incurred to place one additional order.

2. Carrying costs—costs incurred to carry one additional unit in inventory for the period.

D. Economic Order Quantity Model (EOQ) minimizes the total of short-term ordering costs plus short-term carrying costs for the period.

1. EOQ model is based on several assumptions.

a. Demand is uniform throughout the year.

b. Lead-time is constant throughout the year.

c. Entire order is received at the same time.

d. No quantity discounts are available.

e. Inventory size is not limited.

f. Batch-related, product-sustaining, and facility-sustaining storage costs are irrelevant.

2. Reorder point—inventory level that, when reached, indicates the need to place an order for additional inventory.

a. Reorder point = (daily demand x lead time) + Safety stock

E. Just-in-Time Model (JIT)—long-run model based on the principle that inventory should arrive just as needed for production in the quantities needed.

1. The best decision is to maintain zero or minimal inventories.

2. Is a pull system in that production is determined by customer demand and the need for raw materials is determined by production.

3. Implications of a JIT model.

a. Sales estimates must be accurate.

b. Production must be with zero defects.

c. Must have a strong relationship with suppliers.

d. Must have a good relationship with employees.

e. Production often arranged in cells with smaller production runs.

f. Must have a good relationship with and understand customers.

4. Goals of JIT are as follows:

a. Eliminate disruptions in production.

b. Reduce or eliminate nonvalue-added activities.

c. Minimize inventory.

III. Employee compensation packages are a significant aspect of the expenditure process.

A. Companies pay their employees using a variety of plans.

1. Piece-rate pay—employee receives compensation based on the number of items completed.

2. Commission pay—usually a percentage of net sales or contribution margin.

3. Hourly pay—employee is paid a certain amount per hour with, perhaps, more per hour for overtime.

4. Salary pay—compensation based on a fixed amount per period, typically per month.

5. Plans may be used in combination.

B. Gross pay—full amount the employee earns.

1. Net pay—employee's take-home pay.

a. Gross pay less federal and state income taxes, FICA withholdings, voluntary withholdings, pensions, charitable contributions, medical and life insurance, and union dues.

C. Health and life insurance is offered by companies to recruit and retain better employees at a lower overall cost to the company.

D. Paid leave is offered to help attract and retain better employees.

1. Includes sick leave, vacations, and family leave.

E. Bonus—is a fringe benefit, or a part of the company's compensation plan, that is contingent on the occurrence of some future event.
  1. Sales employees may be given bonuses if sales targets are met or exceeded.
  2. Production employees may be given bonuses if production quotas are met.
  3. Upper-level managers are based on broader organizational measures such as net income.
      a. Bonus rate—percentage the bonus will pay.
      b. Bonus base—the form of income the bonus rate is applied to.
      c. Bonus based on income before bonus or income taxes.
      d. Bonus based on income before income taxes.
      e. Bonus based on net income.

Problem I

Indicate whether the following statements are either true (T) or false (F).

_____1. As the price for a product is increased, the demand for that product will also increase.
_____2. Under a JIT inventory system, little or no inventory is maintained.
_____3. The level of safety stock will not affect the economic order quantity.
_____4. In a purely competitive market, a company will be a price taker.
_____5. The most common form of compensation is commission pay.
_____6. A life-cycle pricing strategy may result in losses in the early stages of the product's life.
_____7. Bonuses are forms of compensation contingent on the occurrence of some specified future event.
_____8. Under piece-rate pay, employee compensation is based on the number of items completed.
_____9. When hourly pay is used, compensation is dependent of the amount of work completed.
_____10. The economic order quantity model assumes that demand is uniform throughout the year.

Problem II

Indicate the correct answer by circling the appropriate letter.

1. An environment in which a few firms control the types or distribution of products and services is a/an _____.
   - a. monopoly
   - b. oligopoly
   - c. cartel
   - d. none of the above

2. Which of the following is not a primary influence on a company's selling price?
   - a. competition
   - b. legal constraints
   - c. product costs
   - d. all of the above are primary influences

3. Glutton Motor Company uses a cost-based pricing policy in determining the sales prices of its cars. Glutton requires of all of its salespersons a minimum markup of 20 percent. If a new Ford Explorer cost Glutton $27,000, what is the minimum sales price that will be approved by management?
   - a. $27,000
   - b. $28,500
   - c. $29,460
   - d. $32,400

4. Inflex Corporation has finished the design of a new high-resolution computer monitor. To gain market share, Inflex intends to sell the monitor below its cost of production. After a 5 percent market share has been attained, it will raise its price. What price setting strategy is Inflex practicing?
   - a. penetration pricing
   - b. life-cycle pricing
   - c. target pricing
   - d. none of the above

5. Richie Rich is paid a bonus equal to 3 percent of income before taxes. If the company's income before taxes and the bonus was $3,000,000, Richie's bonus will be _____.
   - a. $90,000
   - b. $83,600
   - c. $87,379
   - d. $91,348

Study Guide: Introduction to Accounting, An Integrated Approach

6. Which of the following is not true about compensation in the form of salary pay?
    a. The amount is fixed per pay period.
    b. The amount of pay is independent of the hours worked.
    c. The amount of pay is independent of the amount of work completed.
    d. The amount is usually based on the amount of revenue generated.

7. Mary Minter receives a bonus each year equal to 6 percent of income before income taxes. During the year, the company reported income before taxes (and the bonus) of $600,000. The company's effective income tax rate is 40 percent. What will Mary receive as a bonus for the year?
    a. $36,000
    b. $21,600
    c. $32,841
    d. $33,962

8. Which of the following is not a reason for a company to maintain inventory?
    a. To meet customer demand.
    b. To smooth production scheduling
    c. To reduce warehouse costs.
    d. To take advantage of quantity discounts.

9. Assume that a company's annual demand for its product is 200,000 units, the ordering cost is $175 per order, and the carrying cost is $10 per unit in inventory per year. What is the economic order quantity?
    a. 2,646
    b. 3,189
    c. 1,756
    d. 5,276

Problem III

The following is a list of important ideas and key concepts from the chapter. To test your knowledge of these terms, match the term with the definition by placing the number in the space provided.

_____	Bonus	_____	Oligopoly
_____	Commission pay	_____	Penetration pricing
_____	Dumping	_____	Piece-rate pay
_____	Kanban system	_____	Predatory pricing
_____	Lead time	_____	Price fixing
_____	Life-cycle pricing	_____	Price gouging
_____	Markup	_____	Pure competition
_____	Monopolistic competition	_____	Skimming pricing
_____	Monopoly	_____	Target pricing

1. Selling products below cost in a foreign market

2. The environment where a few firms control the types of products and services and their distribution

3. A pricing strategy where a company sets its initial selling price low in an attempt to gain a share of the market from its competitors

4. A pull system that uses cards to visually signal the need for inventory

5. Payment for services rendered based on the number of items completed

6. A pricing strategy where the company first determines the selling price of the product and then decides whether to enter the market

7. A company that has exclusive control over a product, service, or geographic market

8. The number of days elapsing from the time an order is placed until the order is received

9. An environment where a large number of sellers produce and distribute virtually identical products and services

10. A pricing strategy where the company attempts to set a selling price for the life of the product based on its total life-cycle costs

11. The practice of setting excessively high prices

Study Guide: Introduction to Accounting, An Integrated Approach

12. An additional amount over cost that is added to determine selling price

13. A pricing strategy in which the company sets its initial selling price high in an attempt to appeal to those individuals who want to be the first to have the product and who are not concerned about price

14. An environment in which there are many companies whose products/services are similar but not identical

15. A fringe benefit contingent on the occurrence of some future event

16. When a group of companies agree to limit supply and charge identical prices

17. Payment for services rendered based on a percentage of revenue generated

18. The practice of selling products below cost in an attempt to drive out competition, control the market, and then raise prices

Problem IV

Complete the following sentences by filling in the correct response.

1. As the price for a company's product is decreased, the demand for the product will
_____.

2. In a purely competitive market, prices are a function of _____ and _____.

3. Legal constraints are more likely to be imposed on industries whose competitive environment
is either a _____ or an _____.

4. Group health insurance rates will typically be _____ than individual rates.

5. Commission pay is usually based on _____ or _____.

6. In the long run, a company must set a price that covers its _____ and provides a
_____ to the owners.

7. A _____ discount is a reduced purchase price due to volume.

8. The economic order quantity model is a mathematical model that minimizes the total of short-
term _____ and _____ costs for the period.

Problem V

Use the following information to calculate the bonus under the assumptions given:

Income before income taxes	$2,200,000
Effective income tax rate	35%
Bonus rate	5%

1. The bonus is based on income before the bonus or income taxes.

2. The bonus is based on income before income taxes.

3. The bonus is based on net income.

Solutions for Chapter 5

Problem 1

1. F	6. T
2. T	7. T
3. T	8. T
4. T	9. F
5. F	10. T

Problem II

1. b	6. d
2. d	7. d
3. d	8. c
4. a	9. a
5. c	

Problem III

15	Bonus	2	Oligopoly
17	Commission pay	3	Penetration pricing
1	Dumping	5	Piece-rate pay
4	Kanban system	18	Predatory pricing
8	Lead time	16	Price fixing
10	Life-cycle pricing	11	Price gouging
12	Markup	9	Pure competitions
14	Monopolistic competition	13	Skimming pricing
7	Monopoly	6	Target pricing

Problem IV

1. increase
2. supply, demand
3. monopoly, oligopoly
4. lower
5. net sales, contribution margin
6. costs, profit
7. quantity
8. ordering, carrying

Problem V

1. $2,200,000 X .05 = $110,000

2. ($2,200,000 - B) X .05 = B
   $110,000 - .05B = B
   $110,000 = 1.05B
   Bonus = $104,762

3. B = ($2,200,000 - B - T) X .05

   T = ($2,200,000 - B) X .35
   T = $770,000 - .35B

   B = ($2,200,000 - B - $770,000 + .35B) X .05
   B = $71,500 - .0325B
   1.0325B = $71,500
   Bonus = $69,249

Chapter 6
Planning, the Balanced Scorecard, and Budgeting

Chapter Overview

Budgets are an important part of the planning process. This chapter explains why companies use budgets and describes the benefits and costs associated with the budgeting process. It also describes various budgeting strategies used by companies. In addition, the chapter illustrates the types of budgets used by companies in the revenue, conversion, and expenditure processes.

There is no need to feel overwhelmed when you study the many different budgets illustrated in this chapter. You should not attempt to memorize the budgets themselves. You should learn the purpose of each budget and which types of information appear on each. Focus on the interrelationships among the budgets and understand how they link together with the planning process and the balanced scorecard. You may need to be able to construct the various budgets, but try to learn how to complete one type of budget at a time. Tackle the exercises that first focus on one or two of the budgets. Then try a problem that covers a linked set of budgets. It may take some time before you are comfortable with the budgets, but studying the budgeting process will help you better understand how businesses do their planning.

Read and Recall Questions

Learning Objective:
LO.1 Describe the purposes, strategies, and approaches to budgeting.

Briefly describe the budgeting process.

What is the primary purpose of a budget?

Identify the benefits and costs associated with the budgeting process.

Define budgetary slack. Why are employees motivated to introduce slack into budgets?

Distinguish between mandated and participatory budgeting.

Define the following terms:

- Ideal standard

- Normal standard

Briefly discuss the advantages and disadvantages of incremental budgeting.

Briefly discuss the advantages and disadvantages of zero-based budgeting.

Briefly describe the master budget.

Identify the first step in revenue process planning.

Explain how the customer perspective of the balanced scorecard impacts a company's planning process and goal setting.

Describe the information that appears in a sales budget.

101

What is the purpose of a cash receipts schedule?

What is an accounts receivable schedule? How is the ending accounts receivable balance calculated?

What is the purpose of the marketing and distribution budget?

Learning Objective:
LO. 3 Discuss the process of conversion process planning and prepare the resulting budget.

How can efficiency and quality goals be measured?

Briefly describe how to prepare a production budget.

Identify two internal process and learning and growth goals for the expenditure process.

Which costs appear on the administrative budget?

What is the purpose of the direct labor and manufacturing overhead budget?

Briefly describe the direct materials purchases budget.

Explain the purpose of the cash disbursements schedule.

Why doesn't depreciation appear on the cash disbursement schedule?

What is the purpose of the accounts payable schedule. How is the estimated ending balance in accounts payable determined?

Outline of Key Concepts

I. Budgeting—the process of expressing a company's goals and objectives from its balanced scorecard perspectives in quantitative terms.
  A. Budget—plan for the future expressed in quantitative terms.
      1. Primary purpose is to present and describe the financial ramifications of plans for the future.
  B. Benefits, costs, and effects of budgeting.
      1. Aids communication and coordination among divisions or functions to enhance the company's ability to operate effectively and efficiently.
      2. Aids resource allocation by ensuring that information is available to help managers determine which activities should receive the limited resources of the company.
      3. Serves as a benchmark against which to evaluate and control actual performance.
          a. When budgeted and actual performance differs, management looks for the causes of the variation.
      4. Budgeting is time consuming and consumes large amounts of human capital.
      5. Rigid adherence to the budget can inhibit a company's ability to respond quickly to changes in the environment.
      6. Affects the motivation and behavior of individuals.
          a. Budgetary slack—deliberately introduced bias by those who fear the consequences of not meeting the budget.
          b. Overestimate the time or cost to complete an activity to protect themselves from unanticipated cost increases.
          c. Budget manipulation arises from incentives tied to meeting the budget or anticipation of budget adjustments by upper management.
          d. Employees may resist the budget if it is perceived to be unrealistic.
  C. There are several approaches to budgeting.
      1. Mandated budgeting—known as top-down budgeting because top management develops the budget and passes them down the organizational hierarchy without input from lower levels of management and employees.

a. Ideal standard—can be achieved if operating conditions are almost perfect; no allowance for operating inefficiencies.

b. Normal standard—can be achieved under practical operating conditions and allows for normal operating inefficiencies.

c. Eliminates the problem of budgetary slack and better aligns company goals and activities to achieve those goals.

d. Employees may resist mandated budgets.

2. Participatory budgeting—known as bottom-up budgeting because the budgeting process begins at lower levels of the organizational hierarchy and continues up through the organization to top management.

a. Provides a wealth of information from throughout the organization.

b. Budgetary slack may be a problem.

c. Usually increases employee motivation.

3. Incremental budgeting—strategy that uses the prior period's budget as a starting point in preparing this period's budget.

a. May lead to increasing budget requests each period.

4. Zero-based budgeting—strategy that begins each budget period with a zero budget and requires consideration of every activity undertaken by the department or segment.

D. Master budget—the compilation of all the budgets and schedules prepared in planning for the revenue, conversion, and expenditure processes.

1. Culminates with the budgeted financial statements.

II. Revenue process planning begins with an estimate of sales volume given the expected selling price.

A. Companies measure the customer perspective of the balanced scorecard along two dimensions.

1. Customer satisfaction—measured by increasing the number of customers, increasing market share, and enhancing company image.

2. Customer loyalty—measured by increasing customer retention and increasing revenue per customer.

B. Sales budget—shows the expected sales for the period in both physical and financial amounts for a particular product line, geographic area, or sales manager.

1. Develop the sales budget in light of the balanced scorecard measures it wants to use.

C. Cash receipts schedule—shows the anticipated cash collections from customers for the period.

1. Must consider what amount will be collected from customers and when it will be collected

D. Accounts receivable schedule—indicates the changes expected in the balance of accounts receivable during the budget period.

1. Planning and controlling accounts receivable is an aspect of the internal perspective.
   E. Marketing and distribution budget—indicates the planned expenditures for marketing, advertising, and selling activities.
      1. Plans in this area are part of the internal process perspective.

III. Conversion process planning includes goals related to efficiency and quality.
   A. These goals are part of the internal process perspective.
      1. Efficiency can be monitored with customer response time.
      2. Quality can be controlled by planning the relative expenditures for prevention and appraisal quality costs versus internal and external failure quality costs.
   B. Production budget—uses information from the sales budget plus the company's desired ending inventory level to determine the quantity of finished goods to produce each period.
      1. After the production budget is completed, the company can prepare its cost of goods sold and finished goods schedule.

IV. Expenditure process planning considers the use and payment for services and goods.
   A. Administrative budget—reflects the expected administrative costs, including administrative labor.
      1. Reflects the costs of activities not considered in the revenue or conversion process.
   B. Direct labor and manufacturing overhead budget—reflects the expected costs of the conversion process.
   C. Direct materials purchases budget—shows the expected quantity and cost of direct materials purchases for the period.
      1. Information from the production budget is a key input to this budget.
   D. Cash disbursements schedule—shows the expected cash outflows during the period.
      1. Before preparing this schedule, the company must determine how much money is owed and when it is due.
      2. Depreciation is an allocation of cost and does not require a cash payment.
   E. Accounts payable schedule—indicates the expected changes in the balance of accounts payable during the period.
      1. Items may be purchased on one period and paid for in a different period.

Problem I

Indicate whether the following statements are either true (T) or false (F).

_____1. The primary purpose of a budget is to present and describe the financial ramifications of plans for the future.
_____2. Budgeting is unnecessary for not-for-profit entities.
_____3. The budgeting process promotes communication and coordination among divisions or departments within a company.
_____4. An ideal standard can be achieved under practical operating conditions.
_____5. Upper management sets mandated budgets.
_____6. Incremental budgeting tends to be less time consuming than zero-based budgeting.
_____7. Every budgeting process has both benefits and costs.
_____8. The purpose of mandated budgets is to set operating budgets that are in line with goals of upper management.
_____9. Participatory budgeting in known as the top-down approach.
_____10. The production budget is developed as a part of the revenue process planning.

Problem II

Indicate the correct answer by circling the appropriate letter.

Use the following information for the first three questions:

Alnon Inc. manufactures and sells aluminum gates. Each gate requires 10 pounds of high-grade cast aluminum. The quarterly production budget for the first year of operations is as follows:

	1st Qtr	2nd Qtr	3rd Qtr	4th Qtr
Gates to be produced	11,000	15,000	12,000	9,000

1. Alnon has no raw materials on hand at the beginning of the first quarter. Alnon's policy is to maintain an ending inventory equal to 10% of the next quarter's estimated production. How many pounds of aluminum must Alnon purchase in the second quarter?

    a. 147,000 lbs.
    b. 150,000 lbs.
    c. 167,000 lbs.

107

d. 135,000 lbs.

2. High-grade aluminum costs $1 per pound. Alnon pays for 50% of its purchases within the discount period (2/10,n/30) and another 30% are paid within the same quarter but after the discount period. The remaining 20% of the quarterly purchases are paid in the next quarter. Budgeted raw materials cash disbursements for the first quarter are _____.

    a. $98,750
    b. $100,000
    c. $110,000
    d. $122,500

3. The projected balance in accounts payable at the end of the second quarter will be _____.

    a. $31,600
    b. $26,700
    c. $48,000
    d. $29,400

Use the following information for the next three questions:

All-Tire manufacturing company projects sales of 10,000, 14,000, and 18,000 tires, respectively, in its first three months of operations. All-Tire's bills customers on the first of the following month and credit terms are 3/10,n/30 from the invoice date. Forty percent of its customers are expected to pay within the discount period. An additional 50 percent will pay within 30 days (but after the discount period) and the remaining 10 percent will pay within 60 days. Tires sell for $50 each.

4. What is All-Tire's expected cash receipts for the second month?

    a. $444,000
    b. $450,000
    c. $397,000
    d. $500,000

5. What is All-Tire's expected cash receipts for the third month?

    a. $1,028,600
    b. $900,000
    c. $671,600
    d. $593,560

6. What is All-Tire's projected accounts receivable balance at the end of the second month?

    a. $1,200,000
    b. $750,000
    c. $1,150,000
    d. $450,000

Study Guide: Introduction to Accounting, An Integrated Approach

7. Which of the following is not a primary benefit of budgeting?

    a. more effective planning
    b. improved communication and coordination between departments
    c. enhanced resource allocation
    d. all of the above are primary benefits of budgeting

8. Ajax Company produces high-grade titanium baseball bats that sell for $300. January sales are estimated to be 2,000 bats with sales increasing by 10 percent per month for the first year of operations. What is the estimated sales revenue for the second quarter of the year?

    a. $3,245867
    b. $2,643,366
    c. $1,800,000
    d. $2,987,345

9. Flexlink estimates sales of $600,000, $500,000 and $900,000 for the first three months of operations. Flexlink's management estimates the following collection pattern:

    40 percent in the month of the sale
    50 percent in the month following the sale
    8 percent in the second month after the sale
    2 percent uncollectible

What are the expected cash collections for the third month of operations?

    a. $712,000
    b. $623,000
    c. $456,000
    d. $658,000

Problem III

Following is a list of important ideas and key concepts from the chapter. To test your knowledge of these terms, match the term with the definition by placing the number in the space provided.

_____ Budgeting   _____ Normal standard
_____ Budgetary slack   _____ Participatory budgeting
_____ Ideal standard   _____ Production budget
_____ Incremental budgeting   _____ Sales budget
_____ Master budgeting   _____ Zero-based budgeting

1. The compilation of all the budgets/schedules prepared in planning for the revenue, conversion, and expenditure process

2. The difference between a chosen estimate of revenues or expenses and a realistic estimate

3. A budget that uses information from the sales budget plus the company's desired ending inventory level to determine the quantity of finished goods to produce each period

4. A budgeting strategy in which the company begins each budget period with a zero budget and must consider all its activities proposed for the budget

5. The process of expressing the company's goals and objectives in quantitative terms

6. A budget that shows the expected sales for the period in both physical and financial amounts

7. A standard that can be achieved only if operating conditions are almost perfect

8. A budgeting approach that allows individuals who are affected by the budget to have input into the budgeting process; bottom-up budgeting

9. A budgeting strategy in which a company uses the prior period's budget as the starting point in preparing this period's budget

10. A standard that can be achieved under practical operating conditions

Study Guide: Introduction to Accounting, An Integrated Approach

Problem IV

Complete the following sentences by filling in the correct response.

1. Employee motivation normally increases in a _____ budgeting environment because employees believe that upper management values their ideas.

2. A budget serves as a useful benchmark against which to _____ and _____ actual performance.

3. _____ activities should be reduced or eliminated.

4. _____ budgeting is a top-down approach in which upper-level management sets budget levels.

5. An _____ standard does not allow for operating inefficiencies.

6. The sales budget shows expected sales in both _____ and _____ amounts.

7. The _____ _____ schedule shows the anticipated cash collections from customers for the period.

8. A budget is a plan for the future expressed in _____ terms.

9. The difference between reported budget numbers and realistic budget numbers is referred to as _____ _____.

10. _____ budgeting allows individuals affected by the budget to have input into the budgeting process.

Problem V

The following sales budget has been prepared for Bill's merchandising firm for the first three months of operation:

Sales Budget for the Period January -- March			
	January	February	March
Sales (units)	5,000	7,000	6,000
Sales (dollars)	$50,000	$70,000	$60,000

Cash sales are estimated to be 20 percent. Credit sales are billed on the first of the following month. Bill offers a 1 percent cash discount for any credit sales paid within 10 days of the billing date. Sixty percent of credit sales are paid within the discount period and another 15 percent are paid in the billing month. The remaining 5 percent of credit sales are paid in the month after billing. Bill estimates that marketing costs will average 5 percent of sales and distribution costs will be $8,000 per month and 3 percent of sales.

Required: Prepare the cash receipts schedule and the marketing and distribution budget for the first three months of the year.

Cash Receipts Schedule

	January	February	March
Cash sales (20%)			
Charge sales paid in discount period (60%)			
Charges sales paid in billing month (15%)			
Charge sales paid in month after billing (5%)			
Total cash receipts			
Cash discounts given			

Marketing and Distribution Costs Budget

	January	February	March
Marketing costs (5%)			
Variable distribution costs (3%)			
Fixed distribution costs			
Total estimated marketing and distribution costs			

Study Guide: Introduction to Accounting, An Integrated Approach

Solutions for Chapter 6

Problem 1

1. T	6. T
2. F	7. T
3. T	8. T
4. F	9. F
5. T	10. F

Problem II

1. a
2. a
3. d
4. a
5. c
6. b
7. d
8. b
9. d

Problem III

5	Budgeting	10	Normal standard
2	Budgetary slack	8	Participatory budgeting
7	Ideal standard	3	Production budget
9	Incremental budgeting	6	Sales budget
1	Master budgeting	4	Zero-based budgeting

Problem IV

1. participatory
2. evaluate, control
3. Nonvalue-added
4. Mandated
5. ideal
6. physical, financial
7. cash receipts
8. quantitative
9. budgetary slack
10. Participatory

Problem V

Cash Receipts Schedule

	January	February	March
Cash sales (20%)	$10,000	$14,000	$12,000
Charge sales paid in discount period (60%)	0	$29,700	$41,580
Charges sales paid in billing month (15%)	0	$ 7,500	$10,500
Charge sales paid in month after billing (5%)	0	0	$ 2,500
Total cash receipts	$10,000	$51,200	$66,580
Cash discounts given	0	$ 300	$ 420

Marketing and Distribution Costs Budget

	January	February	March
Marketing costs (5%)	$ 2,500	$ 3,500	$ 3,000
Variable distribution costs (3%)	$ 1,500	$ 2,100	$ 1,800
Fixed distribution costs	$ 8,000	$ 8,000	$ 8,000
Total estimated marketing and distribution costs	$12,000	$13,600	$12,800

Study Guide: Introduction to Accounting, An Integrated Approach

Chapter 7
Accounting Information Systems

Chapter Overview

Chapter 7 explains the process of identifying, analyzing, measuring, classifying, and reporting accounting events in a manual accounting system. The chapter examines the effect of accounting events on the financial statements. In addition, Chapter 7 compares and contrasts manual and computerized accounting systems.

In this chapter you will study how to identify, analyze, and record many different kinds of accounting events. Do not try to memorize these accounting events. Learn to apply general analytical principles to determine the effects of accounting events on the accounting equation and specific asset, liability, owners' equity, revenue, and expense accounts. Become familiar with the steps in the accounting cycle. Spend extra time on adjusting entries. Learn why they are necessary and be able to distinguish between accrued revenues/expenses and deferred revenues/expenses. Take the time to trace the effect of accounting events to the financial statements. The concepts you learn in this chapter form the foundation for much of the analysis you will perform in the following chapters. Time spent learning this chapter's concepts and completing homework will be rewarded in these later chapters.

Read and Recall Questions

Learning Objective:
LO. 1 Explain the impact of accounting events on the accounting equation and demonstrate how to make and post journal entries.

What is the accounting equation?

Describe a double-entry accounting system.

Identify the three characteristics of an accounting event.

If an asset decreases, identify three possible changes that must occur in the accounting equation to keep the equation in balance.

Define the term "account".

Briefly describe a chart of accounts.

Define the terms "debit" and "credit".

For each transaction, why must the debits equal the credits?

Study Guide: Introduction to Accounting, An Integrated Approach

What is the increase side of an asset? Of a liability? Of owners' equity?

What are retained earnings?

What effect does revenue have on net income? On which side are revenues increased?

What effect do expenses have on net income? On which side are expenses increased?

Define the following terms:

- Journalizing

- Journal entry

- General journal

- General ledger

- Posting

Why is an accounting event recorded in both the general journal and in the general ledger?

What is the normal balance of an asset account? A liability account? An owners' equity account?

Learning Objective:
LO.2 Describe the impact of adjusting events on the accounting equation and demonstrate how to make and post adjusting journal entries.

What is the accounting cycle?

What is an adjusting entry?

Study Guide: Introduction to Accounting, An Integrated Approach

Explain a revenue accrual.

What is the impact of a revenue deferral?

What is the impact of an expense accrual?

Explain an expense deferral.

Learning Objective:
LO. 3 Discuss the impact of closing events on the accounting equation and demonstrate how to make and post closing journal entries.

What is a trial balance? Why is a trial balance prepared?

What is the purpose of a closing entry?

Which types of accounts require closing entries?

Define a permanent account. Which types of accounts are permanent accounts?

What is a post-closing trial balance?

Learning Objective:
LO. 4 Explain and show how accounting events are reported on the financial statements.

Identify the four primary financial statements.

Explain the relationship between the income statement and the statement of retained earnings.

Study Guide: Introduction to Accounting, An Integrated Approach

Explain the relationship between the statement of retained earnings and the balance sheet.

Identify the cash flows classifications that appear on the statement of cash flows.

Explain the relationship between the statement of cash flows and the balance sheet.

<table>
<tr><td>Learning Objective:
LO. 5 Compare and contrast manual accounting systems to computer-based transaction systems and database systems.</td></tr>
</table>

Identify the shortcomings of a manual accounting system.

Identify four advantages of a computerized transaction-based accounting system.

How does a relational database system differ from the asset = liabilities + owners' equity method of organizing accounting information?

Identify the benefits of a database system.

Outline of Key Concepts

I.   Double-entry accounting is the foundation of a manual accounting system based on the accounting equation: Assets = Liabilities + Owners' Equity
   A. Accounting events have three characteristics.
      1. The event must be specific to the entity for which the accounting records are kept.
      2. The event must be measurable in monetary terms.
      3. The event must impact the entity's assets, liabilities, and/or owners' equity.
   B. Account—place where the results of events affecting that item are recorded.
      1. Chart of accounts—an organized listing of accounts used by an entity.
         a. Assets are listed first, followed by liabilities and owners' equity.
            i. Revenue and expense accounts are listed after owners' equity because they measure net income and net income is a part of owners' equity.
      2. Debit means left side of the account and credit means right side of the account.
      3. Increases to assets are recorded on the debit or left side of the account.
      4. Increases to liability and owners' equity accounts are recorded on the credit or right side of the accounts.
      5. Decreases to asset accounts are recorded on the credit or right side of the accounts.
      6. Decreases to liability and owners' equity accounts are recorded on the debit or left side of the accounts.

Study Guide: Introduction to Accounting, An Integrated Approach

7. Revenues increase net income, which increases owners' equity, therefore, revenues are increased on the credit or right side of the account.
8. Expenses decrease net income, which decreases owners' equity, therefore, expenses are increased on the debit or left side of the account.
9. The accounting equation must remain in balance after each event is recorded, and the debits must equal the credits.

C. Journalizing—recording accounting events in chronological order.
   1. Journal entry—the outcome of journalizing.
   2. General journal—record in which both the accounts to be debited and the accounts to be credited are recorded in chronological order.
   3. General ledger—a collection of specific asset, liability, and owners' equity accounts.
      a. The normal balance side of an account is the increase side of the account.
   4. Posting—process of recording the appropriate part of a journal entry to the affected account.

D. Adjusting entry—an entry that is required to update accounts for internal events and events not supported by source documents.
   1. Revenue accrual—recorded when revenues are earned in one accounting period and payment is received in a later period.
   2. Revenue deferral—occurs when a company has been paid in advance by a client or customer for services to be performed in the future.
   3. Expense accrual—recorded when expenses incurred in one accounting period and payment is made in a later period.
   4. Expense deferral—occurs when a company uses previously purchased assets in an attempt to generate revenue in future periods.

E. Trial balance—a listing of all general ledger accounts and their respective balances to ensure that debits equal credits.

F. Closing entry—prepared to close (zero-out) income statement accounts.
   1. Transfers the balance of an income statement account to an owners' equity account.
   2. Post-closing trial balance is prepared after closing entries are posted to ensure that debits equal credits to begin the new accounting period.

G. Four financial statements are required.
   1. Income statement
   2. Statement of cash flows
   3. Statement of owners' equity (retained earnings)
   4. Balance sheet

II. A review—the eight steps in the accounting cycle
A. Identify, analyze, and record events in the general journal.
B. Post general journal entries to the general ledger.
C. Prepare a trial balance.

D. Enter adjusting entries in the general journal and post them to the general ledger.
E. Prepare an adjusted trial balance.
F. Prepare financial statements.
G. Enter closing entries in the general journal and post them to the general ledger.
H. Prepare a post-closing trial balance.

III. Computer-based transaction systems are widely used.
   A. Manual accounting systems suffer from several problems.
      1. Labor intensive and inefficient.
      2. Error prone.
   B. Computerized accounting systems offer a number of advantages.
      1. Transactions can be quickly posted to the appropriate accounts, bypassing the journalizing process.
      2. Detailed listings of transactions can be printed for review at any time.
      3. Internal controls and edit checks can be used to prevent and detect errors.
      4. A wide variety of reports can be prepared.

IV. Relational database systems depart from the assets = liabilities + owners' equity method of organizing information.
   A. Information is stored in a data warehouse.
      1. The company, not the accounting equation, determines which events to record.
   B. Database systems offer a number of advantages.
      1. Reduce inefficiencies that exist in a transaction-based system.
      2. Eliminate redundancies in the company's information system.
      3. Recognize business events rather than just accounting events.

Study Guide: Introduction to Accounting, An Integrated Approach

Problem I

Indicate whether the following statements are either true (T) or false (F).

_____ 1. A credit entry to a liability account will increase the balance of the account.
_____ 2. Total debits must always equal total credits.
_____ 3. The normal balance of an asset is a debit balance.
_____ 4. A trial balance ensures that the correct accounts have been debited and credited.
_____ 5. An accrual is the result of collecting cash prior to revenue being earned or cash paid prior to the expense being incurred.
_____ 6. Total assets of a company will always equal liabilities plus owners' equity.
_____ 7. Financial statements are prepared from information provided in the adjusted trial balance.
_____ 8. All income statement accounts must be closed (zeroed out) at the end of the accounting period.
_____ 9. The income statement lists the assets, liabilities and owners' equity at the end of the accounting period.
_____ 10. A database accounting system eliminates redundancies in the accounting information system.

Problem II

Indicate the correct answer by circling the appropriate answer.

1. On June 6, Mirex Company purchased supplies to be used in the business. As a result of this accounting event, _____.
   a. assets will increase and equities will increase
   b. assets will decrease and equities will decrease
   c. assets will increase and decrease by the same amount
   d. assets will decrease and equities will increase

2. All of the following accounts will be closed at the end of the accounting period except _____.
   a. rent expense
   b. accumulated depreciation
   c. service fees
   d. interest income

3. John Q. Jones, CPA performs various tax services for clients. When will John record revenues earned in his tax practice?
   a. at the time the service is performed
   b. when the cash is received
   c. when John accepts the client
   d. all of the above are correct

4. On April 1, Ace Corporation issued stock for $200,000 cash. As a result of this accounting event, _____.
   a. assets will increase and owners' equity will increase
   b. assets will decrease and owners' equity will decrease
   c. assets will increase and decrease by the same amount
   d. assets will increase and liabilities will increase

5. Ace Corporation purchased land for $100,000 on December 2, 20X1 by paying $20,000 and issuing a note payable for the balance due. Interest is payable annually at a rate of 6 percent. What journal entry will Ace record on the date of the purchase (December 2, 20X1)?

   a. Cash   20,000
      Land   80,000
          Notes payable   100,000
   b. Land   100,000
          Cash   20,000
          Notes payable   80,000
   c. Land   100,000
          Cash   100,000
   d. Land   100,000
      Interest expense   6,000
          Cash   26,000
          Notes payable   80,000

6. Vectar Inc. received a $20,000 payment from a customer for product sold and recorded in the previous month. What journal entry will Vectar make for the receipt of the payment?
   a. debit cash and credit sales
   b. debit sales and credit cash
   c. debit accounts receivable and credit sales
   d. debit cash and credit accounts receivable

7. At the end of the accounting period, ABC Company estimates that it has used $3,500 of water and electricity since the receipt of its last bill. What adjusting entry will be required to ensure that all revenues and expenses have been recorded for the period?
   a. debit utilities expense and credit cash
   b. debit utilities expense and credit accounts payable
   c. debit cash and credit accounts payable
   d. debit accounts payable and credit utilities expense

8. Jill Jones operates several rental apartments throughout the city. On November 1st, one of her renters paid her $3,000 rent for the months of November, December and January. Jill credited unearned rent at the time of the receipt of payment. What adjusting should Jill make if she prepares financial statements every December 31st?
   a. debit unearned rent and credit rental revenue for $2,000
   a. debit rental revenue and credit cash for $2,000
   b. debit cash and credit rental revenue for $3,000
   c. debit unearned rent and credit rental revenue for $1,500

9. On June 1, JJ Company paid $5,400 for a three-year insurance policy. At the time of the payment, prepaid insurance was debited for that amount. Assuming that JJ Company prepares its financial statements on a calendar-year basis, what adjusting will need to be made at the end of the first year?
   a. debit insurance expense and credit prepaid insurance for $1,800
   b. debit insurance expense and credit prepaid insurance for $ $1,050
   c. debit cash and credit insurance expense for $2,300
   d. debit insurance expense and credit cash for $3,250

10. Which of the following would not be included in a company's post-closing trial balance?
   a. cash
   b. accounts payable
   c. retained earnings
   d. rent expense

11. Which of the following statements lists the assets, liabilities, and owners' equity at the end of the accounting period?
   a. income statement
   b. balance sheet
   c. statement of changes in owners' equity
   d. cash flow statement

12. On December 21, XYZ Company borrowed $500,000 from a local bank. As a result of this accounting event, _____.
    a. assets will increase and owners' equity will increase
    b. assets will decrease and owners' equity will decrease
    c. assets will increase and decrease by the same amount
    d. assets will increase and liabilities will increase

13. Which of the following would not be considered an accounting event?
    a. The company purchases supplies on account.
    b. The company pre-pays next month's advertising expense.
    c. The company's chief competitor reduces prices by ten percent.
    d. Office equipment is purchased on account.

14. Jax Company collected $500 cash from a customer who had been billed in the previous month. As a result of this accounting event, _____.
    a. assets will increase and revenues will increase
    b. assets will decrease and expenses will increase
    c. assets will increase and decrease by the same amount
    d. assets will decrease and liabilities will decrease

15. ABC Company performed services for a customer and sent them a bill for the appropriate amount. As a result of this accounting event, _____.
    a. assets will increase and revenues will increase
    b. assets will decrease and expenses will increase
    c. assets will increase and decrease by the same amount
    d. assets will decrease and liabilities will decrease

Study Guide: Introduction to Accounting, An Integrated Approach

Problem III

Following is a list of important ideas and key concepts from the chapter. To test your knowledge of these terms, match the term with the definition by placing the number in the space provided.

_____ account
_____ accounting cycle
_____ adjusting entry
_____ business event
_____ closing entry

_____ expense accrual
_____ expense deferral
_____ revenue accrual
_____ revenue deferral
_____ trial balance

1. An adjusting entry that occurs when revenues are earned in one accounting period and payment is received in a later period

2. An event that management wants to plan and evaluate

3. A listing of all general ledger accounts and their respective balances to ensure that debits equal credits

4. A place where the results of events affecting that item are recorded

5. An entry made to close out a temporary account, transfer the balance to retained earnings, and determine net income

6. An adjusting entry that occurs when a company uses previously purchased assets in an attempt to generate revenue in future periods

7. An internal entry made to adjust the accounts for internal events prior to preparing financial statements

8. An adjusting entry that occurs when a company has been paid in advance for services to be performed in a future period

9. The time period between financial statements

10. An adjusting entry that occurs when expenses are incurred in one accounting period and payment is made in a later period

Problem IV

For each of the following, indicate whether a debit entry or a credit entry will increase or decrease the balance in the account. The first account is done as an example.

	Increased by	Decreased by
Land	debit	credit
Cash	_____	_____
Prepaid insurance	_____	_____
Rent expense	_____	_____
Retained earnings	_____	_____
Capital stock	_____	_____
Supplies	_____	_____
Utilities expense	_____	_____
Inventory	_____	_____
Notes payable	_____	_____
Accumulated depreciation	_____	_____
Patents	_____	_____
Salaries payable	_____	_____

Study Guide: Introduction to Accounting, An Integrated Approach

Problem V

The following accounting events occurred during the first period of operations of Centaur Corporation, a service firm.

a) The owners invested $300,000 in exchange for capital stock.
b) Centaur purchased $40,000 of equipment by issuing a three-year note payable. The interest rate is 10 percent and is payable semi-annually.
c) Centaur purchased $2,000 of supplies on account.
d) Customers pay $41,000 to Centaur for services provided during the period.
e) Employees are paid $12,000 for services provided to Centaur during the period.
f) The semi-annual interest expense of $2,000 is paid on the note payable.
g) Centaur paid for the supplies purchased in (c) above.
h) Customers are billed $12,000 for services provided during the period (payment has not been received).
i) At the end of the period, Centaur recognizes $4,000 or 1/10 of the cost ($40,000 x 1/10= $4,000) of the equipment as depreciation expense.
j) Another $1,200 of the interest on the note payable was incurred but not paid.
k) Centaur used $500 of the supplies purchased earlier in the period.
l) Centaur purchased land for $10,000.

1. Using the matrix provided, determine the effect of each of the preceding events on the accounting equation.

2. Prepare the journal entries to record each of these events.

3. Prepare an income statement, statement of changes in retained earnings and a cash flow statement.

1.　　　 Assets 　　 = 　Liabilities 　+ 　Owners Equity
a)
b)
c)
d)
e)
f)
g)
h)
i)
j)
k)
l)

Problem V (continued)

2.

General Journal

Event	Account Title	Debit	Credit

3.

Centaur Corporation
Income Statement

Study Guide: Introduction to Accounting, An Integrated Approach

Problem V (continued)

Centaur Corporation
Statement of Changes in Retained Earnings

Centaur Corporation
Statement of Cash Flows

Problem VI

The following events occurred during the first month of operations of Clean-em-up Janitorial Services, Inc. Create and label the T-accounts necessary to record the transactions. Enter the transactions into the T-accounts and prepare an unadjusted trial balance as of the end of the first month of operations. Use the letters to label the transactions in the T-accounts.

a) Issued capital stock for $50,000.
b) Purchased cleaning supplies for $15,000 on account.
c) Paid $1,500 for the first three months rent on an office building.
d) Paid a $1,200 insurance premium in advance.
e) Purchased cleaning equipment for $8,000 by paying 10% down and issuing a note payable for the balance.
f) Received $4,000 for cleaning services performed.
g) Paid employees' salaries of $1,800.
h) Paid $10,000 of the amount owed for the purchase in (b) above.
i) Billed clients $8,000 for services performed.
j) Paid a $2,000 dividend to owners.

T-Accounts:

Problem VI (continued)

Clean-em-up Janitorial Services, Inc.
Unadjusted Trial Balance
End of Month One

	Debit	Credit

Problem VII

The unadjusted trial balance for Rolex, Inc. is presented below, together with information to complete any necessary adjusting entries:

Rolex, Inc.
Unadjusted Trial Balance
December 31, 20X1

	Debits	Credits
Cash...	22,000	
Accounts receivable....................................	75,000	
Supplies...	9,000	
Prepaid insurance......................................	12,000	
Equipment..	125,000	
Accumulated depreciation.............................		20,000
Accounts payable......................................		18,000
Capital stock...		150,000
Retained earnings (balance at beginning of year).......		31,000
Service revenue earned.................................		95,000
Rent expense...	24,000	
Utilities expense.......................................	7,000	
Salaries expense..	32,000	
Miscellaneous expense..................................	8,000	
Totals	314,000	314,000

Adjustment Data:
a) Unused supplies on hand at the end of the year were $2,400.
b) Prepaid insurance consists of a two-year policy paid on July 1, 20X1.
c) Depreciation expense for the year is $5,000.
d) Salaries earned by employees but not paid at year-end were $1,400.

Required: Prepare the adjusting entries for the year in general journal form (you may omit explanations). Prepare T-accounts for the accounts affected by the adjusting entries and post the appropriate amounts. Prepare an adjusted trial balance, an income statement, statement of changes in retained earnings, and a balance sheet. Prepare any necessary closing entries.

Problem VII (continued)

Adjusting Entries:

General Journal

Date	Account Title	Debit	Credit

T-accounts

Problem VII (continued)

Rolex, Inc.
Adjusted Trial Balance
December 31, 20X1

	Debit	Credit
_____	_____	_____
_____	_____	_____
_____	_____	_____
_____	_____	_____
_____	_____	_____
_____	_____	_____
_____	_____	_____
_____	_____	_____
_____	_____	_____
_____	_____	_____
_____	_____	_____
_____	_____	_____
_____	_____	_____
_____	_____	_____
_____	_____	_____
_____	_____	_____
_____	_____	_____
_____	_____	_____
_____	_____	_____
_____	_____	_____

Problem VII (continued)

Rolex, Inc.
Income Statement
For the year ended December 31, 20X1

Rolex, Inc.
Statement of Changes in Retained Earnings
For the year ended December 31, 20X1

Problem VII (continued)

Rolex, Inc.
Balance Sheet
December 31, 20X1

Closing Entries:

General Journal

Date	Account Title	Debit	Credit

Study Guide: Introduction to Accounting, An Integrated Approach

Solutions for Chapter 7

Problem I

1. T
2. T
3. T
4. F
5. F
6. T
7. T
8. T
9. F
10. T

Problem II

1. c
2. b
3. a
4. a
5. b
6. d
7. b
8. a
9. b
10. d
11. b
12. d
13. c
14. c
15. a

Problem III

4   account
9   accounting cycle
7   adjusting entry
2   business event
5   closing entry

10   expense accrual
6   expense deferral
1   revenue accrual
8   revenue deferral
3   trial balance

Problem IV

	Increased by	Decreased by
Land	debit	credit
Cash	debit	credit
Prepaid insurance	debit	credit
Rent expense	debit	credit
Retained earnings	credit	debit
Capital stock	credit	debit
Supplies	debit	credit
Utilities expense	debit	credit
Inventory	debit	credit
Notes payable	credit	debit
Accumulated depreciation	credit	debit
Patents	debit	credit
Salaries payable	credit	debit

Problems V

1.

	Assets	=	Liabilities	+	Owners Equity
a)	Increased				Increased
b)	Increased		Increased		
c)	Increased		Increased		
d)	Increased				Increased
e)	Decreased				Decreased
f)	Decreased				Decreased
g)	Decreased		Decreased		
h)	Increased				Increased
i)	Decreased				Decreased
j)			Increased		Decreased
k)	Decreased				Decreased
l)	Increased				
	Decreased				

Study Guide: Introduction to Accounting, An Integrated Approach

Problem V (continued)

2.

General Journal

Event	Account Title	Debit	Credit
a)	Cash	$300,000	
	Capital Stock		$300,000
b)	Equipment	$40,000	
	Notes Payable		$40,000
c)	Supplies	$ 2,000	
	Accounts Payable		$ 2,000
d)	Cash	$41,000	
	Service Revenue		$41,000
e)	Salary Expense	$12,000	
	Cash		$12,000
f)	Interest Expense	$ 2,000	
	Cash		$ 2,000
g)	Accounts Payable	$ 2,000	
	Cash		$ 2,000
h)	Accounts Receivable	$12,000	
	Service Revenue		$12,000
i)	Depreciation Expense	$ 4,000	
	Accumulated Depreciation		$ 4,000
j)	Interest Expense	$ 1,200	
	Interest Payable		$ 1,200
k)	Supplies Expense	$ 500	
	Supplies		$ 500
l)	Land	$10,000	
	Cash		$10,000

3.

Centaur Corporation
Income Statement
For the Current Period

Service Revenue		$53,000
Expenses:		
Salary Expense	12,000	
Interest Expense	3,200	
Depreciation Expense	4,000	
Supplies Expense	500	
Total Expenses		19,700
Net income		$33,300

Problem V (continued)

Centaur Corporation
Statement of Retained Earnings
For the Current Period

Beginning balance	$ -0-
Add net income	33,300
Ending balance	$33,300

Centaur Corporation
Cash Flow Statement
For the Current Period

Cash Flows From Operating Activities:	
Cash collected from customers	$ 41,000
Cash payments for expenses	<16,000>
Cash provided by operations	25,000
Cash Flows From Investing Activities:	
Cash paid for land	<10,000>
Cash Flows From Financing Activities:	
Issuance of capital stock	300,000
Increase in cash for period	$315,000
Beginning cash balance	0
Ending cash balance	$315,000

Problem VI

Cash					Accounts Receivable			Supplies	
(a)	50,000	(c)	1,500		(i) 8,000			(b) 15,000	
(f)	4,000	(d)	1,200						
		(e)	800						
		(g)	1,800						
		(h)	10,000						
		(j)	2,000						
	36,700								

Problem VI (continued)

Prepaid Rent	Prepaid Insurance	Equipment
(c) 1,500	(d) 1,200	(e) 8,000

Accounts Payable	Notes Payable	Capital Stock
(h) 10,000 | (b) 15,000	(e) 7,200	(a) 50,000
5,000		

Dividends	Service Revenue	Salaries Expense
(j) 2,000	(f) 4,000	(g) 1,800
	(i) 8,000	
	12,000	

Clean-em-up Janitorial Services, Inc.
Unadjusted Trial Balance
End of Month One

	Debit	Credit
Cash	36,700	
Accounts receivable	8,000	
Supplies	15,000	
Prepaid rent	1,500	
Prepaid insurance	1,200	
Equipment	8,000	
Accounts payable		5,000
Notes payable		7,200
Capital stock		50,000
Dividends	2,000	
Service revenue		12,000
Salaries expense	1,800	
Totals	74,200	74,200

145

Problem VII

General Journal

Date	Account Title	Debit	Credit
12/31	Supplies expense	6,600	
	Supplies		6,600
12/31	Insurance expense	3,000	
	Prepaid insurance		3,000
12/31	Depreciation expense	5,000	
	Accumulated depreciation		5,000
12/31	Salaries expense	1,400	
	Salaries payable		1,400

T-accounts

Supplies			Supplies Expense		Prepaid Insurance	
Bal. 9,000	Adj. 6,600		Adj. 6,600		Bal. 12,000	Adj. 3,000
2,400					9,000	

Insurance Expense		Depreciation Expense		Accumulated Depreciation	
Adj. 3,000		Adj. 5,000			Bal. 20,000
					Adj. 5,000
					25,000

Salaries Expense		Salaries Payable	
Bal. 32,000			Adj. 1,400
Adj. 1,400			
33,400			

Problem VII (continued)

Rolex, Inc.
Adjusted Trial Balance
December 31, 20X1

	Debit	Credit
Cash..	22,000	
Accounts receivable.....................................	75,000	
Supplies...	2,400	
Prepaid insurance.......................................	9,000	
Equipment..	125,000	
Accumulated depreciation..............................		25,000
Accounts payable.......................................		18,000
Salaries payable..		1,400
Capital stock...		150,000
Retained earnings (balance at beginning of year).......		31,000
Service revenue earned.................................		95,000
Rent expense...	24,000	
Utilities expense.......................................	7,000	
Salaries expense..	33,400	
Miscellaneous expense..................................	8,000	
Supplies expense.......................................	6,600	
Insurance expense......................................	3,000	
Depreciation expense...................................	5,000	
Totals	320,400	320,400

Rolex, Inc.
Income Statement
For the year ended December 31, 20X1

Revenues:		
Service revenue earned		$95,000
Expenses:		
Rent expense	$24,000	
Utilities expense	7,000	
Salaries expense	33,400	
Miscellaneous expense	8,000	
Supplies expense	6,600	
Insurance expense	3,000	
Depreciation expense	5,000	87,000
Net Income		8,000

Problem VII (continued)

Rolex, Inc.
Statement of Changes in Retained Earnings
For the year ended December 31, 20X1

Beginning balance	$31,000
Add: Net income	8,000
Deduct: Dividends paid	- 0 -
Ending balance	$39,000

Rolex, Inc.
Balance Sheet
December 31, 20X1

Assets

Current assets:		
Cash		$ 22,000
Accounts receivable		75,000
Supplies		2,400
Prepaid insurance		9,000
Total current assets		$108,400
Long-term assets:		
Equipment	$125,000	
Less: Accumulated depreciation	25,000	$100,000
Total assets		$208,400

Liabilities

Current liabilities:		
Accounts payable		$ 18,000
Salaries payable		1,400
Total current liabilities		$ 19,400

Stockholders' Equity

Capital stock	$150,000	
Retained earnings	39,000	189,000
Total liabilities and stockholders' equity		$208,400

Study Guide: Introduction to Accounting, An Integrated Approach

Problem VII (continued)

Closing Entries:

	General Journal		
Date	*Account Title*	*Debit*	*Credit*
12/31	Service Revenue Earned	$95,000	
	Retained Earnings		$95,000
12/31	Retained Earnings	$87,000	
	Rent Expense		$24,000
	Utilities Expense		$ 7,000
	Salaries Expense		$33,400
	Miscellaneous Expense		$ 8,000
	Supplies Expense		$ 6,600
	Insurance Expense		$ 3,000
	Depreciation Expense		$ 5,000

Chapter 8
Purchasing/Human Resources/Payment Process: Recording and Evaluating Expenditure Process Activities

Chapter Overview

This chapter examines how expenditure process activities are recorded in the accounting system. Chapter 8 first focuses on how the purchase and use of inventory is recorded using either a perpetual inventory method or a periodic inventory method. The chapter also explains how employee compensation is recorded and reported in the accounting system. In addition, the chapter illustrates the accounting for other operating expenses.

In this chapter, you must learn the differences between the perpetual and periodic inventory methods. Carefully trace the chapter examples to the accounting system illustrations. When reading the section related to payroll, link the discussion to your own experiences with paychecks and taxes. Take extra time to study the accounting for expenses when cash payment precedes the expense and when the expense precedes the payment of cash. Adjusting entries may be associated with these events so you will need to think through these events thoroughly to record and report them correctly in the accounting system. Also, you will need to trace the effects of expenditure process activities to the financial statements.

Read and Recall Questions

Identify the expenditure process activities.

Why do accountants use special journals?

What is the purpose of a subsidiary ledger, such as an accounts receivable subsidiary ledger?

Distinguish between the perpetual inventory system and the periodic inventory system.

Briefly describe the use of the following accounts in a periodic inventory system.

- Purchases

- Purchase Returns and Allowance

- Purchase Discounts

Explain how sales, returns of inventory, and discounts on inventory affect the balance of the inventory account in a perpetual inventory system?

Study Guide: Introduction to Accounting, An Integrated Approach

Describe the gross price method to record a purchase discount. When would a company use this method?

Describe the net price method to record a purchase discount. When would a company use this method?

When the gross price method is used, the inventory is recorded at a higher amount. Does this mean the inventory is worth more when the gross price method is used and worth less when the net price method is used?

How is cost of goods sold determined when a periodic inventory system is used?

Identify the typical withholdings from employees' earnings.

Identify the three primary employer payroll taxes.

What is the salary and wage expense for a company: Gross pay or net pay?

On which financial statement are the cash payments to employees reported?

Explain how to account for a cash payment that precedes the expense.

Explain how to account for an expense that is incurred before the cash payment occurs.

Explain how to account for an expense that is incurred concurrently with the cash payment.

On which statement are a company's expenses reported?

On which statements are a company's cash payments for inventory purchases and human resources reported?

Learning Objective:
LO. 5 Describe how expenditure process activities are reported on the financial statements.

Explain how the cash paid for inventory purchases during a period can be estimated.

How can the amount of cash paid for prepaid operating expenses be estimated?

How can the amount of cash paid for accrued operating expenses be estimated?

Outline of Key Concepts

I. Expenditure process activities must be captured in the accounting system.
    A. The expenditure process consists of four primary activities.
        1. Determine the need for goods/services.
        2. Select suppliers and order goods/services.
        3. Received goods/services.
        4. Pay suppliers of goods/services.
    B. Some companies use special journals and subsidiary ledgers.
        1. Special journal—used to record types of entries that occur again and again throughout the period.
            a. Cash disbursements journal
            b. Cash receipts journal
            c. Purchases journal
            d. Sales journal
        2. Subsidiary ledger—records the details for a specific general ledger account. The total of the subsidiary ledger must equal the general ledger account total.
            a. Accounts payable subsidiary ledger
            b. Accounts receivable subsidiary ledger
            c. Inventory subsidiary ledger

Study Guide: Introduction to Accounting, An Integrated Approach

II.   Two types of inventory systems account for the purchase and sale of inventory.
    A. Perpetual inventory system—keeps a running balance of the cost of inventory available for sale and the cost of goods sold during the period.
        1. Purchases of inventory are recorded as increases in the inventory account.
        2. Sales, returns of, discounts on, and allowances for inventory are recorded as decreases in the inventory account.
    B. Periodic inventory system—determines the balance in inventory and the cost of goods sold only at specific points in time, such as the end of the accounting cycle.
        1. Purchases account—temporary account used to record the purchase of inventory.
        2. Purchases Returns and Allowances—temporary account used to record the return of inventory or a reduction in the cost of inventory.
        3. Purchase Discounts—temporary accounts used to record cash discounts when the gross method is used.
        4. An adjusting entry is required at the end of the period to update the inventory account.

III.   Suppliers offer cash discounts to encourage customers to pay their bills promptly.
    A. Gross price method—the purchase of the inventory is recorded at its full or gross price.
        1. Assumption is that discounts, when received, are reductions in the purchase price of the inventory. A purchase discount is recorded, if and only if, it is taken.
        2. Highlights purchase discounts taken.
    B. Net price method—the purchase of the inventory is recorded at its discounted or net price.
        1. Assumption is that all discounts should be taken; the cost of the inventory is the minimum amount due to the supplier.
            a. If the company fails to take the discount, the additional amount paid is essentially a financing charge.
        2. Highlights purchase discounts not taken.
    C. Inventory purchases are not directly reported on any financial statement.
        1. Balance sheet indicates the inventory on hand at the end of the period.
            a. In a perpetual system, the inventory balance may need to be updated if the physical count of inventory does not agree with the accounting records.
            b. In a periodic system, a physical count determines the ending inventory, and cost of goods sold must be determined.

                Beginning inventory balance
              + Net purchases
              = Cost of goods available for sale
              - Cost of goods sold
              = Ending inventory balance

2. Cost of Goods Sold is reported on the income statement.
3. Cash paid for inventory is reported on the statement of cash flows.

IV. Accounting for payroll is a complicated process.
A. Employees may have a number of withholdings from their gross pay.
1. Federal Insurance Contribution Act (FICA) requires most companies to withhold amounts from employees' earnings for social security and Medicare.
2. Federal, state, and local income taxes may be withheld.
a. Based on amount employee earns, length of the pay period, and the number of exemptions claimed by the employee.
3. Voluntary withholdings include charitable contributions, retirement savings, union dues, etc.
B. Employers are responsible for payroll taxes.
1. Employer must match the FICA tax withheld from the employees' earnings.
2. Federal Unemployment Tax Act (FUTA) and State Unemployment Tax Act (SUTA) are employer taxes to fund the support of the administration of unemployment benefits.
C. Salary and wage expense equals the employees' gross pay.
1. Amounts withheld from the employees represent liabilities that the employer must remit to the proper authorities.
D. Payroll events affect the financial statements.
1. Amounts paid to employees are reported on the statement of cash flows.
2. Salary and wage expenses for nonmanufacturing employees are reported on the income statement.
3. Payroll-related liabilities are reported on the balance sheet as current liabilities.

V. Companies must record and report many expenditure process activities.
A. Cash outflow before expense:
1. The company acquires a good or service that is not used immediately.
2. Creates the future right or asset.
3. Once the good or service is used in an effort to generate revenue, the asset must be reduced and the expense recognized.
B. Expense before cash outflow:
1. The company uses a good or service but does not pay for it at the time.
2. Creates a liability.
C. Expense concurrent with payment:
1. The company uses a good or service and immediately pays for it.
2. Since the right will be used up in the current period, the company should recognize an expense and a cash payment.

D. Expenditure process activities are reported on the financial statements.
   1. Ending balance of any related asset or liability is reported on the balance sheet.
   2. Associated expenses are reported on the income statement.
   3. Related cash payments are reported in the operating section of the statement of cash flows.
E. Cash flows for expenditure cycle activities may need to be estimated.
   1. Estimating cash paid for inventory:
      Beginning inventory balance
      + Net purchases on account
      = Inventory available for sale or use
      - Cost of goods sold
      = Ending inventory
      then
      Beginning accounts payable balance
      + Net purchases on account
      = Maximum amount owed to suppliers
      - Cash paid to suppliers
      = Ending accounts payable balance
   2. Estimating cash paid for prepaid operating expenses:
      Prepaid expenses, beginning balance
      + Cash paid for prepaid expenses
      = Maximum prepaid assets available for use
      - Operating expenses incurred
      = Prepaid expenses, ending balance
   3. Estimating cash paid for accrued operating expense:
      Accrued expense, beginning balance
      + Operating expense incurred
      = Maximum amount owed
      - Cash paid
      = Accrued expense, ending balance
F. A company must compare its expenditure process results against goals from their balanced scorecard.

Problem I

Indicate whether the following statements are either true (T) or false (F).

_____1. Under a perpetual inventory system, cost of goods sold is recorded after every sale.
_____2. The cost to ensure inventory in transit is included in the inventory account.
_____3. Under the gross price method, purchases discounts lost are considered finance charges.
_____4. Deductions from gross pay become a liability of the employer at the time they are withheld.
_____5. If a company assumes that all discounts should be taken, it should use the net price method.
_____6. Purchases discounts lost will increase the cost of inventory included on the balance sheet.
_____7. A periodic inventory system is used by companies that are capable of keeping a running balance of the cost of goods available for sale and cost of goods sold during a period.
_____8. The employer is required to match FICA taxes withheld from the employee.

Problem II

Indicate the correct answer by circling the appropriate letter.

1. Amjay uses a perpetual inventory system and the gross price method to account for its inventory. Amjay purchased 1,000 items of inventory at a price of $3 each. Terms of the sale were 2/10, n/30, FOB shipping point. Shipping charges were $200. Due to an oversight in the accounting department, the invoice was not paid within the discount period. As a result of the above transactions, the inventory account will increase by _____.
   a. $3,000
   b. $2,940
   c. $3,140
   d. $3,200

2. Lex Systems maintains a periodic inventory system and had a beginning inventory of $25,000. During the year, the company purchased $400,000 of inventory and reported cost of goods sold of $365,000 on the income statement. What will Lex Systems report as inventory on the balance sheet at the end of the year?
   a. $25,000
   b. $60,000
   c. $45,000
   d. $35,000

Study Guide: Introduction to Accounting, An Integrated Approach

3. Which of the following is not a payroll tax levied against the employer?
   a. FICA
   b. FUTA
   c. SUTA
   d. all are payroll taxes levied against the employer

4. Amtech uses a perpetual inventory system and the net price method to account for its inventory. Amtech purchased 2,000 items of inventory at a price of $5 each. Terms of the sale were 2/10, n/30, FOB shipping point. Shipping charges were $500. Due to an oversight in the accounting department, the invoice was not paid within the discount period. As a result of the above transactions, the inventory account will increase by _____.
   a. $9,800
   b. $10,000
   c. $10,300
   d. $10,500

5. Lex Corp. reported utilities expense of $125,000 on the 20X1 income statement. Utilities Payable had a beginning balance of $4,000 and an ending balance of $3,000. What is the estimated amount paid for utilities?
   a. $125,000
   b. $129,000
   c. $126,000
   d. $124,000

6. The Lectern Corporation had cost of goods sold of $640,000 for the year and the following account balances related to the purchase of inventory:

	Beginning of year	End of year
Inventory	$54,000	$36,000
Accounts payable	$13,000	$21,000

How much cash did Lectern Corporation pay for inventory during the year?
   a. $614,000
   b. $586,000
   c. $723,000
   d. $634,000

7. On December 23, 20X1, HOK Corporation paid $12,000 rent for the first three months of 20X2. What entry will HOK record to account for the $12,000 payment?
   a. debit cash and credit prepaid rent
   b. debit rent expense and credit prepaid rent
   c. debit prepaid rent and credit cash
   d. debit rent expense and credit cash

161

8. The Lucern Corporation reported insurance expense of $40,000 for the year. The balances in the prepaid insurance account were as follows:

	Beginning of year	End of year
Prepaid insurance	$9,000	$3,000

How much cash did Lucern Corporation pay for insurance during the year?
   a. $46,000
   b. $31,000
   c. $43,000
   d. $34,000

9. Milex reported rent expense of $18,000 on the 20X1 income statement. Prepaid rent had a beginning balance of $2,000 and an ending balance of $8,000. What is the estimated amount paid for rent?
   a. $18,000
   b. $8,000
   c. $12,000
   d. $24,000

10. JK Systems maintains a periodic inventory system and had a beginning inventory of $45,000. During the year, JK purchased $350,000 of inventory and had an ending inventory of $32,000. JK's cost of goods sold will be _____.
   a. $350,000
   b. $395,000
   c. $363,000
   d. $427,000

   Study Guide: Introduction to Accounting, An Integrated Approach

Problem III

The following is a list of important ideas and key concepts from the chapter. To test your knowledge of these terms, match the term with the definition by placing the number in the space provided.

_____ gross price method	_____	purchases
_____ net price method	_____	purchases discounts
_____ periodic inventory system	_____	special journal
_____ perpetual inventory system	_____	subsidiary journal

1. A journal used for transactions that occur frequently and in the same manner

2. A system used by companies that need to determine the balance in inventory and the cost of goods sold only at specific points in time

3. A ledger used to record details for specific general ledger accounts

4. A temporary account used to record purchase discounts taken

5. A method used to record inventory purchases at the discounted price

6. A system used by companies that want to keep a running balance of the cost of inventory available for sale and the cost of goods sold during the period

7. A temporary account used to record the purchase of inventory

8. A method used to record inventory purchases at the full price

Problem IV

Following is a list of selected transactions for the Ectar Corporation:

a. Purchased $35,000 of raw materials from a supplier. Terms 2/10, n/30.
b. Received and paid a $2,500 bill for advertising.
c. Purchased $75,000 of raw materials from a supplier. Terms 1/15, n/60.
d. Paid the supplier within the discount period for the purchase in (a) above.
e. Returned $5,000 of defective raw materials purchased in (c) above.
f. Purchased $400 of office supplies on account.
g. Paid the balance due on the purchase in (c) above. Due to a cash shortage, the payment was not made within the discount period.

Assume that Ectar uses a perpetual inventory system and the net price method to account for raw materials inventory purchases. Prepare the necessary journal entries to record the transactions.

General Journal

Date	Account Title	Debit	Credit

Study Guide: Introduction to Accounting, An Integrated Approach

Problem V

Following is a list of selected transactions for the Ace Corporation:

a. Purchased $100,000 of raw materials from a supplier. Terms 3/10, n/30.
b. Purchased $80,000 of raw materials from a supplier. Terms 2/15, n/90.
c. Paid the supplier within the discount period for the purchase in (a) above.
d. Returned $4,000 of defective raw materials purchased in (b) above.
e. Paid the balance due on the purchase in (b) above. Due to an oversight in the accounting department, the payment was not made within the discount period.

Assume that Ace uses a periodic inventory system and the gross price method to account for raw materials inventory purchases. Prepare the necessary journal entries to record the transactions.

General Journal

Date	Account Title	Debit	Credit

Solutions for Chapter 8

Problem I

1. T   5. T
2. T   6. F
3. F   7. F
4. T   8. T

Problem II

1. d
2. b
3. d
4. c
5. c
6. a
7. c
8. d
9. d
10. c

Problem III

8 gross price method   7 purchases
5 net price method   4 purchases discounts
2 periodic inventory system   1 special journal
6 perpetual inventory system   3 subsidiary journal

Problem IV

	General Journal		
Date	Account Title	Debit	Credit
a.	Raw Materials Inventory	$34,300	
	Accounts Payable		$34,300
b.	Advertising Expense	$2,500	
	Cash		$2,500
c.	Raw Materials Inventory	$74,250	
	Accounts payable		$74,250
d.	Accounts Payable	$34,300	
	Cash		$34,300
e.	Accounts payable	$4,950	
	Raw Materials Inventory		$4,950
f.	Office Supplies	$400	
	Accounts Payable		$400
g.	Accounts Payable	$69,300	
	Discount Lost	700	
	Cash		$70,000

Problem V

General Journal

Date	Account Title	Debit	Credit
a.	Purchases	$100,000	
	Accounts Payable		$100,000
b.	Purchases	$80,000	
	Accounts Payable		$80,000
c.	Accounts Payable	$100,000	
	Cash		$97,000
	Purchase Discount		$ 3,000
d.	Accounts Payable	$4,000	
	Purchase Returns and Allow.		$4,000
e.	Accounts Payable	$76,000	
	Cash		$76,000

Study Guide: Introduction to Accounting, An Integrated Approach

Chapter 9
Recording and Evaluating Conversion Process Activities

Chapter Overview

Chapter 9 presents the accounting system for conversion process activities. The chapter explains the three inventory accounts (raw materials, work-in-process, and finished goods) that reflect the events occurring in the conversion process. The flow of materials, labor, and other manufacturing costs through these accounts is illustrated. In addition, the chapter explains how to calculate cost of goods manufactured.

You may have little or no direct knowledge about the activities involved in manufacturing a product. Therefore, many of the terms and cost flow illustrations may not make intuitive sense to you. If this is the case, you may want to think through the steps of a simple manufacturing example that you are likely familiar with: making chocolate chip cookies. What are the significant raw materials used? How would you determine direct labor? Which materials and items are necessary to make the cookies but are too difficult or inexpensive to directly trace to the batch of cookies (salt and electricity, for example)? You might try to apply the accounting system described in this chapter by accounting for the cost of a batch of cookies.

Whether you try the above exercise or not, you should become familiar with the cost flows illustrated in Chapter 9. Do not try to memorize the journal entries, but focus on the exhibits that illustrate the cost flows through the accounts. If you understand the cost flows, you should be able to figure out most journal entries and calculate cost of goods manufactured.

Read and Recall Questions

Identify the four conversion process activities.

Briefly describe the following conversion process internal controls documents.

- Production order

- Materials requisition

- Job cost record

Identify the three types of inventory accounts maintained by manufacturing firms.

Briefly describe the cost flows through the various manufacturing inventory accounts.

Distinguish between direct materials and indirect materials.

Study Guide: Introduction to Accounting, An Integrated Approach

In which account is the purchase of raw materials recorded?

Where does the cost of direct materials flow when they are requisitioned into production?

Distinguish between direct labor and indirect labor.

In which account is the cost of direct labor recorded? In which account is the cost of indirect labor recorded?

Learning Objective:
LO. 3 Explain the process of applying manufacturing overhead and record these activities.

What is the purpose of the manufacturing overhead account?

171

How are actual manufacturing overhead costs recorded in the accounting system?

Why aren't manufacturing overhead costs recorded in the Work-in-Process Inventory account?

Define applied manufacturing overhead.

Why is applied rather than actual manufacturing overhead assigned to Work-in-Process Inventory?

Define activity-based costing (ABC).

Identify the six steps in the ABC manufacturing overhead application process.

Study Guide: Introduction to Accounting, An Integrated Approach

Define the following:

- Underapplied overhead

- Overapplied overhead

Describe what is done with a balance in the Manufacturing Overhead account at the end of the accounting period.

Learning Objective:
LO. 4 Discuss the purpose of and prepare a cost of goods manufactured statement.

Define cost of goods manufactured.

What is full-absorption costing, and why is it required for external reporting?

Explain the purpose of the cost of goods manufactured report.

What is a variance?

What are the possible explanations for a difference between budgeted and actual direct labor costs?

What is a direct labor price variance? When is a direct labor price variance favorable? When is it unfavorable?

What is a direct labor usage variance? When is a direct labor usage variance favorable? When is it unfavorable?

Study Guide: Introduction to Accounting, An Integrated Approach

What are the possible explanations for the difference between the budgeted and actual amount of direct materials?

What is a direct material price variance? When is a direct material price variance favorable? When is it unfavorable?

What is a direct material usage variance? When is a direct material usage variance favorable? When is it unfavorable?

What is a direct materials inventory variance? When is a direct materials inventory variance favorable? When is it unfavorable?

Outline of Key Concepts

I.   Conversion process activities are internal to the organization.
 A. Conversion process consists of four activities.
      1. Schedule production.
      2. Obtain raw materials (internal transfer).
      3. Use labor and other manufacturing resources to convert raw materials into finished goods.
      4. Store finished goods until sold.
 B. Internal controls documents are important in the conversion process.
      1. Production order—issued by the production function, prenumbered, production cannot begin without this document.
      2. Materials requisition—issued by the production function, verified by the inventory control functions, materials are released only when the requisition is received.
      3. Job cost record—maintained by the accounting function, updated daily, verified with the general ledger records and the production function.
 C. Manufacturing firms maintain three types of inventory accounts in the general ledger.
      1. Raw materials inventory—the costs incurred to purchase and receive raw materials.
      2. Work-in-process inventory—the costs of products started but not yet completed.
      3. Finished goods inventory—the costs of products completed but not yet sold.

II. Cost flows mirror the physical flow of resources through the production process.
 A. Recording raw material activities:
      1. Purchases of materials are recorded in Raw Materials Inventory.
      2. Cost of direct materials issued into production is transferred from Raw Materials Inventory to Work-in-Process Inventory.
      3. Cost of indirect materials issued into production is transferred from Raw Materials Inventory to Manufacturing Overhead.
 B. Recording labor activities:
      1. Cost of direct labor used in production is recorded in the Work-in-Process Inventory.
      2. Cost of indirect labor used is recorded in Manufacturing Overhead.
 C. Recording Manufacturing Overhead events:
      1. Manufacturing Overhead—temporary account used to reflect the indirect manufacturing overhead costs of the period.
         a. Actual manufacturing overhead—amount of overhead cost incurred during the period and recorded as debits to the Manufacturing Overhead account.
      2. Manufacturing overhead costs are assigned to Work-in-Process Inventory.

Study Guide: Introduction to Accounting, An Integrated Approach

a. Applied manufacturing overhead—amount of overhead assigned to Work-in-Process during the period and recorded as credits to the Manufacturing Overhead account.

b. Manufacturing overhead is applied to production because it is convenient and better matches costs with production activities.

3. Activity-based costing (ABC)—a system for assigning overhead costs to Work-in-Process Inventory based on the consumption of cost drivers. There are six steps:

   a. Identify and classify production activities by level and group costs into cost pools.

   b. Determine the appropriate cost driver for each activity by selecting a driver as closely related as possible to the activity.

   c. Estimate the amount of overhead related to each cost driver.

   d. Estimate the amount of each cost driver to be used.

   e. Determine the predetermined overhead rate for each cost driver.

      i. Rate used throughout the period as the estimate of manufacturing overhead per unit of cost driver.

   f. Apply manufacturing overhead to Work-in-Process Inventory using the predetermined overhead rate.

4. Rarely will actual overhead equal applied overhead.

   a. Underapplied overhead—amount of overhead applied to Work-in-Process Inventory throughout the period was not as much as the actual amount of manufacturing overhead cost incurred to produce the products.

      i. Cost of the products manufactured during the period is understated.

   b. Overapplied overhead—amount of overhead applied to Work-in-Process Inventory is greater than the actual amount of overhead incurred to produce the products.

      i. Cost of the products manufactured during the period is overstated.

   c. If the balance in the Manufacturing Overhead account is small, it is closed to Cost of Goods Sold.

D. As products are completed, the cost of manufacturing the products is transferred from Work-in-Process Inventory to Finished Goods Inventory.

   1. Cost of goods manufactured—cost of completed products; includes direct materials, direct labor, and applied manufacturing overhead.

   2. Full-absorption costing—costing system in which all production costs are applied to the products manufactured during the period.

      a. Required for external reporting.

   3. When products are sold, the cost is transferred from Finished Goods Inventory to Cost of Goods Sold.

E. Cost of goods manufactured report—shows the changes that occurred in the Raw Materials Inventory and Work-in-Process Inventory accounts during the period.
1. Allows the comparison of the cost of manufacturing products with the budgeted production costs.

III. In the conversion process, efficiency and quality are evaluated.
A. Variance—difference between the standard and actual amounts of inputs.
1. Used to evaluate the efficiency of the conversion process.
B. Direct labor variances have three possible explanations.
1. The wage rate per hour differs from the standard.
2. The number of hours used differs from the standard allowed for the actual level of production.
3. Both the wage rate and the number of hours allowed differs from the standard.
C. Direct labor price variance—indicates the difference in labor cost due to a change in the average wage rate paid to direct labor workers.
1. (Actual price per hour – Standard price per hour) x Actual number of hours worked.
   a. If the actual price is greater than the standard price per hour, the variance is unfavorable.
   b. If the actual price is less than the standard price per hour, the variance is favorable.
D. Direct labor usage variance—indicates the difference in labor cost is due to a change in the number of hours worked per unit produced.
1. (Actual hours worked – Standard hours allowed for the actual number of units produced) x Standard price.
   a. If the actual hours worked are greater than the standard hours allowed, the variance is unfavorable.
   b. If the actual hours worked are less than the standard hours allowed, the variance is favorable.
E. Direct materials variances have four possible explanations.
1. Amount paid to purchase materials differs from the standard price.
2. Amount of materials used differs from the standard amount allowed for the actual number of units produced.
3. Amount of materials purchased differs from the amount used.
4. Some combination of the above.
F. Direct material price variance—indicates the difference in material cost due to a change in the amount paid to purchase materials.
1. (Actual price per item purchased – Standard price per item purchased) x Actual amount of material purchased
   a. If the actual price is greater than the standard price, the variance is unfavorable.

Study Guide: Introduction to Accounting, An Integrated Approach

   b. If the actual price is less than the standard price, the variance is favorable.

 G. Direct material usage variance—indicates the difference in material cost due to a change in the amount of materials used per unit produced.

   1. (Actual amount of materials used – Standard amount of materials allowed for the actual number of units produced) x Standard purchase price

    a. If the actual amount of materials used is greater than the standard amount of materials allowed, the variance is unfavorable.

    b. If the actual amount of materials used is less than the standard amount allowed, the variance is favorable.

 H. Direct materials inventory variance—indicates the change in direct materials cost due to purchasing a different quantity of materials than what was used.

   1. (Actual amount of materials purchased – Actual amount of materials used in production) x Standard purchase price

    a. If the actual amount of materials purchased is greater than the actual amount of materials used, the variance is unfavorable.

Problem I

Indicate whether the following statements are either true (T) or false (F).

_____1. A manufacturing firm typically maintains three types of inventory accounts.

_____2. Efficiency is measured by comparing actual outputs to expected outputs.

_____3. If the actual materials used in production exceed the standard, there will be a favorable direct materials usage variance.

_____4. Direct materials are physically traceable to the final product.

_____5. Janitorial services in the factory would be classified as direct labor.

_____6. The direct labor usage variance indicates whether workers are producing products in the amount of time allowed.

_____7. The direct materials price variance is the responsibility of the production department.

_____8. Manufacturing overhead is considered a permanent account.

_____9. A cost pool is a group of costs that change in response to the same cost driver.

_____10. Predetermined overhead rates are based on actual overhead costs incurred during the year.

Problem II

Indicate the correct answer by circling the appropriate letter.

1. Under an activity-based costing system, testing the product will typically occur in the _____ _____ activity level.
   a. facility-sustaining
   b. product-sustaining
   c. batch-related
   d. unit-related

2. Under an activity-based costing system, ordering parts for use in production will typically occur in the _____ _____ activity level.
   a. facility-sustaining
   b. product-sustaining
   c. batch-related
   d. unit-related

3. During the year, Fx Company paid $35,000 for utilities at the production facility. What journal entry did Fx make related to the utilities?
   a. debit Manufacturing Overhead and credit Cash
   b. debit Work-in-Process Inventory and credit Cash
   c. debit Cash and credit Utilities Expense
   d. debit Utilities Expense and credit Cash

4. Under an activity based costing system, building maintenance costs will typically occur in the _____ _____ activity level.
   a. facility-sustaining
   b. product-sustaining
   c. batch-related
   d. unit-related

5. Based on budgeted data, the assembly department should use 2,000 direct labor hours in the accounting period. Indirect labor costs are expected to be $100,000. Using direct labor hours as the cost driver, what amount will be added to work-in-process inventory if 300 direct labor hours are used in the first quarter of operations?
   a. $ 300
   b. $ 3,000
   c. $15,000
   d. $30,000

Study Guide: Introduction to Accounting, An Integrated Approach

6. Under an activity-based costing system, assembling the units produced will typically occur in the _____ _____ activity level.
   a. facility-sustaining
   b. product-sustaining
   c. batch-related
   d. unit-related

Use the following information for the next four questions:

Information for the most recent month of operations is provided below:

   10,000 pounds of raw materials were purchased for $9,200
   6,300 pounds of raw materials were used in production
   14,000 hours of direct labor costing $310,800 were used in production
   Standard quantity allowed for actual production was 6,000 pounds of raw materials
   Standard quantity of labor allowed for production was 15,000 hours
   Standard direct labor rate is $25.00 per hour
   Standard price is $1.00 per pound of raw materials

7. The direct materials price variance is _____.
   a. $800 unfavorable
   b. $800 favorable
   c. $240 unfavorable
   d. $240 favorable

8. The direct materials usage variance is _____.
   a. $300 unfavorable
   b. $800 favorable
   c. $400 unfavorable
   d. $600 unfavorable

9. The direct labor price variance is _____.
   a. $16,500 unfavorable
   b. $26,300 favorable
   c. $31,800 unfavorable
   d. $39,200 favorable

10. The direct labor usage variance is _____.
   a. $10,000 unfavorable
   b. $14,000 unfavorable
   c. $43,000 favorable
   d. $25,000 favorable

Use the following information for the next two questions:

The Manufacturing Overhead - Machining account had a credit balance of $29,000 at the end of the accounting period. Other account balances were as follows:

Work-in-process inventory	$ 100,000
Finished goods inventory	$ 300,000
Cost of goods sold	$1,600,000

11. If the overapplied manufacturing overhead is considered by management to be small, cost of goods sold will be _____.
    a. increased by $29,000
    b. decreased by $29,000
    c. increased by $23,200
    d. decreased by $23,200

12. If the overapplied manufacturing overhead is considered by management to be significant, cost of goods sold will be _____.
    a. increased by $29,000
    b. decreased by $29,000
    c. increased by $23,200
    d. decreased by $23,200

13. During the week, Boxtell Manufacturing's employees submitted time cards indicating that it had incurred $93,000 in direct labor and $21,000 in indirect labor. As a result of the preceding activity, Boxtell should make the following journal entry:

a.	Work-in-Process Inventory	$93,000	
	Salaries Expense	$21,000	
	Wages Payable		$114,000
b.	Salaries Expense	$114,000	
	Wages Payable		$114,000
c.	Salaries Expense	$93,000	
	Manufacturing Overhead	$21,000	
	Wages Payable		$114,000
d.	Work-in-Process Inventory	$93,000	
	Manufacturing Overhead	$21,000	
	Wages Payable		$114,000

Study Guide: Introduction to Accounting, An Integrated Approach

Problem III

Following is a list of important ideas and key concepts from the chapter. To test your knowledge of these terms, match the term with the definition by placing the number in the space provided.

_____ Activity-based costing   _____ Full absorption costing
_____ Actual manufacturing overhead   _____ Manufacturing overhead
_____ Applied manufacturing overhead   _____ Predetermined overhead rate
_____ Cost of goods manufactured   _____ Variance
_____ Cost pool

1. A costing system in which all production costs are applied to the products manufactured during the period

2. The total cost of products manufactured during the period

3. The difference between the standard and actual amounts of inputs

4. A system for assigning costs to cost objects

5. The amount of overhead incurred during the period

6. The estimated amount of overhead divided by the estimated amount of cost driver; used to apply overhead to work-in-process

7. The amount of overhead applied to work-in-process during the period

8. A group of costs that change in response to the same cost driver

9. A temporary account used to reflect the indirect manufacturing costs of the period

Problem IV

Complete the following sentences by filling in the correct response.

1. If the actual price paid for materials is greater than the standard price, there will be a/an _____ materials price variance.

2. Poor quality of direct materials may cause a/an _____ material price variance but result in a/an _____ materials usage variance.

3. If the actual direct labor hours used are less than the standard direct labor hours, there will be a/an _____ direct labor usage variance.

4. The estimated cost of an input is determined by multiplying the _____ _____ by the _____ _____.

5. The direct materials inventory variance is the difference between the quantity of direct materials _____ and the quantity _____ in production, times the _____ price.

6. A manufacturing firm typically maintains _____ _____, _____ and _____ _____ inventories.

7. Costs cannot be combined into a _____ _____ unless they are represented by the same _____ _____.

8. Underapplied overhead occurs when _____ overhead costs exceed the _____ overhead costs.

Study Guide: Introduction to Accounting, An Integrated Approach

Problem V

The following information is available for Lextar manufacturing for the month of August:

10,000 board feet of lumber were purchased for $4,500
5,700 board feet were used in production
800 hours of direct labor costing $5,800 were used in production
Standard quantity of lumber allowed for actual production was 6,000 board feet
Standard quantity of labor allowed for production was 750 hours
Standard direct labor rate is $8.00 per hour
Standard price is $.40 per board foot

Calculate the following variances for the month of August:

Direct materials price variance:

Direct materials usage variance:

Direct labor price variance:

Direct labor usage variance:

Problem VI

Clarion Manufacturing makes computer consoles for use in college classrooms. Using the following legend, classify the costs incurred by Clarion.

DM   Direct materials cost
DL   Direct labor cost
MOH   Manufacturing overhead
SA   Selling and administrative cost

_____1. Sheet plastic used for the console outer shell
_____2. Salary for the production shift supervisor
_____3. Wiring cable for the console
_____4. Commission paid to sales staff
_____5. Salary paid to production line workers
_____6. Rent on production facility
_____7. Advertising
_____8. Utilities on production facility
_____9. Utilities on office building

Study Guide: Introduction to Accounting, An Integrated Approach

Problem VII

The following information is provided for the Linder Manufacturing Company:

Raw Materials Inventory:		Work-in-Process Inventory	
Beginning-of-year	$ 12,000	Beginning-of-year	$ 38,000
End-of-year	$ 16,000	End-of-year	$ 11,000
Raw materials purchased	$345,000	Indirect materials used	$ 32,000
Direct labor used	$115,000	Manufacturing overhead applied	$103,000

Required: Prepare the Cost of Goods Manufactured report for Linder Manufacturing.

Linder Manufacturing
Cost of Goods Manufactured

Problem VIII

D Company manufactures a specialty mulching product from certain pulp woods. Selected transactions for D company are presented below:

a. Purchased $50,000 of raw materials with terms 2/10, n/30 (use the net price method).

b. Raw materials costing $18,000 are transferred into the production process. Of this amount, $16,000 is considered direct materials and $2,000 is considered indirect materials.

c. Employee's salaries (ignore withholding) paid were $5,000 for direct labor (400 hours), $1,000 for indirect labor, and $3,000 for selling and administrative.

d. Depreciation for the month was $12,000 on production equipment and $3,500 on office equipment.

e. Expired insurance costs (prepaid in the previous period) on coverage related to production facilities and office facilities were $2,000 and $1,000, respectively.

f. D Company maintains only one cost pool and applies its overhead based on $10 per direct labor hour.

Required: Prepare the entries in general journal form to record the preceding events.

	General Journal		
Date	Account Title	Debit	Credit

Study Guide: Introduction to Accounting, An Integrated Approach

Problem VIII (continued)

General Journal

Date	Account Title	Debit	Credit

Solutions for Chapter 9

Problem I

1. T	6. T
2. T	7. F
3. F	8. F
4. T	9. T
5. F	10. F

Problem II

1. b
2. c
3. a
4. a
5. c
6. d
7. b
8. a
9. d
10. d
11. b
12. d
13. d

Problem III

4	Activity-based costing	1	Full absorption costing
5	Actual manufacturing overhead	9	Manufacturing overhead
7	Applied manufacturing overhead	6	Predetermined overhead rate
2	Cost of goods manufactured	3	Variance
8	Cost pool		

Problem IV

1. unfavorable
2. favorable, unfavorable
3. favorable
4. standard price, standard quantity
5. purchased, used, standard
6. raw materials, work-in-process, finished goods
7. cost pool, cost driver
8. actual, applied

Problem V

Direct materials price variance:

$$(AP - SP) \times AQp = DMPV \qquad (\$.45 - \$.40) \times 10,000 = \$500 \text{ unfavorable}$$

Direct materials usage variance:

$$(AQu - SQb) \times SP = DMUV \qquad (5,700 - 6,000) \times \$.40 = \$120 \text{ favorable}$$

Direct labor price variance:

$$(AP - SP) \times AQ = DLPV \qquad (\$7.25 - \$8.00) \times 800 = \$600 \text{ favorable}$$

Direct labor usage variance:

$$(AQu - SQb) \times SP = DLUV \qquad (800 - 750) \times \$8.00 = \$400 \text{ unfavorable}$$

Problem VI

1. DM
2. MOH
3. DM
4. SA
5. DL
6. MOH
7. SA
8. MOH
9. SA

Problem VII

Linder Manufacturing
Cost of Goods Manufactured

Beginning balance of raw materials	$ 12,000
Add raw materials purchased during period	345,000
Raw materials available for use	$357,000
Less: Indirect materials used	32,000
ending balance of raw materials	16,000
Direct materials used in production	$309,000
Beginning balance of work-in-process	$ 38,000
Add: Direct materials issued into production	309,000
Direct labor used in production	115,000
Manufacturing overhead applied to production	103,000
Total work-in-process	$565,000
Less ending balance of work-in-process	11,000
Cost of goods manufactured	$554,000

Study Guide: Introduction to Accounting, An Integrated Approach

Problem VIII

General Journal

Date	Account Title	Debit	Credit
a)	Raw materials inventory	49,000	
	Accounts payable		49,000
b)	Work-in-process inventory	16,000	
	Manufacturing overhead	2,000	
	Raw materials inventory		18,000
c)	Work-in-process inventory	5,000	
	Manufacturing overhead	1,000	
	Salaries expense	3,000	
	Cash		9,000
d)	Manufacturing overhead	12,000	
	Depreciation expense	3,500	
	Accumulated Depreciation		15,500
e)	Manufacturing overhead	2,000	
	Insurance expense	1,000	
	Prepaid insurance		3,000
f)	Work-in-process	4,000	
	Manufacturing overhead		4,000

Chapter 10
Marketing/Sales/Collection/Customer Support Process: Recording and Evaluating Revenue Process Activities

Chapter Overview

Chapter 10 discusses the recording and reporting of revenue process activities. The relationship between revenue recognition and cash received is explored in depth. The chapter explores the role of cost flow assumptions in accounting for inventory events. In addition, this chapter examines the problem of recording and reporting uncollectible accounts. The chapter also considers the effects of revenue process activities on the income statement, statement of cash flows, and balance sheet. It concludes by discussing the use of sales revenue variances to evaluate revenue process activities.

As in past chapters, you must familiarize yourself with new vocabulary. Revisit the revenue recognition criteria and learn to apply the criteria to the analysis of revenue process activities. Read the section of the chapter on inventory cost flow methods in depth and trace their effects to the financial statements. You may want to complete several exercises or problems applying these cost-flow methods.

Read and Recall Questions

Identify the five activities in the revenue process.

Learning Objective:
LO. 1 Describe how revenue activities are analyzed and recorded in the accounting system.

Conceptually, when are revenues earned?

Conceptually, when are revenues realized?

Identify the three points in time when revenue can be recognized.

Why do sales returns and allowances arise?

How are sales returns recorded in the accounting system?

Why are sales discounts offered to customers?

If a customer pays within the discount period, how is the sales discount recorded in the accounting system?

Study Guide: Introduction to Accounting, An Integrated Approach

What type of accounts are Sales Returns and Allowances and Sales Discounts?

Describe the specific identification inventory costing method. Why is it difficult to use?

Briefly describe the first-in, first-out (FIFO) inventory costing method.

Briefly describe the last-in, first-out (LIFO) inventory costing method.

In periods of falling prices, which inventory costing method reports the higher net income? Why?

Why may a company adopt the LIFO inventory method even if it produces lower net income?

Why does the Internal Revenue Service (IRS) require a company using LIFO for tax purposes to use LIFO for financial statement reporting purposes?

Learning Objective:
LO. 3 Discuss how uncollectible accounts are recorded.

Why do companies make credit sales when they know some accounts will prove to be uncollectible?

Why are estimates of uncollectible accounts made at the end of each accounting period?

Define the net realizable value of Accounts Receivable.

Why is the estimate of uncollectible accounts recorded in Allowance for Doubtful Accounts rather than subtracted from Accounts Receivable directly?

What type of an account is Allowance for Doubtful Accounts?

What effect does the write-off of an account receivable have on the net realizable value of accounts receivable?

Learning Objective:
LO. 4 Explain how revenue process activities are reported on the financial statements.

On which financial statement are Cost of Goods Sold and Uncollectible Accounts Expense reported?

On which statement is the net realizable value of Accounts Receivable reported?

On which statement is cash received from customers reported?

If not reported directly on the statement of cash flows, how can cash collected from customers be estimated?

Learning Objective:
LO. 5 Discuss how revenue process activities are evaluated internally.

What are the possible explanations for a revenue variance?

What does the sales price variance indicate? When is this variance unfavorable?

What does the sales quantity variance indicate? When is this variance favorable?

Outline of Key Concepts

I.   Accounting for the revenue process is divided into two separate processes: sales and collections.

    A. Revenue process consists of five activities.

        1. Determine marketing and distribution channels.

        2. Receive and accept orders.

        3. Deliver goods and services.

        4. Receive payment from customers.

        5. Provide customer support.

II.   The FASB has stated that revenues are recognized when they have been earned and realized.

    A. Revenues are earned when a company has done everything it has promised to do for the customer.

        1. Delivered products or rendered services to a customer.

    B. Revenues are realized when an exchange has taken place and the company receives cash, a claim to cash, or some other increase in net asset.

        1. Net assets are total assets less total liabilities, so revenue is realized when the company receives some other noncash asset or has its liabilities reduced.

    C. Revenue can be recognized at three points in time.

        1. Revenue can be recognized when cash is received.

            a. Cash and owners' equity are increased.

        2. Revenue can be recognized before cash is collected.

            a. An asset (receivable) and owners' equity are increased.

        3. Revenue may be recognized after cash is received.

            a. Assets are increased and liabilities are increased.

            b. The liability would be reported on the balance sheet as something like Unearned Revenue or Advances from Customers.

    D. Three other events can affect the amount of revenue reported for a given period.

        1. Sales returns

        2. Sales allowances

        3. Sales discounts

    E. Sales Returns and Allowances—a temporary account represents returns by customers and price allowances granted to customers.

        1. Is a contra revenue account and subtracted from gross sales revenue to obtain net sales revenue for presentation on the income statement.

    F. Sales Discounts—a temporary account used to report cash discounts taken by customers.

        1. Is a contra revenue account and subtracted from gross sales revenue to obtain net sales revenue for presentation on the income statement.

201

III. The sale of inventory items creates the need to transfer the cost of the inventory item from the Inventory account to the Cost of Goods Sold account.
   A. Specific identification method—used when a company has heterogeneous inventory items and identifies each inventory item with the date of its purchase or manufacture, and the price to purchase or make the item.
      1. When the item is sold, the cost of the item is transferred to Cost of Goods Sold.
      2. Difficult to use in most businesses.
   B. First-in, First-out (FIFO) Method—costs are charged to cost of goods sold in chronological order.
      1. First inventory costs recorded are the first expensed to Cost of Goods Sold.
      2. Inventory balance consists of the most recent costs.
      3. Usually approximates the physical flow of goods.
   C. Last-in, First-out (LIFO) Method—costs are charged to cost of goods sold in reverse chronological order.
      1. Last inventory costs recorded are the first costs expensed to Cost of Goods Sold.
      2. Inventory balance consists of the oldest inventory costs.
   D. When inventory prices are fluctuating, FIFO and LIFO will produce differing cost of goods sold and inventory balances.
      1. If prices are rising, FIFO will produce a higher ending inventory balance, a lower cost of goods sold, and higher net income than LIFO.
      2. If prices are falling, FIFO will produce a lower ending inventory balance, a higher cost of goods sold, and lower net income than LIFO.
      3. In periods of rising prices, a company may elect to use LIFO because it will result in lower income tax expense, and therefore, less cash outflow.
         a. If LIFO is used for tax purposes, the IRS requires that LIFO be used for external reporting purposes.
      4. Generally accepted accounting principles (GAAP) require consistent application of cost flow assumptions.
         a. Prevents switching back and forth between methods to obtain the best net income result.

IV. When companies make credit sales to customers, some accounts will prove to be uncollectible.
   A. When reporting sales, companies should consider two primary objectives.
      1. Proper income measurement requires matching revenues recognized during a period with all related expenses incurred to earn those revenues.
         a. Matching requires recognizing uncollectible accounts expense in the same period as the revenue earned.
         b. To achieve proper matching, companies will have to estimate the portion of the current year's credit sales anticipated to be uncollectible

and deduct this estimated expense on the current year's income statement.
2. Proper asset valuation requires that Accounts Receivable be reported at the amount expected to be collected from credit customers.
   a. Net realizable value—net dollar amount the company expects to eventually collect after making allowances for estimated uncollectible accounts.
B. The entry to record the estimated uncollectible accounts requires a debit to Uncollectible Accounts Expense and a credit to Allowance for Doubtful Accounts.
   1. Allowance for Doubtful Accounts—a contra asset account that is deducted from Accounts Receivable to report the net realizable value of accounts receivable on the balance sheet.
C. Writing-off an account—when a customer's accounted has been designated as uncollectible, the customer's account balance must be removed from the company's accounting records.
   1. Requires a debit to Allowance for Doubtful Accounts and a credit to Accounts Receivable.
   2. A write-off of an account does not change the net realizable value of accounts receivable.

V.   Revenue process events must be reflected on the financial statements.
A. Net Sales, Cost of Goods Sold, and Uncollectible Accounts Expense will be reported on the income statement.
B. Net realizable value of Accounts Receivable on the balance sheet.
C. Cash collected from customers is reported on the statement of cash flows.
   1. May have to estimate collections from customers.
      Beginning accounts receivable, net
      + Net sales (sales less sales returns & allowances and less sales discounts)
      = Maximum amount owed to the company by customers
      - Cash received from customers
      = Ending accounts receivable, net

VI. Companies monitor their revenue process activities.
A. Compare actual results against goals. Some examples are:
   1. Increase in number of customers.
   2. Increase customer satisfaction.
B. Three reasons that the actual amount of sales revenue may differ from the planned amount of sales revenue.
   1. Selling price differs from budgeted selling price.
   2. Number of units sold differs from number planned.
   3. Both the selling price and the number of units sold differ from the plan.

C. Sales price variance—indicates the difference in revenue due to a change in selling price.
  1. (Actual selling price per unit - Budgeted selling price per unit) x Actual number of units sold
     a. If the actual selling price is greater than the budgeted selling price, the variance is favorable.
     b. If the actual selling price is less than the budgeted selling price, the variance is unfavorable.
D. Sales quantity variance—indicates the difference in revenue due to a change in sales volume.
  1. (Actual number of units sold – Budgeted number of units to sell) x Budgeted selling price
     a. If the actual number of units sold is greater than the budgeted number of units, the variance is favorable.
     b. If the actual number of units sold is less than the budgeted number of units, the variance is unfavorable.

Problem I

Indicate whether the following statements are either true (T) or false (F).

_____1.   Revenues will always increase the net worth of a business.
_____2.   All increases in the net worth of a business are the result of generating revenues.
_____3.   The LIFO cost assumption reflects that costs are charged to cost of goods sold in reverse chronological order.
_____4.   Revenues are earned when the product is sold or the service has been rendered to a customer.
_____5.   In periods of rising prices, the use of a LIFO cost flow assumption will result in a lower net income than FIFO.
_____6.   Under a perpetual inventory system, cost of good sold is recorded after every sale.
_____7.   Unearned revenue is considered a liability account.
_____8.   An increase in the sales discounts account will cause an increase in a company's reported net sales.
_____9.   The write-off of a customer's account as uncollectible will not change the net accounts receivable balance.
_____10. Cost of goods sold would be reported as an asset on the balance sheet.

Study Guide: Introduction to Accounting, An Integrated Approach

Problem II

Indicate the correct answer by circling the appropriate letter.

1. LTD Manufacturing Company transferred 2,000 telkons costing $7.00 each from Work-in-Process Inventory to Finished Goods Inventory on July 23rd. LTD's entry to record the transfer would be _____.

   a. Work-in-Process Inventory $14,000
          Finished Goods Inventory $14,000
   b. Finished Goods Inventory $14,000
          Work-in-Process Inventory $14,000
   c. Raw Materials Inventory $14,000
          Finished Goods Inventory $14,000
   d. Finished Goods Inventory $14,000
          Raw Materials Inventory $14,000

Use the following information for the next two questions:

On December 1, 19X9, Beltway leasing received a $12,000 payment from a customer for rent on a building for December through February.

2. Beltway's entry to record receipt of the payment will be _____.

   a. Cash $12,000
          Unearned rental revenue $12,000
   b. Cash $12,000
          Rental revenue $12,000
   c. Cash $ 1,000
          Rental revenue $ 1,000
   d. Unearned rental revenue $12,000
          Cash $12,000

3. Assuming that Beltway prepares its financial statements on December 31, it will need to make the following adjusting entry:

   a. Unearned rental revenue $8,000
          Cash $8,000
   b. Unearned rental revenue $4,000
          Cash $4,000
   c. Rental revenue $4,000
          Unearned rental revenue $4,000
   d. Unearned rental revenue $4,000
          Rental revenue $4,000

4. On September 3, Flax Company sold a product costing $23,000 to its customer for $35,000. Flax's entry to record the sale will be _____.

a.	Cash	$35,000	
	Cost of goods sold	$23,000	
	Sales		$35,000
	Inventory		$23,000
b.	Cash	$35,000	
	Cost of goods sold		$23,000
	Gain on sale		$12,000
c.	Cash	$35,000	
	Cost of goods sold		$35,000
d.	Cash	$35,000	
	Cost of goods sold		$23,000
	Gain on sale		$12,000

Use the following information for the next three questions:

The following is a chronological record of inventory events for the first month of operations. A perpetual inventory system is used:

	Number of units		Unit	Total
	Bought	Sold	Price	Cost
Purchase	400		$2.00	$800
Sale		300		
Purchase	200		$2.50	$500
Purchase	300		$3.00	$900
Sale		400		

5. If a FIFO cost flow assumption is used, ending inventory shown on the balance sheet will be

_____.

a. $400
b. $600
c. $550
d. $660

6. If a LIFO cost flow assumption is used, ending inventory shown on the balance sheet will be

_____.

a. $400
b. $350
c. $450
d. $600

Study Guide: Introduction to Accounting, An Integrated Approach

7. If a LIFO cost flow assumption is used, cost of goods sold reported on the income statement will be _____.
    a. $1,750
    b. $1,900
    c. $2,100
    d. $1,550

8. Y Company reported $400,000 in net sales in 20X1. Accounts receivable had a $60,000 balance at the beginning of the year and a $40,000 balance at the end of the year. What will Y Company report as cash received from customers on its 20X1 cash flow statement?
    a. $400,000
    b. $420,000
    c. $380,000
    d. $460,000

9. Resex Company collected $1,200 from a customer on a sale made and recorded in the previous month. Resex's entry to record the receipt of the $1,200 will be _____.
    a.   Accounts receivable $1,200
                Sales $1,200
    b.   Cash $1,200
                Sales $1,200
    c.   Cash $1,200
                Accounts receivable $1,200
    d.   Accounts receivable $1,200
                Cash $1,200

10. The net dollar amount that a company expects to collect on its credit sales is called
_____.

    a.   net realizable value
    b.   revenues
    c.   net gain
    d.   uncollectible accounts

Problem III

Prepare journal entries in general journal form to record the following selected transactions for the Ace Company. A perpetual inventory system is used.

June 1   Merchandise, which originally cost Ace Company $2,000, is sold for $3,500.

June 5   Merchandise, which originally cost Ace Company $5,000, is sold for $11,000. Terms of the sale are 1/15, n/60 from the sales date.

June 10   Ace Company received a $20,000 deposit on a special order for an overseas customer. Shipment of the merchandise is expected to be made in July.

June 15   A $500 sale to Hexway Inc. is written-off as uncollectible.

June 19   Merchandise, which originally cost Ace Company $1,000, is sold for $2,100. Terms of the sale are 1/15, n/60 from the sales date.

June 20   Payment is received for the June 5th sale (within the discount period).

June 28 $200 of the merchandise sold on June 19th is returned as defective.

June 30   Ace Company received a $4,000 payment from a credit sale made to a customer in May.

Study Guide: Introduction to Accounting, An Integrated Approach

Problem III (cont.)

General Journal

Date	Account Title	Debit	Credit

Problem IV

The following is a chronological record of inventory events for Extar Corporation:

Date		Number of units Bought	Sold	Unit Price	Total Cost
1/1	Beginning inventory	1,000		$50	$50,000
1/5	Sale		500		
1/12	Purchase	300		$55	$16,500
1/21	Purchase	600		$57	$34,200
1/28	Sale		1,200		

Extar maintains a perpetual FIFO inventory system. The sales price of Extar's product is $100 per unit and all sales and purchases are made on account.

Required: Prepare the journal entries in general journal form for the month of January (you may omit journal entry descriptions).

	General Journal		
Date	Account Title	Debit	Credit

Study Guide: Introduction to Accounting, An Integrated Approach

Solutions for Chapter 10

Problem I

1. T
2. F
3. T
4. T
5. T
6. T
7. T
8. F
9. T
10. F

Problem II

1. b
2. a
3. d
4. a
5. b
6. c
7. a
8. b
9. c
10. a

Problem III

General Journal

Date	Account Title	Debit	Credit
6/1	Cash	3,500	
	Sales		3,500
	Cost of goods sold	2,000	
	Inventory		2,000
6/5	Accounts receivable	11,000	
	Sales		11,000
	Cost of goods sold	5,000	
	Inventory		5,000
6/10	Cash	20,000	
	Deposit		20,000
6/15	Allowance for doubtful accounts	500	
	Accounts receivable		500
6/19	Accounts receivable	2,100	
	Sales		2,100
	Cost of goods sold	1,000	
	Inventory		1,000
6/20	Cash	10,890	
	Sales discounts	110	
	Accounts receivable		11,000
6/28	Sales returns and allowances	200	
	Accounts receivable		200
6/30	Cash	4,000	
	Accounts receivable		4,000

Study Guide: Introduction to Accounting, An Integrated Approach

Problem IV

	General Journal		
Date	Account Title	Debit	Credit
1/5	Accounts receivable	$50,000	
	Sales		$50,000
	Cost of goods sold	$25,000	
	Inventory		$25,000
1/12	Inventory	$16,500	
	Accounts payable		$16,500
1/21	Inventory	$34,200	
	Accounts payable		$34,200
1/28	Accounts receivable	$120,000	
	Sales		$120,000
	Cost of goods sold	$64,300	
	Inventory		$64,300

Chapter 11
Time Value of Money

Chapter Overview

This chapter illustrates the concepts of return of investment and return on investment. Risk is considered when estimating the expected return on investment. The chapter explains three types of risk: inflation risk, business risk, and liquidity risk. The time value of money is examined in depth. The future value and present value of one dollar is illustrated, and the calculation of present and future values of annuities is also presented.

The time value of money may be an unfamiliar concept. Try relating the concept of present value to situations with which you are familiar. For example, assume that your grandparents have offered to give you $1,000 three years from now when you graduate from college or some lesser amount of cash now for meeting school expenses. Since you are very short on cash right now, you decide to take the second option. Assuming your grandparents are earning 10 percent compound interest on their investments, what amount of cash could you ask for today that would be equivalent to $1,000 three years from now. Also, think about the various lotteries. How does a state determine the annual payments for lottery winnings? How does a state determine the payout if a winner elects to receive one lump-sum payment? These questions and many other questions require an understanding of the time value of money so it is well worth your time to work a number of exercises and problems using time value of money concepts. By the way, your grandparents should be happy to give you $750 today.

Read and Recall Questions

Briefly discuss capital resources processes.

Describe investing activities.

Describe financing activities.

When planning, companies first plan their operating processes, then ascertain the needed investments, and finally determine how to finance these investments. The performance phase reverses this order. Why is the order reversed in the performance phase?

Identify three ways companies use operating profits.

Learning Objective:
LO. 1 Explain the risk/return relationship.

Distinguish between return of investment and return on investment.

Explain why return on investment is not adequate for differentiating among investments.

Study Guide: Introduction to Accounting, An Integrated Approach

Define rate of return and indicate how it is calculated.

When do investments have negative rates of return?

Define expected rate of return.

Identify the steps to ascertain the investment's expected rate of return.

Define risk.

Why do people have different attitudes toward risk?

Identify and discuss the three primary sources of risk.

Explain how risk and return are related.

Define the following terms:

- Risk premium

- Risk-adjusted expected rate of return

- Risk-free rate of return

Study Guide: Introduction to Accounting, An Integrated Approach

Briefly explain the concept of time value of money.

Define simple interest. On what does the amount of simple interest depend?

Explain compound interest.

What happens to the amount of interest as the frequency of compounding increases?

Briefly discuss the future value of the amount of $1.

219

Define present value.

Explain what the present value of the amount of $1 represents.

What happens to the present value as the number of compounding periods increases?

What is an annuity?

Briefly explain the future value of an annuity.

Identify the factors that affect the amount of money that accumulates when calculating the future value of an annuity.

Study Guide: Introduction to Accounting, An Integrated Approach

Why is there one less interest period than the number of payments when calculating the future value of an annuity?

Briefly explain the present value of an annuity.

Identify the four-step process for solving time value of money problems.

Outline of Key Concepts

I. Capital resource processes—involve the investing and financing activities of the company.
    A. Investing activities—concern the purchase, use, and sale of long-term assets.
    B. Financing activities—involve raising cash by borrowing, receiving contributions from owners, or from operating profits to pay for investments in assets, to repay monies borrowed from creditors, and to provide a return to owners.
    C. Companies use operating profits in three ways.
        1. To pay the interest on borrowed fund and the borrowed funds when they come due.
        2. To reward owners with dividends.
        3. To reinvest funds in the firm to maintain the existing operational capacity and to finance additional long-term investments in the firm.

II.   The concept of return is associated with investing decisions.
    A. Return of investment—the return of the amount initially invested.
    B. Return on investment—money received in excess of the initial investment.
        1. To differentiate among investments, two additional factors must be considered.
           a. Must consider the length of time of the investments.
           b. Must consider the amount of the initial investments.
           c. Need a common-size measure of performance.
    C. Rate of return—measures the performance of investments on a common-size basis and eliminates any distortion caused by the size of the initial investment.
        1. Dollar amount of return on investment/Dollar amount of initial investment
        2. Investments have a negative return when they do not recover the initial investment.
    D. Expected rate of return—predicted rate of return. To estimate, it is necessary:
        1. Forecast the investment's possible rates of return.
        2. Establish a probability that each forecasted rate of return will occur.
        3. Multiply each forecasted return by its respective probability and sum the resulting products.

III.   Risk—exposure to the chance that an unfavorable outcome will occur at some future point in time.
    A. People have different attitudes toward risk.
        1. Risk seekers—enjoy risky situations.
        2. Risk avoiders—avoid risky situations.
        3. A decision about which investment is better depends on the investor's willingness to accept risk.
    B. There are three primary types of risk.
        1. Inflation risk—the chance of a decline in the purchasing power of the monetary unit during the time money is invested.
        2. Business risk—associated with the ability of a particular company to continue in business.
           a. Rate of interest on borrowed funds increases as the chance of business failure increases.
        3. Liquidity risk—chance that an investment cannot be readily converted into cash.

IV.   Risk and return are directly related; the greater the risk, the greater the return the investor expects.
    A. Risk-free rate of return—rate of return that a virtually risk-free investment produces.
        1. Risk premium—an amount added to the risk-free rate of return to compensate for risk factors associated with a particular investment.
           a. Results in the risk-adjusted expected rate of return.
    B. To earn a higher rate of return, investors must assume more risk.

Study Guide: Introduction to Accounting, An Integrated Approach

C. Managers must assume risk that is consistent with the risk preferences of the firm's owners.

V. Time value of money—assumption that a dollar today, given that it can generate a return on investment over time, is worth more than a dollar one year from today.
  A. Simple interest—calculated only on the amount borrowed.
    1. Depends on the amount loaned or borrowed (principal), the annual interest rate, and the amount of time the principal is used.
        Principal x Rate x Time = Interest
  B. Compound interest—based on a principal amount that includes interest from previous time period.
    1. Compounding—process of adding interest to the principal.
    2. As the frequency of compounding increases, the total amount of interest increases.
  C. Future value of the amount of $1—the amount that $1 becomes at a future date, if invested at a specified annual interest rate and compounded a certain number of times per year over the investment period.
    1. A means of determining the amount of money in the future that is equivalent to an amount today.
  D. Present value of the amount of $1—the amount of money that, if invested today at some compounded interest rate for a specified time period, will equal $1 at the end of that time period.
    1. It is the cash equivalent today of some specified future amount of cash at a specified date in the future.
    2. As the number of compoundings increase, the present value decreases.
  E. Annuity—series of equal cash payments made at equal intervals.
  F. Future value of an annuity—the amount of money that accumulates at some future date as a result of making equal payments over equal intervals of time and earning a specified interest rate over that time period.
    1. The amount of money that accumulates is a function of:
        a. Size of the payments.
        b. Frequency of the payments.
        c. Interest rate used over the life of the annuity.
    2. Annuity assumes that the final payment is made on the future value date.
        a. One less interest period than the number of payments.
  G. Present value of an annuity—the amount of money that, if invested at some interest rate today, will generate a set number of equal periodic payments that are made over equal time intervals.
  H. Use a four-step process for solving time value of money problems.
    1. Determine whether the problem is an annuity.
    2. Determine whether the problem is present or future value.
        a. With annuities, if the lump sum occurs after the periodic payments, it is a future value problem.

223

b. If the lump sum occurs before the periodic payments, it is a present value problem.
3. Identify the missing element.
   a. PV = lump sum payment currently (present value)
   b. FV = lump sum payment in the future (future value)
   c. ANN = equal payments over equal intervals
   d. r = annual interest rate
   e. c = number of compounding/payments per year
   f. n = total number of payments/compoundings over the entire time period
4. Solve for the missing element.

Problem I

Indicate whether the following statements are either true (T) or false (F).

_____1. An investment will have a negative rate of return if the original investment is not recovered.
_____2. The predicted rate of return on an investment is called the annual rate of return.
_____3. People who enjoy taking risks are said to be risk avoiders.
_____4. There is a direct relationship between the uncertainty that an unfavorable outcome will occur and the level of risk of an investment.
_____5. The amount/cost of an investment varies inversely with the change in its risk-adjusted rate of return.
_____6. Inflation risk is factored into every investment decision.
_____7. To earn a higher rate of return, the investor must assume more risk.
_____8. The higher the probability of default on a loan, the lower the interest rate charged on the debt.
_____9. The present value of future cash flows will always be smaller than the sum of those future cash flows.
_____10. Business risk takes into account the likelihood that a company will cease operations.

Study Guide: Introduction to Accounting, An Integrated Approach

Problem II

Indicate the correct answer by circling the appropriate letter.

1. Investment Z cost $5,000 and was sold one year later for $5,900. The investment's rate of return was
    a. 8%
    b. 12%
    c. 14%
    d. 18%

2. Which of the following risk factors will result in a risk premium being included in the risk-adjusted rate of return on an investment?
    a. inflation risk
    b. business risk
    c. liquidity risk
    d. all of the above

3. Max, age 25, wants to retire a millionaire in 20 years. If Max's investments average a 12% rate of return (compounded annually), how much must he invest at the end of each year in order to have $1,000,000 at retirement?
    a. $13,879
    b. $12,679
    c. $15,638
    d. $22,465

4. Mary wants to purchase a new automobile in five years that will cost $30,000. Assuming that she can earn a 6% annual rate of return, how much must she invest today to ensure she will have the $30,000?
    a. $25,674
    b. $21,111
    c. $16,784
    d. $22,419

5. How would your answer change to question (4) if Mary earned 6% compounded semi-annually?
    a. $24,187
    b. $22,345
    c. $22,323
    d. $21,785

6. Yolanda recently inherited $300,000. She intends to invest $100,000 of the inheritance and spend the rest. If her investment earns 4% compounded semi-annually, how much will she have in 15 years?

    a. $181,140
    b. $165,450
    c. $185,680
    d. $220,650

7. Determine the present value of a $10,000 annuity payments made over ten years if the payments are made at the end of each year. The annuity earns an 8% annual rate of return.

    a. $67,101
    b. $63,456
    c. $56,091
    d. $83,423

8. Jean purchased a $25,000 automobile and must make annual payments of $6,595 for the next five years. What annual rate of interest is Jean being charged on the loan?

    a. 6%
    b. 8%
    c. 10%
    d. 12%

9. John plans to invest $20,000 in a certificate of deposit that will earn 5% annually. Approximately how many years will it take to double his investment?

    a. 5
    b. 10
    c. 15
    d. 20

10. Bill and Mary need to borrow $200,000 to purchase a house in the country. If the annual interest rate is 12% and the repayment period is 15 years, their yearly loan payment will be

_____.

    a. $21,894
    b. $31,510
    c. $29,365
    d. $34,321

Study Guide: Introduction to Accounting, An Integrated Approach

Problem III

Following is a list of important ideas and key concepts from the chapter. To test your knowledge of these terms, match the term with the definition by placing the number in the space provided.

_____ business risk	_____ present value of an annuity
_____ compounding	_____ rate of return
_____ expected return	_____ risk-adjusted expected rate of return
_____ future value of an annuity	_____ risk-free rate of return
_____ inflation risk	_____ risk premium
_____ liquidity risk	_____ time value of money

1. The amount of money that accumulates at some future date as a result of making equal payments over equal intervals of time and earning a specified rate of interest over that time period

2. A tool used to solve problems involving the comparison of cash flows that occur at different points in time

3. The process of adding interest to principal for purposes of interest calculation

4. The chance that an investment cannot be readily converted to cash

5. An expected rate of return including the risk premium

6. The chance of a decline in the purchasing power of the monetary units during the time money is invested

7. A summary measure of an investment's performance stated in dollars that is based on the dollar amount of the possible returns on investment and the probability of those returns occurring

8. The rate of return that a virtually riskless investment produces

9. The amount of money that, if invested at some rate of interest today, will generate a set number of equal periodic payments that are made over equal time intervals

10. The risk associated with the ability of a particular company to continue in business

11. A percentage measurement of the performance of investments on a common-size basis

12. An increase in the rate of return expected by an investor for assuming greater investment risk

227

Problem IV

Complete the following sentences by filling in the correct response.

1. Return on investment should not be used to rank investment alternatives because it does not take into account the _____ the investment was held or the _____ of the initial investment.

2. The expected rate of return is based on the _____ rates of return and the _____ of those rates of return occurring.

3. The time value of money is the tool used to solve problems involving cash flows that occur at _____ points in time.

4. The cash equivalent today of some specified amount of cash at a specified date in the future is called the _____ _____ of that future amount.

5. An annuity is a series of _____ cash payments over equal time periods.

6. Investors will choose the investment with the _____ expected return for a given level of _____ .

Problem V

Calculate the expected rate of return on a $200,000 investment with following possible outcomes (returns will occur at the end of one year):

Possible Outcomes	Possible Returns	Probability of Outcome
Robust economy	$ 90,000	.15
Steady growth	20,000	.65
Recession	4,000	.15
Depression	$-70,000	.05

Problem VI

The following information is provided for two investment alternatives:

	Investment X	Investment Y
Amount of investment	$50,000	$50,000
Possible outcomes and (probabilities)	10,000 (.8)	15,000 (.7)
	4,000 (.2)	1,000 (.3)

Calculate the expected rate or return for each investment.

Solutions for Chapter 11

Problem I

1. T	6. T
2. F	7. T
3. F	8. F
4. T	9. T
5. T	10. T

Problem II

1. d
2. d
3. a
4. d
5. c
6. a
7. a
8. c
9. c
10. c

Problem III

10	business risk	9	present value of an annuity
3	compounding	11	rate of return
7	expected return	5	risk-adjusted expected rate of return
1	future value of an annuity	8	risk-free rate of return
6	inflation risk	12	risk premium
4	liquidity risk	2	time value of money

Study Guide: Introduction to Accounting, An Integrated Approach

Problem IV

1. time, amount
2. possible, likelihood
3. different
4. present value
5. equal
6. highest, risk

Problem V

Possible Outcomes	Possible Returns	Rate of Return if Event Occurs	Probability of Outcome
Robust economy	$ 90,000	45%	.15
Steady growth	20,000	10%	.65
Recession	4,000	2%	.15
Depression	$-70,000	-35%	.05

Expected rate of return = (.15 x 45%) + (.65 x 10%) + (.15 x 2%) + (.05 x -35%) = 11.8%

Problem VI

a. Investment X   Expected rate of return = (.8 x 20%) + (.2 x 8%) = 17.6%

   Investment Y   Expected rate of return = (.7 x 30%) + (.3 x 2%) = 21.6%

Chapter 12
Planning Investments: Capital Budgeting

Chapter Overview

Chapter 12 applies the time value of money concepts from Chapter 11 to capital budgeting decisions. Capital budgeting is a process used to decide which investments to acquire and to evaluate performance of the investments after acquisition. The chapter discusses the steps involved in capital budgeting and emphasizes the net present value method for analyzing investment decisions. In addition, the chapter explains the effects of income taxes and depreciation on capital budgeting decisions.

Success in learning Chapter 12 material requires a good understanding of the time value of money concepts presented in Chapter 11. If you do not understand the time value of money, you should review Chapter 11 problems before continuing with this chapter. When completing net present value problems, first focus on determining whether the cash inflows and outflows are lump sum amounts or annuities. Make sure you use the appropriate interest rates and interest compounding periods. Remember that depreciation is not a cash flow, but because depreciation is a tax-deductible expense it reduces income tax payments and thus has cash flow consequences. Although you may be inclined to think that the net present value analysis results tell a manager what investment decision to make, any investment decision must be tempered by sound human judgment.

Read and Recall Questions

Learning Objective:
LO. 1 Explain the concept of and calculate a company cost of capital.

Briefly describe the capital budgeting process.

Identify the four basic processes of the capital budgeting process.

Why do companies make capital investments?

How do companies identify long-term investment opportunities?

Define cost of capital.

What is the purpose of return on investment and how is it calculated?

| **Learning Objective:** |
| LO. 2 Use NPV analysis to make investment decisions for a not-for-profit entity. |

Define net present value (NPV) analysis.

Study Guide: Introduction to Accounting, An Integrated Approach

Using the NPV method, when is an investment an acceptable one?

Identify the four steps in performing an NPV analysis.

Why does a negative NPV indicate that the rate of return is less than the cost of capital?

Discuss the three assumptions underlying NPV analysis.

Identify the typical cash inflows and cash outflows associated with NPV analysis.

Why can income taxes affect capital budgeting decisions?

How are after-tax cash inflows and after-tax cash outflows calculated?

Learning Objective:
LO. 3 Use NPV analysis to make investment decisions assuming uniform depreciation.

Explain the tax shield created by depreciation.

Learning Objective:
LO. 4 Use NPV analysis to make investment decisions assuming tax depreciation.

Briefly describe the modified accelerated cost recovery system (MACRS).

If using the MACRS tables in NPV analysis is more accurate, why do some companies calculate uniform depreciation over the life of the project?

Study Guide: Introduction to Accounting, An Integrated Approach

What are the two sources of cash flow associated with the disposal of an asset?

How can human judgment affect a capital budgeting decision?

Uncertainty is inherent in the capital budgeting process. How can sensitivity analysis be used to deal with this uncertainty?

Define operating leverage.

Explain how qualitative factors affect capital expenditure decisions.

Outline of Key Concepts

I. Capital budgeting—process used for analysis and selection of the long-term investments of a business.
    A. There are four basic processes in capital budgeting.
        1. Identifying long-term investment opportunities.
        2. Selecting appropriate investments.
        3. Financing the selected investments.
        4. Evaluating the investments.
    B. Managers must consider many factors when identifying investment opportunities.
        1. Managers must recognize what is included in the cost of the long-term investment.
        2. Must understand motives for making these investments.
        3. There are four basic reasons for making capital investments.
            a. Need to replace worn-out or unproductive operating assets
            b. Expand the business's operating capacity based on long-term strategic decisions made by the company.
            c. Keep up with changing technology.
            d. Comply with mandates of the government.
        4. Must tie the investments to the organization's strategy.
    C. Any return that is greater than or equal to the company's cost of capital is considered a satisfactory return.
        1. Cost of capital—represents the amount of return that the assets of the company must generate to satisfy both creditors and owners.
            a. Calculated as the weighted-average cost of its debt and equity financing.
            b. Used as the hurdle rate.
        2. When making the investment decision, the cost of capital is compared to the expected return on investment.
            a. If the expected rate of return on a long-term investment exceeds the cost of capital (hurdle rate), the investment satisfies both the creditors' and owners' desire for a satisfactory return.
        3. Managers must estimate the future cash inflows and outflows attributable to the investment.

II. Net Present Value (NPV) analysis—method of evaluating investments that uses the time value of money to assess whether the investment's expected rate of return is greater than the company's cost of capital.
    A. NPV method has four steps.
        1. Identify (estimate) the timing and amount of all cash inflows and outflows associated with the potential investment over its anticipated life.
        2. Calculate the present value of the expected future cash flows using the company's cost of capital as the discount rate.

Study Guide: Introduction to Accounting, An Integrated Approach

3. Compute the net present value by subtracting the initial cash outflows necessary to acquire the asset from the present value of the future cash flows.
4. Decide to make or reject the investment in the capital asset.
   a. If the net present value is zero or positive, the proposed investment is acceptable.
   b. If the net present value is negative, the company should reject the project.

B. Three assumptions underline NPV analysis.
   1. All cash flows are known with certainty.
   2. Cash flows are assumed to occur at the end of the time period.
   3. Cash inflows are immediately reinvested in another project that earns a return for the company equal to the cost of capital.

C. Initial cash outflows include:
   1. Acquisition costs.
   2. Increase in working capital.

D. Cash inflows occur during the investment's life.
   1. A decrease in operating expenses is considered a cash inflow.
   2. Revenues.
   3. Release of working capital.
   4. Investment sold for salvage.

E. Income taxes change both the amount of cash inflows and outflows used in the capital budgeting decision.
   1. After-tax cash inflows—difference between the taxable cash inflow and the amount of tax paid on it.
      a. Cash inflow x (1 – Tax rate)
   2. After-tax cash outflows—difference between the tax-deductible cash outflow and the amount of tax savings because of it.
      a. Cash outflow x (1 – Tax rate)

F. Depreciation does not directly decrease cash, but it reduces income subject to tax and the related amount of income taxes due on income.
   1. Creates a tax shield that keeps the company from being taxed on the recovery of the cost of their investments.
   2. Modified Accelerated Cost Recovery System (MACRS)—the current tax depreciation system.
      a. Allows more depreciation in the first years of the asset's life, creating larger tax shields earlier in the asset's life and smaller tax shields later in the asset's life.
      b. Assets are classified according to the period of time over which the IRS requires these assets to be depreciated.

G. The disposal of assets can produce two cash flows.
   1. Proceeds of the sale.
   2. Change in the amount of taxes due when the asset is sold for a gain or loss.

      a. Gain on disposal occurs if the proceeds from the sale of an asset exceed its book value at the date of disposal.

      b. Loss on disposal occurs if the proceeds from the sale of an asset are less than its book value at the date of the sale.

H. The investment decision is ultimately based on human judgment, uncertainty, and other qualitative factors.

    1. Goal incongruence—arises because an employee acts in his or her own best interests even if that action is not in the company's best interest.

    2. Sensitivity analysis can be used to deal with uncertainty and human perceptions.

    3. Operating leverage—proportion of fixed costs associated with a project.

      a. The higher the proportion of fixed costs, the higher the risk if sales are less than expected.

      b. If a company believes it has high operating leverage, it may use a higher hurdle rate to compensate for the increased risk.

    4. The nature of the investment will influence the investment decision.

    5. Must consider whether the investment links with the company's balanced scorecard goals.

I. Capital investment decisions affect the budgeted financial statements.

    1. Initial cash outflows would be reported on the budgeted statement of cash flows as an investing activity.

    2. Net annual cash inflows from the project will be reported as operating cash flows on the budgeted statement of cash flows.

    3. The book value of the investment will appear on the budgeted balance sheet.

    4. Depreciation of the investment's assets will impact the budgeted income statement.

Problem I

Indicate whether the following statements are either true (T) or false (F).

_____1. To be acceptable, an investment's rate of return must exceed the company's cost of capital.

_____2. The net present value of an investment is the profit generated by the investment.

_____3. The rate of return used to determine present value is called the hurdle rate.

_____4. A decrease in operating expenses would be considered a cash inflow.

_____5. Discounted cash flow analysis does not take into account the time value of money.

_____6. If the net present value of a project is negative, the investment should not be undertaken.

_____7. After-tax cash outflows are smaller than the pretax cash payment.

_____8. A depreciation tax shield will be treated as a cash inflow.

Problem II

Indicate the correct answer by circling the appropriate letter.

1. Which of the following is not a basic process involved in capital budgeting?
   a. Identifying long-term investment opportunities.
   b. Selecting the appropriate investments.
   c. Financing the selected investments.
   d. Evaluating the investments.
   e. All of the above are basic processes in capital budgeting.

2. Which of the following is not a reason for a company to make a long-term investment?
   a. To replace worn out or unproductive equipment.
   b. To avoid paying dividends on stock.
   c. To expand the business's operating capacity.
   d. To comply with mandates of the government.
   e. All of the above are reasons for making long-term investments.

3. Corporation X is financed by using $3,000,000 of stockholders' equity and $2,000,000 of debt. If the debt has an 8 percent interest rate and stockholders require a 15 percent return on their investment, the cost of capital will be _____.
   a. 12.2 percent
   b. 11.7 percent
   c. 11.5 percent
   d. 23 percent

4. Which of the following is not an assumption underlying net present value analysis?
   a. All cash flows are known with certainty.
   b. Cash flows occur at the beginning of the period.
   c. Cash flows are immediately invested in another project that earns a return meeting or exceeding the cost of capital.
   d. All of the above are assumptions of net present value analysis.

5. Company Z sold a machine for $50,000. The machine had a book value of $70,000 and the company's effective income tax rate was 40 percent. The after-tax cash inflow from the sale was _____.
   a. $46,000
   b. $50,000
   c. $58,000
   d. $70,000

6. Company Z can acquire a machine that will reduce annual operating costs by $20,000 for the next five years. Assuming a cost of capital of 16 percent and ignoring the effect of taxes, what is the maximum price the company would be willing to pay for the machine?
   a. $65,486
   b. $61,785
   c. $83,456
   d. $100,000

7. Company X sold a machine for $100,000. The machine had a book value of $90,000 and the company's effective income tax rate was 30 percent. The after-tax cash inflow from the sale was _____.
   a. $90,000
   b. $93,000
   c. $97,000
   d. $100,000

8. Alpha Corporation is considering a $200,000 investment that will produce annual cash inflows of $30,000 for the next 15 years. Alpha's cost of capital is 12 percent. Ignoring the effect of taxes, the investment's net present value will be _____.
   a. <$25,650>
   b. $1,456
   c. $14,897
   d. $4,327

9. Zeta Company is considering investing in a project that will generate the following cash inflows:

Year	Cash Inflow
1	$35,000
2	$45,000
3	$60,000

Ignoring taxes and assuming a 10 percent cost of capital, what is the maximum price the company would pay for the project?

a. $114,085
b. $116,782
c. $139,789
d. $140,000

10. Company Y has invested in equipment that will generate annual pre-tax operating expense savings of $100,000. Depreciation on the equipment is $20,000 per year. Assuming an effective tax rate of 30 percent, the <u>net</u> annual cash flow from the equipment is _____.

a. $120,000
b. $84,000
c. $76,000
d. $36,000

Problem III

Following is a list of important ideas and key concepts from the chapter. To test your knowledge of these terms, match the term with the definition by placing the number in the space provided.

_____	capital budgeting	_____	net present value analysis
_____	cost of capital	_____	operating leverage
_____	goal incongruence	_____	return on investment
_____	hurdle rate	_____	tax shield

1. Cost of capital

2. A reduction in tax liability by reducing taxable income without affecting pre-tax cash flows

3. A method of evaluating investments that uses the time value of money to assess whether the investment's expected rate of return is greater than the company's cost of capital

4. The process used for analysis and selection of the long-term investments of a business

5. The profit before interest and taxes divided by the asset investment

6. The proportion of fixed costs associated with a project

7. Often the weighted-average cost of debt and equity financing

8. A condition whereby an employee acts in his or her own best interests even if the action is not in the company's best interest

Problem IV

Zectar Corporation is considering investing $500,000 in a machine that will produce annual operating income of $200,000 for five years. Depreciation on the machine would be $60,000 per year. The company's effective tax rate is 30 percent and its discount rate is 16 percent.

    a. Calculate the after-tax cash flows associated with the project.

    b. Calculate the net present value of the investment.

    c. Should the investment be undertaken? Why?

Problem V

Complete the following sentences by filling in the correct response.

1. A firm's cost of capital is the weighted average cost of a firm's _____ and _____ financing.

2. The _____ phase of evaluation involves the comparison of the cash flow projections made in the preacquisition analysis to the _____ cash flows generated by the investment.

3. Under the _____ _____ _____ method, the cost of capital is used as the hurdle rate.

4. The _____ _____ _____ is the return that is necessary to satisfy both creditors and owners.

5. The net present value method only considers the _____ and _____ of an investment's cash flows.

Solutions for Chapter 12

Problem I

1. T
2. F
3. T
4. T
5. F
6. T
7. T
8. T

Problem II

1. e
2. b
3. a
4. b
5. c
6. a
7. c
8. d
9. a
10. c

Problem III

4   capital budgeting   3   net present value analysis
7   cost of capital   6   operating leverage
8   goal incongruence   5   return on investment
1   hurdle rate   2   tax shield

Problem IV

a.   After-tax Cash Flows
Cost of machine	<$500,000>
Annual operating income (1 - .30) x $200,000 =	$140,000
Annual depreciation (.30) x $ 60,000 =	$ 18,000

b.   Net Present Value

Pva (5, 16%) x $140,000	3.2744 x $140,000 =	$458,416
Pva (5, 16%) x $ 18,000	3.2744 x $ 18,000 =	$ 58,939
Net cash inflows		$517,355
Less: Cost of machine		<$500,000>
Net Present Value		$ 17,355

c.   Since the net present value is positive, the company should make the investment. The return on the investment exceeds the cost of the company's capital.

Problem V

1. debt, equity
2. postaudit, actual
3. net present value
4. cost of capital
5. amount, timing

Study Guide: Introduction to Accounting, An Integrated Approach

Chapter 13
Planning Equity Financing

Chapter Overview

Chapter 13 investigates equity financing as a means of raising the capital necessary to run the business and invest in long-term projects. The chapter explores the partnership and corporate forms of equity financing. Terms related to the corporate form of equity financing are discussed in depth. The characteristics of both partnerships and corporate equity instruments are presented. In addition, the chapter discusses the costs and benefits of equity financing versus debt financing.

As you study this chapter, it will be necessary to learn the terms associated with both partnership and corporate forms of equity financing. You should be able to identify the advantages and disadvantages of both of these equity-financing options. In a later chapter you will study how to record and communicate the results of corporate equity financing activities. Therefore, you will be asked to apply what you learn in this chapter to the recording of these activities in the accounting system.

Read and Recall Questions

Learning Objective:
LO. 1 Explain how companies plan for debt versus equity financing.

Define equity financing.

Define debt financing.

Explain financial risk.

Explain the purpose of the debt to equity ratio. How is this ratio calculated?

Discuss the time interest earned ratio and indicate how it is calculated.

Discuss financial leverage. Why may companies find this to be an attractive financing strategy?

What is the purpose of the return on owners' equity ratio? How is this ratio calculated?

Discuss the rewards of equity financing to the owners of the company.

Study Guide: Introduction to Accounting, An Integrated Approach

Describe the risks faced by the providers of equity financing.

What are the sources of equity financing?

Discuss the advantages of the sole proprietorship and partnership forms of business ownership structures.

Discuss the two primary disadvantages of sole proprietorships and partnerships.

Describe the major advantages of the corporate business ownership structure.

Discuss the two primary disadvantages of the corporate ownership structure.

In a partnership, how is the value of each owner's interest in the company determined?

If a partnership agreement is silent on this matter, how is the income of a partnership divided among the partners?

Identify five commonly used methods for dividing the earnings of a partnership.

Why may partners agree to split earnings according to the ratio of capital account balances?

Why may a salary allowance be used to allocate partnership earnings to one or more partners?

Why may an interest allowance on capital balances be used to allocate partnership earnings?

Study Guide: Introduction to Accounting, An Integrated Approach

Besides company earnings, what events may cause changes in a partner's capital account balance during a period?

Learning Objective:
LO. 3 Discuss the process of raising capital through equity financing in a corporation.

Discuss the rights or benefits that common stock provides owners.

Describe the characteristics of common stock.

Describe the following five features associated with preferred stock.

- Cumulative preferred stock

- Participating preferred stock

- Callable preferred stock

- Redeemable preferred stock

- Convertible preferred stock

Explain what return on common equity represents. How is it calculated?

Define the following terms that describe the status of shares of stock.

- Authorized shares

- Issued shares

- Treasury stock

- Outstanding shares

Study Guide: Introduction to Accounting, An Integrated Approach

- Retired shares

Describe the following terms related to the value of shares of stock.

- Par value

- Legal capital

- No-par stock

- No-par, stated value stock

- Market value

What is the purpose of a dividend?

Briefly discuss three forms of dividends.

Identify and describe the four dates related to dividends.

Define a stock split. Why would a company enter into a stock split?

How does a stock split differ from a stock dividend?

Outline of Key Concepts

I.   Companies raise capital using equity financing or debt financing.

    A. Debt financing—obtain funds in exchange for a liability to repay the borrowed funds.

        1. Financial risk—the chance that a company will fail because it defaults on its debt.

            a. Default—unable to meet either the interest or principal payments.

        2. Debt to equity ratio—measures the relationship between the amount of debt and the amount of owners' equity used to finance the company.

            a. The larger the debt to equity ratio, the greater the amount of debt used to finance the company and the greater the financial risk.

        3. Times interest earned ratio—measures a company's ability to service its debt by comparing earnings before deducting interest and taxes to the amount of interest expense for the period.

        4. Financial leverage—financing strategy designed to increase the rate of return on owners' investment by generating a greater return on borrowed funds than the cost of using the funds.

    B. Equity financing—obtain funds in exchange for ownership interest in the company and when management elects to reinvest the company's earnings in the company.

        1. Return on owners' equity ratio—measures the performance of the company in terms of the owners' investment.

            a. Net income/Owners' equity

            b. The higher the return, the more the owners are earning, and the better their investment.

        2. In addition to financial rewards, owners may receive psychic rewards.

        3. Risks include not earning a satisfactory return or losing some or all of the investment.

II.   Ownership structures have advantages and disadvantages.

    A. Sole proprietorships and partnerships have similar advantages and disadvantages.

        1. These ownership structures have three advantages.

            a. Ease of formation.

            b. Income is taxed only once.

            c. Are more likely to be managed by the owners.

        2. These structures share two disadvantages.

            a. Risk associated with unlimited liability.

            b. Inability to raise large amount of capital.

        3. Partnerships also have the disadvantage of mutual agency.

    B. Corporations have different advantages and disadvantages.

        1. Advantages of the corporate structure.

            a. Limited liability.

            b. Ability to raise large amounts of capital.

            c. Unlimited life

257

       2. Disadvantages of the corporate structure.
          a. Time and money to incorporate and satisfy regulatory requirements.
          b. Double taxation.

III.   Determining the equity of each partner is important.
    A. Partnership income can be allocated to partners in a variety of ways.
       1. If the partnership agreement is silent, profits and losses are divided equally.
       2. Divided on a fixed ratio.
       3. Ratio of capital account balances—used when the net income is closely related to the amount invested by the individual partners.
       4. Salary allowance—allocate partnership earnings based on the amount of time respective partners spend operating the business.
          a. It is not an expense of the business but a mean of dividing income.
       5. Interest allowance on capital balances—uses an interest rate multiplied by each partner's capital balance to allocate partnership earnings.
          a. It is an incentive designed to reward partners who invest capital and maintain capital in the business.
       6. May use a combination of salary and interest allowance and then divide the remainder of the profits on an agreed upon ratio.
    B. Other factors change the equity of each partner.
       1. Partners may make additional investments.
       2. Partners may make withdrawals of cash and other assets from the business.

IV.   Corporations may issue shares of stock to indicate an owner's interest in the business.
    A. Common stock—represents the basic ownership unit of the corporation.
       1. Common stock bestows certain rights to stockholders.
          a. Right to vote on significant events that affect the corporation.
          b. Right to declared dividends.
          c. Right to residual assets upon liquidation of the corporation.
          d. Right to dispose of the shares by sale or gift.
          e. Preemptive right—right to maintain their percentage ownership interest in the corporation when it issues new shares of common stock.
    B. Preferred stock—represents an ownership interest in a corporation with special privileges or preferences as to liquidation and dividends.
       1. Preferred stock bestows specific rights to stockholders.
          a. Upon liquidation of the corporation, preferred stockholders are paid before the common stockholders.
          b. Entitled to receive dividends before common stockholders receive dividends.
       2. In exchange for their rights, preferred stock makes some concessions.
          a. Usually give up the right to vote.
          b. Dividends they receive are usually limited to a set amount per share of stock.

Study Guide: Introduction to Accounting, An Integrated Approach

3. Five features may be associated with preferred stock.
   a. Cumulative preferred stock—accumulates unpaid dividends over time (dividends in arrears) and then when dividends are declared and paid in later years, the accumulated amount plus current dividends are paid before common stockholders receive any dividends.
   b. Participating preferred stock—allows preferred stockholders the right to receive an amount in excess of the stated dividend rate or amount.
   c. Callable preferred stock—gives the corporation the right to repurchase its preferred stock at a stipulated price.
   d. Redeemable preferred stock—gives the stockholder the option to turn in the stock for cash at the stockholder's option (at a guaranteed minimum price).
   e. Convertible preferred stock—gives the stockholders the right to exchange shares for other forms of capital, as stated in the corporate charter, at the option of the preferred stockholder.

C. Return on common equity—represents the portion of income available to provide a return from common stockholders.
   1. (Net income – Preferred stock dividends)/(Stockholders' equity – Liquidating value of preferred stock)

D. There are several terms that refer to the number of shares associated with a corporation.
   1. Authorized shares—the total number of shares the state has approved for a corporation to sell.
   2. Issued shares—the number of authorized shares a corporation has sold to stockholders.
      a. Treasury stock—the shares of a corporation's issued stock that the corporation has repurchased and intends to reissue at a later date.
         i. Reduces the number of shares outstanding but not issued.
   3. Outstanding shares—the number of shares issued less the number of shares of treasury stock held by the corporation.
   4. Retired shares—repurchased issued shares that the corporation will never reissue; number of shares issued and outstanding are decreased.

E. Monetary values are attached to shares of stock.
   1. Par value—arbitrary value assigned to shares of capital stock that is approved by the state in which the business is incorporated.
      a. Legal capital—the portion of stockholders' equity required by state law to be retained for the protection of the corporation's creditors.
      b. Amount of proceeds in excess of the par value of the stock is called paid-in capital in excess of par.
   2. No-par stock—does not have a minimum price assigned to each share of stock.

3. No-par, stated value stock—has a minimum price or stated value established by the corporation's board of directors but no par value specified in the charter.
4. Market value—the price agreed to by an unrelated willing buyer and seller.

F. Dividends are a distribution of the assets of the corporation to the owners of the corporation.
   1. Cash dividend—cash distribution paid by sending checks to stockholders as of a certain date.
   2. Stock dividend—a distribution of additional shares of the corporation to existing stockholders.
      a. Each investor has more shares, but his or her percentage interest in the corporation does not change.
   3. Property dividends—involves the distribution of specific noncash assets.
   4. There are four dates related to dividends.
      a. Date of declaration—date on which the board of directors announces its decision to pay a dividend.
      b. Date of record—the date on which it is determined who is eligible to receive the corporation's dividends.
      c. Ex-dividend date—occurs two or three days prior to the date of record and is the last date when an individual can buy the stock of the corporation and still receive the corporation's declared dividend.
      d. Date of payment—date that the company pays the dividends to stockholders of record.

G. Stock split—a corporation calls in its old shares of stock and issues a larger number of new shares of stock in their place.
   1. Par or stated value is reduced to reflect the new number of shares issued and outstanding.
   2. Each stockholder retains the same percentage interest in the corporation.
   3. Stock splits are often used to reduce the market price of the stock to make the price more affordable to investors.
   4. Reverse stock split—corporation calls in its old shares and replaces them with a reduced number of shares with a higher par value.

Problem I

Indicate whether the following statements are either true (T) or false (F).

_____1. Reinvestment of a company's earnings is considered equity financing.
_____2. The risk to owners of a corporation is limited to the amount invested.
_____3. Callable preferred stock gives the shareholder the right to turn in the stock for cash at the stockholder's option.
_____4. Par value of stock is the price agreed to by an unrelated willing buyer and seller.
_____5. A stock dividend will not change an investor's percentage ownership interest in the corporation.
_____6. Partners have unlimited liability for the debts of the partnership.
_____7. Corporations are subject to double taxation.
_____8. In absence of an agreement to the contrary, partners will share profits and losses in the same ratio as their capital contributions.
_____9. Owners may use financial leverage to increase the rate of return to shareholders.
_____10. Outstanding shares are the number of shares issued less the number of shares repurchased and held as treasury stock.

Problem II

Indicate the correct answer by circling the appropriate letter.

1. Which of the following is not a right normally associated with the ownership of common stock?
   a. Preference over creditors to assets in liquidation.
   b. Preemptive right.
   c. Right to vote on significant events that affect the corporation
   d. All of the above are rights of a common stock shareholder.

2. X Corporation will issue 500,000 shares of additional common stock on December 1. Janet currently owns 2% of X Corporation's outstanding stock. Janet has the first option to purchase _____ shares of the stock.
   a. - 0 -
   b. 10,000
   c. 100,000
   d. 500,000

3. Preferred stock shareholders will generally have which of the following rights?
 a. Right to receive dividends before common stock shareholders.
 b. Right to assets in liquidation before common stock shareholders.
 c. Right to assets in liquidation before creditors.
 d. Both a and b.

4. Y Corporation has 10,000 shares of $5, noncumulative, $100 par, preferred stock outstanding. If a dividend is declared, what amount will preferred stock shareholders receive before common stock shareholders receive any dividend?
 a. $50,000
 b. $100,000
 c. $250,000
 d. none of the above

5. Z Corporation has cumulative preferred stock outstanding that carries a normal dividend of $200,000. The corporation is 3 years in arrears on dividend payments. What amount will common stock shareholders receive if a $1,000,000 dividend is paid in the current year?
 a. - 0 -
 b. $200,000
 c. $400,000
 d. $800,000

6. With respect to a cash dividend, a legal liability (obligation) is created on the following date:
 a. The date of declaration
 b. The date of record
 c. The ex-dividend date
 d. Date of payment

7. Which of the following is not an advantage of a sole proprietorship or partnership.
 a. limited liability
 b. ease of formation
 c. income is only taxed once
 d. none of the above is an advantage of a sole proprietorship or partnership

8. Jack, Jerry and Jane formed a partnership and agreed to share profits in a fixed ratio of 3:2:1, respectively. If the partnership earned $36,000 during the year, Jack's capital account will be increased by _____.
 a. $6,000
 b. $12,000
 c. $18,000
 d. $36,000

Study Guide: Introduction to Accounting, An Integrated Approach

9. The M&M Partnership is owned by Max and Mary. Since Mary will manage daily operations, she receives a salary allocation of $35,000 each year. Any remaining profits or losses are shared equally. M&M reported net income of $25,000 for the year. Mary's capital account will increase by _____.
    a. $17,500
    b. $30,000
    c. $35,000
    d. $40,000

10. Which of the following is not an advantage of a corporation.
    a. limited liability
    b. ability to raise large amounts of money
    c. unlimited life
    d. income only taxed once

Use the following information for the next two questions:

At the end of the current period, Roenick Corporation provided the following selected financial information:

Income before interest and taxes	$120,000	Total stockholders' equity	550,000
Total assets	950,000	Interest expense	42,000
Total liabilities	400,000	Income taxes	$ 35,000

11. Roenick's debt-to-equity ratio is _____.
    a. 0.727
    b. 1.375
    c. 0.300
    d. 0.421

12. Roenick's times interest earned is _____.
    a. 3.9
    b. 8.1
    c. 2.9
    d. 0.2

13. Which of the following will affect a company's financial risk?
    a. The company's debt-to-equity ratio.
    b. The volatility of a company's sales
    c. Both a and b are correct
    d. None of the above are correct

Problem III

Following is a list of important ideas and key concepts from the chapter. To test your knowledge of these terms, match the term with the definition by placing the number in the space provided.

_____ authorized shares   _____ legal capital
_____ callable preferred stock   _____ par value
_____ common stock   _____ participating preferred stock
_____ convertible preferred stock _____ preemptive right
_____ cumulative preferred stock _____ retired shares
_____ date of payment   _____ stock dividend
_____ dividends in arrears   _____ stock split
_____ ex-dividend date   _____ treasury stock

1. The shares of a corporation's issued stock that the corporation has repurchased and intends to reissue at a later date

2. The amount of cumulative preferred stock dividends not paid in full when stipulated

3. A right of common stockholders that allows them to maintain their percentage interest in the corporation when it issues new shares of common stock

4. The last date when an individual can buy the stock of the corporation and still receive the corporation's declared dividend

5. Repurchased issued shares that the corporation will never reissue

6. Preferred stock that gives the issuing corporation the right to repurchase the preferred stock at a stipulated price

7. The total number of shares the state has approved for a corporation to sell

8. The distribution of additional shares of the corporation's stock to existing stockholders

9. The basic ownership unit of a corporation

10. The date on which the corporation formally pays dividends to stockholders of record

11. The portion of stockholders' equity required by state law to be retained for the protection of the corporation's creditors

Study Guide: Introduction to Accounting, An Integrated Approach

12. Preferred stock that gives the stockholder the right to convert (exchange) the preferred shares for other forms of capital, as stated in the corporate charter, at the option of the preferred stockholder

13. Preferred stock that allows preferred stockholders the right to receive an amount in excess of the stated dividend rate or amount

14. The corporation's recall of its old shares of stock and issuance of a larger number of new shares in their place

15. Preferred stock that accumulates unpaid dividends over time

16. An arbitrary value assigned to shares of capital stock that is approved by the state in which the business is incorporated

Problem IV

Complete the following sentences by filling in the correct response.

1. _____ stock represents the basic ownership unit of the corporation.

2. The _____ right allows common stock shareholders to maintain their percentage ownership interest in a corporation.

3. _____ preferred stock indicates the corporation has the right to repurchase the stock at a predetermined price.

4. The portion of stockholders' equity required by state law to be retained for the protection of the corporation's creditors is referred to as _____ _____.

5. _____ are distributions of assets of the corporation to shareholders and typically are made from the _____ of the company.

6. A _____ dividend is the distribution of non-cash assets to the stockholders of a company.

7. When a company obtains funds in exchange for a liability to repay the borrowed funds it is referred to as _____ financing.

8. When a company obtains funds in exchange for an ownership interest in the firm it is referred to as _____ financing.

10. The larger the debt-to-equity ratio, the greater the amount of _____ used to finance the company's operations, and the greater the _____ risk.

Problem V

The average capital balances for ABC Partnership are provided below:

A, capital	$50,000
B, capital	$40,000
C, capital	$10,000

Allocate the current period's net income of $80,000 under each of the allocation agreements below:

1. Income and losses are allocated in the ration of 4:3:1.

2. Income and losses are allocated in the ratio of the capital account balances.

Study Guide: Introduction to Accounting, An Integrated Approach

3. A is to receive a salary of $30,000 with remaining profits allocated in the ratio of the capital account balances.

4. Interest of 6 percent is paid on the average capital account balance with remaining profits and losses shared in a ratio of 3:2:1.

Solutions for Chapter 13

Problem I

1. T
2. T
3. F
4. F
5. T
6. T
7. T
8. F
9. T
10. T

Problem II

1. a
2. b
3. d
4. a
5. b
6. a
7. a
8. c
9. b
10. d
11. a
12. c
13. c

Problem III

7	authorized shares	11	legal capital
6	callable preferred stock	16	par value
9	common stock	13	participating preferred stock
12	convertible preferred stock	3	preemptive right
15	cumulative preferred stock	5	retired shares
10	date of payment	8	stock dividend
2	dividends in arrears	14	stock split
4	ex-dividend date	1	treasury stock

Problem IV

1. Common
2. preemptive
3. Callable
4. legal capital
5. Dividends, earnings
6. property
7. debt
8. equity
9. debt, financial

Problem V

1. A 4/8 X $80,000 = $40,000
   B 3/8 X $80,000 = $30,000
   C 1/8 X $80,000 = $10,000

2. A $50,000/$100,000 X $80,000 = $40,000
   B $40,000/$100,000 X $80,000 = $32,000
   C $10,000/$100,000 X $80,000 = $ 8,000

3.

Item	A	B	C	Amount Distributed	Amount Remaining
Net income					$80,000
Salary Allowance	$30,000	$ - 0 -	$ - 0 -	$30,000	50,000
Remainder	25,000	20,000	5,000	50,000	- 0 -
	$55,000	$20,000	$5,000	$80,000	- 0 -

4. Interest Allocation:

   A $ 50,000 X .06 = $3,000
   B $ 40,000 X .06 = $2,400
   C $ 10,000 X .06 = $ 600
   Total $100,000 X .06 = $6,000

Item	A	B	C	Amount Distributed	Amount Remaining
Net income					$80,000
Interest Allowance	$ 3,000	$ 2,400	$ 600	$ 6,000	74,000
Remainder	37,000	24,667	12,333	74,000	- 0 -
	$40,000	$27,067	$12,933	$80,000	- 0 -

269

Chapter 14
Planning Debt Financing

Chapter Overview

Chapter 14 explores the use of debt financing to raise the capital necessary to operate a business and to enable a business to invest in long-term projects. The chapter explains periodic payment, lump-sum payment, and interest-bearing notes; and, it offers guidance on how to determine which type of note best fits the company's financing needs. The chapter also illustrates the effect that the proposed financing alternatives will have on cash flows, income, and financial position.

As in previous chapters, it is necessary that you become familiar with the new terms presented. You will be drawing upon your knowledge of the time value of money once again. Present value calculations are an integral part of determining the issue price of interest-bearing notes and recognizing interest expense. If needed, you may review Chapter 11 as you study this chapter. In addition to understanding the calculations presented, you should develop an understanding of the potential benefits of debt financing versus equity financing. Conceptually, you should try to link Chapters 13 and 14 together as alternative approaches in the process of raising capital for a business.

Read and Recall Questions

> **Learning Objective:**
> LO. 1 Describe and calculate the impact of a periodic payment note payable on the company's budgeted financial statements.

Why do lenders impose covenants on borrowers?

Explain the difference between the face rate of interest and the market rate of interest.

What is a periodic payment note?

What is the amount of the future value of a periodic payment note?

Explain what happens to the carrying value of a periodic payment note over time.

Learning Objective:
LO. 2 Discuss and calculate the impact of a lump-sum payment note payable on the company's budgeted financial statements.

Discuss the characteristics of a lump-sum payment or noninterest-bearing note.

On a five-year lump-sum payment note, what are the amounts of cash flows shown on the statement of cash flows in years 2, 3, and 4?

Explain what happens to the carrying value of lump-sum payment notes over time.

Discuss the characteristics of a periodic and lump-sum payment (interest-bearing) note.

Explain the impact on initial cash flows, interest payments, interest expense, and carrying value of issuing an interest-bearing note at a discount.

What are the effects on initial cash flows, interest payments, interest expense, and carrying value of issuing an interest-bearing note at a premium?

At the issue date, what is the present value of an interest-bearing note when its market and face rates of interest are equal?

When a company has issued an interest-bearing note, explain how the interest payments and principal payments are classified on the statement of cash flows.

Discuss the factors that a financial planner should consider when deciding which type of long-term debt instruments the company should issue.

Other Debt Financing Issues:

Why may creditors require borrowers to secure their debt with collateral?

What is a lease? Distinguish between an operating lease and a capital lease.

Study Guide: Introduction to Accounting, An Integrated Approach

What are bonds?

Bonds may be issued with repayment provisions. Briefly discuss the following types of bonds with special repayment provisions:

- Callable bonds

- Convertible bonds

- Serial bonds

Bonds may be issued with security provisions. Briefly describe the following types of bonds with security provisions:

- Secured bonds

- Unsecured bonds

- Subordinated bonds

Outline of Key Concepts

I. Debt financing—a means for a company to obtain funds, goods, and/or services in exchange for a liability to repay the borrowed funds.
   A. Terms of the debt should be formalized between the lender and borrower.
      1. Covenants—restrictions placed on the borrower by the lender to protect the lender's interests.
      2. Notes are written promises that describe the cash flows the borrower is willing to pay in return for the use of the lender's funds.
      3. Maker of the note—the borrower.
      4. Holder of the note—the lender.
      5. Face value of the note—the amount that the note's maker will ultimately pay the note's holder for the principal.
      6. Face rate of interest on the note—determines the amount of cash interest that the note's maker will periodically pay the holder of the note.
      7. Market or effective interest rate—actual interest rate charged for the use of the proceeds of the note.
      8. Proceeds—amount of cash raised from the issuance of the debt.
   B. Managers must consider how the debt will impact the income statement (interest expense), statement of cash flows (initial receipt of cash and repayment of debt, and the balance sheet (carrying value of the liability).

II. Periodic payment note—a debt instrument that contains a promise to make a series of equal payments consisting of both interest and principal at equal intervals over a specified time period; typically called installment notes.
   A. This note involves a present value of an annuity.
      1. Difference between the total amount repaid and the face amount of the note is the interest expense for the term of the note.
      2. The carrying value of the note decreases over time, the payment is the same over time, and the interest portion of the payment decreases while the principal portion of the note payment increases over time.
      3. Future value of the note is zero.

4. Interest expense for a given period is equal to the carrying value x market rate x time.

III. Lump-sum payment note—debt instrument that contains a promise to pay a specific amount of money at the end of a specific period of time; often called a noninterest-bearing note.
   A. Note does not have a face rate of interest.
      1. Specifies only the amount the borrower promises to pay back at a future date.
      2. Face value depends on the amount of money the borrower wants to use and the market interest rate the borrower and lender agree upon.
         a. Face value is the future value of the note.
      3. Interest expense for a given period is equal to carrying value x market rate x time.
      4. Initial carrying value is the present value of the note.
         a. Increases over time because the interest and principal are not paid until the end of the life of the note.

IV. Periodic payment and lump-sum note—debt instrument that combines periodic cash payments and a final lump-sum cash payment; also called an interest-bearing note.
   A. Has a face rate of interest and a face value that indicates the maker promises to make periodic cash interest payments and a lump-sum payment on the date the note matures.
      1. Periodic cash interest payment = face rate of interest x face value of note.
      2. Market rate of interest determines the proceeds of the note.
   B. When the market rate of interest is greater than the face rate of interest, the proceeds of the note will be less than the face value of the note.
      1. Discount—difference between the face value and proceeds.
      2. Determine the proceeds by calculating the present value of the face value of the note plus present value of the cash interest payments.
         a. Based on the market interest rate.
      3. Interest expense for a period is equal to carrying value x market rate x time.
         a. Interest expense will be greater than the periodic cash interest payments.
      4. Carrying value increases over time.
   C. When the market rate of interest is less than the face rate of interest, the proceeds of the note will be greater than the face value of the note.
      1. Premium—amount by which the present value of the note exceeds the face value of the note.
      2. Determine the proceeds by calculating the present value of the face value of the note plus present value of the cash interest payments.
         a. Based on the market interest rate.
      3. Interest expense for a period is equal to carrying value x market rate x time.

a. Interest expense will be less than the periodic cash interest payments.
4. Carrying value decreases over the life of the note.

D. When the market rate of interest is the same as the face rate, the proceeds of the note will be the same as the face value of the note.
1. No premium or discount.
2. Interest expense will be equal to the cash interest payments.

V. Long-term debt financing is available from a number of sources.

A. Nonpublic financing—company enters into an agreement with a person or institution to borrow funds.
1. Collateral—an asset or group of assets to which the creditor has a claim if the borrower fails to comply with the terms of the note.
   a. Mortgage—long-term note secured with real estate.

B. Leases—an agreement to convey the use of a tangible asset from one party to another in return for rental payments.
1. Operating lease—rental agreement for a period of time that is substantially shorter than the economic life of the leased asset.
2. Capital lease—the lessee (user) acquires such a substantial interest in the leased asset that the lessee company, for all practical purposes, owns the asset.
   a. Recognition of an asset and liability.

C. Bonds—long-term debt instruments issued by corporations to raise money from the public.
1. Usually take the form of periodic payment and lump-sum notes.
2. Bond issue—consists of a group of $1,000 face value notes with a specified interest rate, often paid semiannually, that mature in 10 or more years.
3. Bond indenture—bond contract that specifies the amount of the bond issue, the life of the bond, the face value of each bond, and the face interest rate of the bond issue.
4. Bond provisions relate to ownership, repayment, and security.
   a. Registered bonds—numbered and made payable in the name of the bondholder.
   b. Bearer bonds—made payable to the bearer or person who has physical possession of the bond; no longer issued.
   c. Callable bonds—the company issuing the bonds has the right to buy them back before the maturity date at a specified price.
   d. Convertible bonds—allow bondholders to exchange their bonds for common or preferred stock.
   e. Serial bonds—bond issue that has specified portions of the bond issue coming due periodically over the life of the bond issue.
   f. Secured bonds—have some part of the issuing company's assets serving as security for the loan.

g. Unsecured bonds—do not have any specific assets pledged as security against their repayment. Rest on the general creditworthiness of the issuing company.
   i. Called debenture bonds.
h. Subordinated bonds—unsecured bonds whose rights to repayment are ranked after some other group of creditors or persons.

Problem I

Indicate whether the following statements are either true (T) or false (F).

_____ 1. Restrictions on the borrowing company are called covenants.
_____ 2. Face value is the amount that must ultimately be repaid by the borrower.
_____ 3. A noninterest–bearing note will be issued at a premium.
_____ 4. The interest portion of an installment payment becomes larger with each subsequent payment.
_____ 5. When the market rate of interest on a note is less than the face rate, a note will be issued at a premium.
_____ 6. Interest expense is the cost of using borrowed funds.
_____ 7. For most businesses, nonpublic financing is the most common source of long-term debt.
_____ 8. When the market rate equals the face rate, the cash proceeds will equal the face value of the note.
_____ 9. A periodic payment note will consist of equal amounts of interest and principal repayments over the life of the note.
_____ 10. A capital lease is typically for a period of time that is shorter than the economic life of the asset being leased.

Problem II

Indicate the correct answer by circling the appropriate letter.

Use the following information for the next two questions:

Jinger Corporation borrowed $200,000 from a local bank. The loan is a periodic payment note with an interest rate of 10 percent. The annual payment is $32,509.

1. What is the interest portion of the first payment?
   a. $12,000
   b. $20,000
   c. $32,509
   d. $16,345

2. What is the loan balance after the first payment?
   a. $200,000
   b. $167,491
   c. $180,000
   d. $187,491

Use the following information for the next two questions:

On August 1, X Corporation issued a 10-year, $400,000 note payable with a face rate of interest of 9% payable annually. The market rate of interest was 12% and the cash proceeds of the note were $332,197.

3. What is the amount of the annual cash payment?
   a. $36,000
   b. $18,000
   c. $48,000
   d. $24,000

4. What is interest expense for the first period?
   a. $39,864
   b. $36,000
   c. $48,000
   d. $41,739

Study Guide: Introduction to Accounting, An Integrated Approach

5. On January 1, X Corporation borrowed $100,000 agreeing to pay interest at a rate of 6%. Compute the periodic payment if the note is to repaid over the next 10 years.
   a. $13,587
   b. $10,000
   c. $8,931
   d. $12,794

6. On July 1, Z Corporation issued a 10-year, $200,000 note payable with a face rate of interest of 4%. Assuming a market rate of interest of 5% and annual payments, what will be the cash proceeds on the note?
   a. $200,000
   b. $191,784
   c. $167,352
   d. $184,554

7. On June 1, X Corporation issued a 5-year, $800,000 note payable with a face rate of interest of 8% payable semi-annually. The market rate of interest was 6%. What are the cash proceeds on the note?
   a. $756,984
   b. $812,539
   c. $868,242
   d. $891,006

Problem III

Following is a list of important ideas and key concepts from the chapter. To test your knowledge of these terms, match the term with the definition by placing the number in the space provided.

_____ bearer bond	_____ face value of note
_____ bond	_____ holder of note
_____ bond indenture	_____ lease
_____ callable bond	_____ lump-sum payment note
_____ capital lease	_____ mortgage bond
_____ carrying value of debt	_____ operating lease
_____ collateral	_____ registered bonds
_____ convertible bond	_____ secured bond
_____ covenants	_____ serial bond
_____ debenture bonds	_____ unsecured bond

1. A bond that is secured with real estate

2. A bond feature that allows bondholders to exchange their bonds for common or preferred stock

3. A bond that has some part of the issuing corporation's assets serving as security for the loan

4. A rental agreement for a period of time substantially shorter than the economic life of the leased asset

5. A bond that does not have any specific assets pledged as security against its repayment

6. An asset or group of assets specifically named in a debt agreement to which the creditor has claim if the borrower fails to comply with the terms of the note

7. Bonds that are numbered and made payable in the name of the bondholder

8. A debt instrument that contains a promise to pay a specific amount of money at the end of a specified period of time

9. The bond contract

10. A lease in which a company acquires such a substantial interest in the leased property that, for all practical purposes, the lessee company owns the asset

11. The lender

12. An agreement to convey the use of a tangible asset from one party to another in return for rental payments

13. A long-term debt instrument issued by corporations to raise money from the public

14. A bond issue that has specified portions of the bond issue coming due periodically over the life of the bond issue

15. Restrictions that lenders place on the borrowing company to protect the lender's interest

16. A bond that is payable to the bearer or person who has physical possession of the bond

17. Remaining liability on the pro forma balance sheet

18. A bond that gives the company issuing the bond the right to buy it back before the maturity date at a specified price

Study Guide: Introduction to Accounting, An Integrated Approach

19. The amount the borrower will repay the lender for principal

20. Unsecured bonds; bonds with no specific assets pledged as collateral

Problem IV

Complete the following sentences by filling in the correct response.

1. The _____ of a note refers to the cash received by the borrower whereas the _____ _____ refers to the amount the borrower must repay.

2. When the market rate of interest is _____ than the face rate of interest, the proceeds of the note will be less than the face value of the note.

3. The contract that specifies the terms and conditions related to a bond is called the _____ _____.

4. A _____ bond is secured by a company's real estate whereas a _____ bond is unsecured.

5. Firms use _____ liabilities to finance assets such as buildings, equipment, land and patents.

Problem V

Y Corporation issued a five-year, $50,000 face value, noninterest-bearing note payable on January 1, 20X1. The effective rate of interest on the note was 8% compounded semiannually.

a. What amount will Y Corporation receive on January 1, 20X1?

b. What amount will Y Corporation repay on the maturity date?

c. What amount of interest will be incurred by the borrower for 20X1?

Study Guide: Introduction to Accounting, An Integrated Approach

Problem VI

On September 1, 20X1, Lintner Company borrowed $300,000 from the bank. Under the terms of the loan, Lintner will make five annual payments of interest and principal. The interest rate on the note is 8 percent. Prepare an amortization schedule for the periodic note payable (see Exhibit 14.3).

Problem VII

Vectar Corporation issued a $2,000,000, 20-year bond payable on March 1, 20X1. The bond carries a face rate of 9 percent payable annually. The market rate was 7 percent on the date the bond was issued and the cash proceeds of the bond were $2,423,760.57. Prepare the bond amortization schedule for the first three years of the bond (see Exhibit 14.4).

Solutions for Chapter 14

Problem I

1. T
2. T
3. F
4. F
5. T
6. T
7. T
8. T
9. F
10. F

Problem II

1. b
2. d
3. a
4. a
5. a
6. d
7. c

Problem III

16	bearer bond	19	face value of note
13	bond	11	holder of note
9	bond indenture	12	lease
18	callable bond	8	lump-sum payment note
10	capital lease	1	mortgage bond
17	carrying value of debt	4	operating lease
6	collateral	7	registered bonds
2	convertible bond	3	secured bond
15	covenants	14	serial bond
20	debenture bonds	5	unsecured bond

Problem IV

1. proceeds, face value
2. greater
3. bond indenture
4. mortgage, debenture
5. long-term

Problem V

a. $50,000 x PV(4%, 10) = cash proceeds

   $50,000 x .6756 = $33,780

b. The face value of the note ($50,000) must be repaid at maturity.

c. Interest for first 6 months:

   $33,780 x .08 x 6/12 = $1,351.20

   Interest for last 6 months:

   ($33,780 + $1,351.20) x .08 x 6/12 = $35,131.20 x .08 x 6/12 = $1,405.25

   Total interest expense for the year:

   $1,351.20 + $1,405.25 = $2,756.45

Problem VI

Periodic Payment Annuity X PVA(5,8%) = $300,000
Annuity X 3.9927 = $300,000
Annuity = $75,137.13

Date	(a) Payment	(b) Interest Expense [.08 x (d)]	(c) Principal [(a) - (b)]	(d) Loan Balance [(d) - (c)]
9/1/X1				$300,000.00
9/1/X2	$75,137.13	$24,000.00	$51,137.13	$248,862.87
9/1/X3	$75,137.13	$19,909.03	$55,228.10	$193,634.77
9/1/X4	$75,137.13	$15,490.78	$59,646.35	$133,988.42
9/1/X5	$75,137.13	$10,719.07	$64,418.06	$ 69,570.36
9/1/X6	$75,137.13	$ 5,566.77*	$69,570.36	$ - 0 -

* rounding

Problem VII

Date	(a) Payment [.09 x $2,000,000]	(b) Interest [.07 x (e)]	(c) CV Adjustment [(a) - (b)]	(d) Carrying Value [(d) - (c)]
3/1/X1				$2,423,760.57
3/1/X2	$180,000.00	$169,663.24	$10,336.76	$2,413,423.81
3/1/X3	$180,000.00	$168,939.67	$11,060.33	$2,402,363.48
3/1/X4	$180,000.00	$168,165.44	$11,834.56	$2,390,528.92

Study Guide: Introduction to Accounting, An Integrated Approach

Chapter 15
Recording and Evaluating Capital Resource Process
Activities: Financing

Chapter Overview

In the two preceding chapters, planning for equity and debt financing was presented. This chapter extends the discussion on equity and debt financing by examining the process for recording and communicating these activities. The chapter illustrates the accounting process for recording corporate equity and debt financing events.

As you study this chapter, it may be necessary to review the terms and concepts presented in Chapters 13 and 14. Make sure you understand the equity financing events; don't try to memorize all the journal entries associated with these accounting events. You will only become confused. As you study the debt financing events, carefully analyze the amortization tables. Notice the effect that the amortization of bond discounts and premiums have on the interest cost of using debt financing and on the carrying value of the bonds. Also seek to understand the cash flow effects of each type of note illustrated. This chapter will require focused study time and a lot of practice completing exercises and problems.

Read and Recall Questions

Learning Objective:
LO. 1 Explain, record, and report equity financing activities for a corporation.

Why does corporate accounting separate the contributions made by stockholders from the undistributed earnings of the firm?

If stock has a par value, what amount is always credited to the common stock account?

What does the account Paid-in Capital in Excess of Par represent? When is it used?

If no-par stock is issued, what amount appears in the capital stock account? If no-par stated value stock is issued, what amount appears in the capital stock account?

If stock is issued for assets other than cash, at what amount will the transaction be recorded?

Define retained earnings. What is the normal account balance for the account, Retained Earnings?

What does a deficit in the Retained Earnings account represent?

How does net income change the Retained Earnings account? How does a loss change the Retained Earnings account?

What effect does the declaration of dividends have on the balance of the Retained Earnings account? What effect does the entry on the date of payment have on the balance of the Retained Earnings account?

What is a small stock dividend? What value is used to record a small stock dividend?

What type of account is Stock Dividends Distributable?

What is a large stock dividend? What value is used to record a large stock dividend?

What type of account is Treasury Stock? What is its normal balance?

When is the Paid-in Capital from Treasury Stock account used? Would this account ever be debited? Explain.

291

Would the Retained Earnings account ever be debited when reissuing treasury stock? Explain.

On which statement are the changes in retained earnings reported?

How is cash resulting from owners' equity activities classified on the statement of cash flows?

<table>
<tr><td>**Learning Objective:**
LO. 2 Describe, record, and report debt financing activities for a corporation.</td></tr>
</table>

Explain what the total amount of each payment of an installment note represents.

How is the principal of an installment note reported on the balance sheet?

How is the payment on an installment note classified on the statement of cash flows?

Study Guide: Introduction to Accounting, An Integrated Approach

What determines the face value of a lump-sum payment note?

When accounting for lump-sum payment notes, what does the account Discount on Note Payable represent? What type of account is Discount on Note Payable?

As the Discount on Note Payable account is reduced, what happens to the carrying value of the lump-sum payment note payable?

When do the cash flows associated with a lump-sum payment note occur?

If the market interest rate is greater than the face rate of interest, will the proceeds be equal to, greater than, or less than the face value of the bonds? Explain.

If the market interest rate is greater than the face rate of interest, will the interest expense be equal to, greater than, or less than the cash interest paid? Explain.

What does the account Discount on Bonds Payable represent? What type of account is Discount on Bonds Payable?

How are bonds issued at a discount reported on the balance sheet?

If the market interest rate is less than the face rate of interest, will the proceeds be equal to, greater than, or less than the face amount of the bonds? Explain.

If the market interest rate is less than the face rate of interest, will interest expense be equal to, greater than, or less than the cash interest paid? Explain.

What does the account Premium on Bonds Payable represent? What type of account is Premium on Bonds Payable?

How are bonds issued on a premium reported on the balance sheet?

Study Guide: Introduction to Accounting, An Integrated Approach

If the market interest rate equals the face rate of interest, are the proceeds of the bond issue equal to, greater than, or less than the face value of the bonds? Explain.

If the market interest rate equals the face rate of interest, is the interest expense equal to, greater than, or less than the cash interest paid? Explain.

On which financial statement is interest expense reported?

Outline of Key Concepts

I. When accounting for equity financing events, corporations must separate owner contributions from the retained earnings of the company.
    A. When accounting for par value stock, the amount of the par value is credited to the capital stock account regardless of the amount paid for the shares.
        1. Paid-in Capital in Excess of Par—account which represents the additional net assets that owners contribute above the par value of the stock.
    B. With no-par stock, the amount received for the shares is the amount credited to the capital stock account.
        1. If the stock has a stated value, the stated value of the stock is credited to the capital stock account.
    C. Retained Earnings—account which represents the amount of the corporation's earnings since its inception less all dividends distributed.
        1. Appears on the balance sheet as part of stockholders' equity.
        2. Has a normal credit balance.
        3. Deficit balance (debit)—occurs when the cumulative total of net losses plus dividends declared exceeds the cumulative total of net income.

D. Cash dividends declared reduce retained earnings and create a liability.
   1. When the dividends are paid, the liability and cash are decreased.
E. Small stock dividends—the additional number of shares to be issued is from 20 to 25 percent or less of the shares issued.
   1. Retained Earnings is debited for the fair market value of the stock multiplied by the number of new shares issued.
   2. Stock Dividends Distributable—account credited on the date of declaration.
      a. Credited for the par value of the shares.
      b. Excess of market value over par is credited to the Paid-in Capital in Excess of Par.
      c. It is a contributed capital account, not a liability.
F. Large stock dividend—one that is greater than 25 percent of the number of shares issued.
   1. The dividend is recorded at the par value rather than the market value of the stock.
G. Treasury Stock account represents the amount paid to reacquire its own shares of stock with the intent to reissue them at a later date.
   1. The account is reported as a contra equity account that reduces total stockholders' equity on the balance sheet. It is NOT an asset.
   2. The account is debited when shares are reacquired.
   3. When shares are reissued, Treasury Stock is credited. Any amount received in excess of the acquisition price is credited to Paid-in Capital from Treasury Stock.
   4. When Treasury stock is reissued for less than the acquisition cost, the difference is first debited to Paid-in Capital from Treasury Stock, and if this account is inadequate, Retained Earnings will be debited.

II.   Regardless of the type of debt instrument, debt is initially recorded at its face value.
   A. Accounting for periodic payment long-term notes (installment notes) requires timely recognition of the interest expense on the notes.
      1. The note is recorded at the present value of the annuity payments.
      2. A repayment schedule shows the portion of each payment that covers the interest on the loan and the portion that reduces the principal of the note.
         a. Journal entries mirror the repayment schedule.
         b. Cash payments remain constant, but the interest expense and the decrease to Notes Payable change each month.
      3. Interest expense will be reported on the income statement.
      4. Interest payments will be reported in the operating section of the statement of cash flows.
      5. Payments applied to the principal will be reported in the financing section of the statement of cash flows.
      6. Carrying value of the note will be reported as a liability on the balance sheet.

a. The portion of the note due in the coming year is classified as a current liability.

B. Noninterest-bearing notes do not have a face rate of interest.

1. Face value of the note depends on the market interest rate.
2. The market rate is used to calculate the present value of the note payable.
3. The note is recorded at the face amount and a discount account is used to offset or reduce the liability so that it reflects the carrying value of the note.
4. Entries to reflect interest involve a credit to Discount on Notes Payable and a debit to Interest Expense.
5. As the discount account is reduced, the carrying value of the note payable increases.
6. At maturity, the carrying value of the note will equal the face amount of the note.
7. Interest expense will be reported on the income statement.
8. The only cash flows will occur at the time the note is issued and when the note is repaid at maturity. Reported as financing cash flows on the Statement of Cash Flows.
9. Carrying value of the note is reported on the balance sheet.

C. Bonds—if the market interest rate is greater than the face rate of interest on the bond issue, the proceeds from the sale of the bonds are less than the face value of the bonds.

1. The resulting discount is amortized over the life of the bonds.
2. Discount on Bonds Payable—a contra liability account subtracted from Bonds Payable to show the bonds' carrying value on the balance sheet.
3. The amortization of the discount results in a higher amount of interest expense being reported on the income statement than cash interest payments being reported on the statement of cash flows.
4. At the maturity date, the discount will be fully amortized so that the carrying value of the bonds equals the face value of the bonds.

D. Bonds—if the market interest rate is less than the face interest rate of the bond issue, the proceeds from the sale of the bonds are greater than the face value of the bonds.

1. The resulting premium is amortized over the life of the bonds.
2. The balance in Premium on Bonds Payable is added to Bonds Payable to determine the carrying value of the bonds on the balance sheet.
3. The amortization of the premium results in a lesser amount of interest expense being reported on the income statement than the cash interest payments reported on the statement of cash flows.
4. At the maturity date, the premium will be fully amortized so that the carrying value of the bonds equals the face value of the bonds.

E. Bonds—if the market interest rate and the face interest rate are equal at the time the bonds are issued, the proceeds of the sale of the bonds equal the face value of the bonds.

1. Interest expense equals the amount of cash interest paid.

III. Management must evaluate the results of financing activities.
 A. Compare against the goals set in the balanced scorecard.
  1. Might calculate several ratios:
   a. Debt to equity ratio
   b. Times interest earned ratio
   c. Return on equity
   d. Return on common equity

Problem I

Indicate whether the following statements are either true (T) or false (F).

_____1. A periodic payment note is recorded at the present value of the annuity payments.
_____2. Interest payments will be shown in the financing section of the cash flow statement.
_____3. The market rate of interest is used to calculate the present value of a note payable.
_____4. Repayment of the principal portion of a note payable will be shown in the financing section of the cash flow statement.
_____5. The carrying value of a lump-sum note payable will get larger each time the company records interest expense.
_____6. A credit balance in retained earnings would be considered a deficit in retained earnings.
_____7. Stock dividends cause a corporation's net assets to decrease.
_____8. At maturity, the carrying value of a note is equal to its face value.
_____9. A corporation is not considered a separate legal entity.
_____10. Once a cash dividend has been declared, a liability for payment exists for the corporation.
_____11. Dividends are not paid on treasury stock.
_____12. For corporations, contributions made by stockholders are separated from reinvested earnings.
_____13. If common stock is sold for more than its par value, the corporation will recognize a gain.
_____14. A "small" stock dividend will be recorded at the stock's fair market value.
_____15. Treasury stock is considered an asset of the corporation.

Study Guide: Introduction to Accounting, An Integrated Approach

Problem II

Indicate the correct answer by circling the appropriate letter.

1. On December 1, 20X1 Z Corporation purchased equipment by issuing a 5-year $400,000 non-interest bearing note payable. The market rate of interest was 8 percent. The entry to record the purchase of the equipment will include a _____.
   - a. debit to the equipment account of $400,000
   - b. debit to the equipment account of $272,240
   - c. debit to notes payable of $400,000
   - d. credit to notes payable of $272,240

Use the following information for the next three questions:

On January 1, 20X1, Y Corporation purchased $100,000 of equipment by issuing an installment note payable. The note payable pays interest of 12 percent and is to be repaid in equal installments over the next ten years. Payments will be made each December 31.

2. What is the periodic payment that Y Corporation must make to repay the $100,000 loan?
   - a. $17,698
   - b. $15,690
   - c. $21,335
   - d. $17,211

3. What amount of interest expense will Y Corporation report in 20X1?
   - a. $9,000
   - b. $8,456
   - c. $12,000
   - d. $11,700

4. What will Y Corporation report as a liability on its balance sheet on December 31, 20X1?
   - a. $100,000
   - b. $98,000
   - c. $93,140
   - d. $94,302

5. On an installment note payable, interest expense will _____.
   - a. become larger each year
   - b. become smaller each year
   - c. remain the same throughout the life of the note payable
   - d. none of the above

Use the following information for the next two questions:

Box Inc. issued 20-year bonds with a $3,000,000 face value and a 6 percent face rate. At the time of the issue, the market rate of interest was 8 percent. Interest is paid annually.

6. What is the annual cash payment made by Box Inc.?
   a. $180,000
   b. $240,000
   c. $300,000
   d. $200,000

7. Which of the following entries would have been made on the issue date of the bond?

a.	Cash	3,000,000	
	Bonds Payable		3,000,000
b.	Cash	2,410,758	
	Discount on Bonds Payable	589,242	
	Bonds Payable		3,000,000
c.	Cash	3,000,000	
	Premium on Bonds Payable		589,242
	Bonds Payable		2,410,758
d.	none of the above		

8. X Corporation issued 200,000 shares of its $20 par value common stock. The issue price was $30 per share. The journal entry made by X Corporation on the issue date would be _____.

a.	Cash	6,000,000	
	Common Stock		4,000,000
	Paid-in Capital in Excess of Par - Common Stock		2,000,000
b.	Cash	6,000,000	
	Common Stock		6,000,000
c.	Cash	6,000,000	
	Common Stock		4,000,000
	Gain on sale of Common Stock		2,000,000
d. none of the above			

9. On July 1, Y Corporation declared a 30 percent stock dividend. On the date declared, there were 10,000 shares of $20 par value common stock outstanding. The fair market value per share prior to the declaration of the dividend was $35. The entry on July 1 will include _____.
   a. a debit to cash of $60,000
   b. a debit to cash of $105,000
   c. a credit to stock dividends distributable of $105,000
   d. a credit to stock dividends distributable of $60,000

Study Guide: Introduction to Accounting, An Integrated Approach

10. On January 16, Z Corporation declared a 5 percent stock dividend. On the date declared, there were 20,000 shares of $10 par value common stock outstanding. The fair market value per share prior to the declaration of the dividend was $17. The entry on January 16 to record the declaration of the stock dividend is _____.

a.	Retained earnings	$17,000	
	Stock dividend distributable		$10,000
	Paid-in-capital, common stock		$ 7,000
b.	Stock dividend distributable	$10,000	
	Paid-in-capital, common stock	$ 7,000	
	Retained earnings		$17,000
c.	Retained earnings	$10,000	
	Common stock		$10,000
d.	Retained earnings	$17,000	
	Common stock		$10,000
	Paid-in-capital, common stock		$ 7,000

11. During the year, Fasttax Corporation reported net income of $235,000 and paid cash dividends of $85,000. The beginning balance in retained earnings was $400,000. What will Fasttax report as retained earnings on the balance sheet as of the end of the year?

a. $400,000
b. $635,000
c. $165,000
d. $550,000

12. A cash dividend will reduce retained earnings on the _____.

a. declaration date
b. ex-dividend date
c. date of record
d. date of distribution

13. Which of the following will not reduce total stockholders' equity?

a. The purchase of treasury stock.
b. The company reported a net loss for the year.
c. The company paid a cash dividend.
d. The company issued a stock dividend.

14. A cash dividend will be shown in the _____ section of the cash flow statement.

a. cash flows from operations
b. cash flows from financing activities
c. cash flows from investing activities
d. non-cash activities

15. The purchase of treasury stock will be shown in the _____ section of the cash flow statement.
    a. cash flows from operations
    b. cash flows from financing activities
    c. cash flows from investing activities
    d. non-cash activities

Problem III

Complete the following sentences by filling in the correct response.

1. On an installment note payable, the annual _____ _____ remains the same but _____ _____ becomes smaller each year.

2. When the market rate equals the face rate, the cash proceeds will equal the _____ value of the bond.

3. Premiums are _____ to and discounts are _____ from the face value of a bond in arriving at its carrying value.

4. When the market rate is greater than the face rate, the bond will be issued at a _____.

5. On the cash flow statement, the proceeds of a bond issue will be shown in the _____ section and the payment of interest expense will be shown in the _____ section.

6. When the face rate is _____ than the market rate, the bond will be issued at a premium.

7. _____ _____ is the amount of corporate earnings since inception that has not been _____ to shareholders as _____.

8. A stock split will change the _____ _____ of the stock and will cause the number of shares outstanding to _____.

9. In a corporation, _____ made by stockholders are kept separate from undistributed _____ of the firm.

    Study Guide: Introduction to Accounting, An Integrated Approach

Problem IV

On May 1, 20X1, the Dialex Corporation issued a 3-year $500,000 note payable. The face rate on the note was 8 percent and interest is paid semi-annually. The market rate of interest was 10 percent. The amortization schedule (rounded to the nearest dollar) is as follows:

Date	Cash Payment (.04 x FV)	Interest Expense (.05 x CV)	Discount Amortized	Discount	Note Carrying Value
5/1/X1				$25,378	$474,622
11/1/X1	$20,000	$23,731	$3,731	$21,647	$478,353
5/1/X2	$20,000	$23,918	$3,918	$17,730	$482,270
11/1/X2	$20,000	$24,114	$4,114	$13,616	$486,384
5/1/X3	$20,000	$24,319	$4,319	$9,297	$490,703
11/1/X3	$20,000	$24,535	$4,535	$4,762	$495,238
5/1/X4	$20,000	$24,762	$4,762	$0	$500,000

Prepare the following entries in general journal form:
   a. The issuance of the note payable on 5/1/X1.
   b. The interest payment on 11/1/X2.
   c. The adjusting entry on 12/31/X3.

General Journal			
Date	Account Title	Debit	Credit

Problem V

Prepare the following selected journal entries for Kirk Company for 20X1:

1/1   Kirk issued a $400,000 three-year noninterest-bearing note payable (annual compounding) for computer equipment. The market rate of interest was 8 percent.

4/1   Kirk made the annual $26,380 payment on a $100,000 installment note payable issued one year earlier. At the time the note was issued, the market rate of interest was 10 percent.

7/1   Kirk issued a $400,000, 8% face rate, 10-year bond payable. The bond pays interest on 7/1 and 12/31 and the market rate of interest is 6%.

12/31   The $16,000 interest payment related to the bond issued on 7/1 was made.

12/31   Prepare the adjusting entry to record interest on the note payable issued on 1/1.

General Journal

Date	Account Title	Debit	Credit

Problem VI.

Events affecting the stockholders' equity section of the Solex Corporation are presented below. On the general journal provided on the following page, prepare all necessary journal entries for the year.

1/11   One thousand shares of no-par, no-stated value common stock were issued for $7 per share.

3/29   Land was purchased by the company by issuing 20,000 shares of no-par, no-stated value common stock. The market price per share was $8.

6/30   The board of directors declared a cash dividend of $1 per share. There were 100,000 shares outstanding on the date of declaration. The date of record is 7/5 and payment date is 7/9.

7/9   Solex paid the cash dividend declared on 6/30.

8/3   Solex repurchased 1,000 shares of its own stock for $7.50 per share.

10/15   The board of directors declared a 5 percent stock dividend to be issued on 10/25. On the date of declaration, there were 99,000 shares outstanding. The market price per share was $8.25.

10/25   The stock certificates related to the stock dividend on 10/15 were distributed.

12/12   The stock repurchased by Solex on 8/3 was resold for $9.50 per share.

Problem VI (continued)

General Journal

Date	Account Title	Debit	Credit

Study Guide: Introduction to Accounting, An Integrated Approach

Solutions for Chapter 15

Problem I

1. T	9. F
2. F	10. T
3. T	11. T
4. T	12. T
5. T	13. F
6. F	14. T
7. F	15. F
8. T	
9. F	

Problem II

1. b
2. a
3. c
4. d
5. b
6. a
7. b
8. a
9. d
10. a
11. d
12. a
13. d
14. b
15. b

Problem III

1. cash payment, interest expense
2. face
3. added, subtracted
4. discount
5. financing, operating
6. greater
7. Retained earnings, distributed, dividends
8. par value, increase
9. contributions, earnings

Problem IV

	General Journal		
Date	*Account Title*	*Debit*	Credit
5/1/X1	Cash	474,622	
	Discount on Note Payable	25,378	
	Note Payable		500,000
11/1/X2	Interest Expense	24,114	
	Discount on Note Payable		4,114
	Cash		20,000
12/31/X3	Interest Expense	8,254	
	Discount on Note Payable		1,587
	Interest Payable		6,667

Adjusting entry on 12/31/X3:

Interest Expense $24,762 \times 2/6 = \$8,254$

Interest Payable $20,000 \times 2/6 = \$6,667$

Study Guide: Introduction to Accounting, An Integrated Approach

Problem V

General Journal		Debit	Credit
Date	Account Title		
1/1	Computer Equipment	317,520	
	Note Payable		317,520
4/1	Note Payable	16,380	
	Interest Expense	10,000	
	Cash		26,380
7/1	Cash	459,520	
	Bonds Payable		400,000
	Premium on Bonds Payable		59,520
12/31	Interest Expense	13,786	
	Premium on Bonds Payable	2,214	
	Cash		16,000
12/31	Interest Expense	25,402	
	Note Payable		25,402

Noninterest-Bearing Note Payable Issued on 1/1
   PV(3,8%) X $400,000 =   .7938 X $400,000 = $317,520

Cash Proceeds on 7/1 Bond Issue:
   PV(20,3%) X $400,000 =   .5537 X $400,000 = $221,480
   PVa(20,3%) X $16,000 = 14.8775 X $16,000 = $238,040
                                                $459,520

Interest Expense on 12/31 Bond Payment:
   $459,520 X .06/2 = $13,786

Adjusting Entry (12/31) on Noninterest-Bearing Note Payable
   $317,520 X .08 = $25,402

Problem VI

General Journal

Date	Account Title	Debit	Credit
1/11	Cash	7,000	
	Common Stock		7,000
3/29	Land	160,000	
	Common Stock		160,000
6/30	Dividends	100,000	
	Dividends Payable		100,000
7/9	Dividends Payable	100,000	
	Cash		100,000
8/3	Treasury Stock	7,500	
	Cash		7,500
10/15	Retained Earnings	40,838	
	Stock Dividends Distributable		40,838
	(99,000 X .05 X $8.25)		
10/25	Stock Dividends Distributable	40,838	
	Common Stock		40,838
12/12	Cash	9,500	
	Treasury Stock		7,500
	Paid-in Capital - Treasury Stock		2,000

Study Guide: Introduction to Accounting, An Integrated Approach

Chapter 16
Recording and Evaluating Capital Resources Process
Activities: Investing

Chapter Overview

This chapter presents information about plant assets, natural resources, and intangible assets. The chapter explores the process of recording and reporting the acquisition, use, and disposal of these assets. Allocating the cost of a plant asset to the periods benefited is called depreciation. For financial reporting purposes, depreciation can be calculated using the straight-line, units-of-production, or declining-balance methods. The expense resulting from the cost of natural resources is called depletion. The cost of intangible assets, which have no physical substance, is allocated through a process called amortization.

As you study this chapter, you should first become familiar with which costs should be included in the acquisition cost of operational assets. You should also learn to compute depreciation using the methods discussed in the chapter. When operational assets are disposed of, the cost of the asset and the related accumulated depreciation must be removed from the accounts. Be sure you learn how to calculate the gain or loss that arises from the sale or exchange of operational assets. You should also focus on how operational assets, their related expenses, and related cash flows are reported in the financial statements.

Read and Recall Questions

Learning Objective:
LO. 1 Explain, record, and report long-term asset purchases.

Identify the three major categories of operational investments.

Define plant assets. Give three examples of plant assets.

How does a company determine whether to categorize a tangible, long-term asset as a plant asset?

Distinguish between capital expenditures and revenue expenditures.

Identify which items are usually included in the acquisition cost of a building.

Identify which items are usually included in the construction cost of a building.

Identify which items are usually included in the acquisition cost of land.

Identify which costs are usually included in the acquisition cost of equipment.

Study Guide: An Introduction to Accounting, An Integrated Approach

On what grounds may a company choose not to capitalize certain capital expenditures?

What is depreciation?

What is accumulated depreciation? What type of account is Accumulated Depreciation?

What factors affect the calculation of depreciation?

What factors cause the useful life of a plant asset, other than land, to be limited?

Define salvage value and depreciable cost.

Briefly discuss straight-line depreciation. How is it calculated?

Briefly discuss the units-of-production method of depreciation.

What advantage does the units-of-production depreciation method have over the straight-line method of depreciation?

What justifies the use of an accelerated depreciation method?

Briefly describe the declining-balance depreciation.

Study Guide: An Introduction to Accounting, An Integrated Approach

How is double-declining balance depreciation calculated?

Why may companies use a midyear convention for assets purchased or disposed of during the year?

How do companies account for the undepreciated cost of an asset when the estimated useful life and/or salvage value of a plant have changed?

Briefly describe extraordinary repairs and betterments.

What are natural resources? Which items are included in the acquisition cost of natural resources?

What is depletion? How is depletion calculated?

315

When does depletion cost become an expense?

Describe the characteristics of intangible assets.

Briefly define the following intangible assets:

- Patent

- Copyright

- Franchise

- Leasehold

- Leasehold improvement

- Trademark

Study Guide: An Introduction to Accounting, An Integrated Approach

- Goodwill

What is amortization of intangible assets?

Identify the three things that the entries associated with the disposal of a plant asset must accomplish.

How is the gain or loss on the sale of a plant asset determined?

On the exchange of dissimilar assets, how is the gain or loss on the transaction calculated?

What value becomes the recorded cost of the newly acquired asset when dissimilar assets are exchanged?

Why are gains on the exchange of similar assets not recognized? Why are losses recognized?

What value is assigned to a new asset acquired through the trade-in of a similar asset?

What information about operational assets will appear on the balance sheet?

What information about operational assets will appear on the income statement?

What information about operational assets will appear on the statement of cash flows?

Study Guide: An Introduction to Accounting, An Integrated Approach

Outline of Key Concepts

I. The acquisition of operational investments involves a capital expenditure.
   A. Plant assets are tangible assets held primarily for use in a business for more than one accounting period.
      1. Includes land, buildings, and equipment.
      2. Also called property, plant, and equipment.
   B. Accounting for capital expenditures and revenue expenditures differs.
      1. Capital expenditures create the expectation of future benefits that apply beyond the current account period.
         a. Are capitalized—add the cost of the plant asset to the asset account rather than expense it immediately.
      2. Revenue expenditures—provide benefits exclusively during the current account period.
         a. Are generally expensed when incurred.
   C. The cost of any purchased plant asset includes all normal, reasonable, and necessary expenditures to acquire the asset and prepare it for its intended use.
      1. When land and depreciable assets are acquired with one purchase price, the buyer must allocate the total purchase price among them.
         a. Allocations are frequently based on appraisal values.
      2. Cost of equipment normally includes the purchase price, freight charges, sales taxes paid, and installation costs.
   D. Materiality relates to whether an item's dollar amount or its inherent nature is significant enough to influence a financial statement user's decisions.
      1. If an amount of a capital expenditure is not material, the expenditure is often expensed.

II. Accounting for the use of plant assets.
   A. Depreciation is the allocation of the acquisition cost of the plant asset over the useful life of the asset.
      1. Asset cost less accumulated depreciation equals the carrying value of the asset.
      2. Carrying value does not represent a decreasing value; it represents the remaining undepreciated cost of the asset.
   B. Four factors affect depreciation calculations.
      1. Cost of the asset.
      2. Useful life—period of time over which a business expects to obtain economic benefits from the use of the plant asset or other operational investment.
      3. Salvage value—expected fair market value of a plant asset at the end of its useful life.
         a. Cost – Salvage value = Depreciable cost
      4. Method of depreciation.

319

C. Companies commonly use three methods of depreciation.
   1. Straight-line method—allocates the depreciable cost of the asset to depreciation expense equally over its useful life.
      a. (Cost – Salvage value)/Estimated years in useful life = Annual depreciation expense
      b. Based on the assumption that benefits derived from an asset are constant during each year of its life.
   2. Units-of-production method—depreciation expense is based on actual usage rather than the passage of time.
      a. Useful life is expressed in terms of expected units of output.
      b. Involves a two-step calculation.
         i. (Cost – Salvage value)/Estimated total output = Depreciation per unit of output.
         ii. Depreciation per unit of output x Actual output for current period = Depreciation expense for the current period.
   3. Accelerated depreciation methods recognize relatively greater expense in the early years of the asset's use and progressively less expense as time passes.
      a. Declining-balance depreciation—reflects depreciation expense for each year based on a constant percentage of a declining balance equal to the remaining undepreciated cost of the asset at the start of each year.
D. There are numerous issues related to the use of plant assets.
   1. Revisions to the original useful life and salvage value assigned to plant assets require the recalculation of depreciation expense for the current and remaining future periods.
   2. Assets may continue to be used after they are fully depreciated.
      a. The company must stop recording annual depreciation expense.
   3. Extraordinary repairs are capital expenditures that extend the remaining useful life of an operational asset.
   4. Betterments represent capital expenditures to improve the asset's performance capabilities.

III. Plant assets may be discarded, sold, or exchanged for another asset.
   A. Disposals of plant assets generally require entries to accomplish three things.
      1. Record partial-year depreciation expense up to the date of disposal.
      2. Remove the cost of the asset and its related accumulated depreciation from the accounting records.
      3. Record any gain or loss on the disposal of the asset.
   B. Companies may exchange plant assets for other noncash assets.
      1. Gain or loss on the exchange of dissimilar assets is calculated as the difference between the carrying value of the asset given up and whichever of the following two values can be determined more objectively.
         a. Fair market value of the asset received in the exchange.

Study Guide: An Introduction to Accounting, An Integrated Approach

        b. Fair market value of the asset given up in the exchange.
    2. The exchange of similar assets is not viewed as the culmination of the earnings process.
        a. As a result, companies do not record any gains determined by a comparison of the fair market value and carrying value of the asset given up.
        b. Losses are recognized and recorded.
        c. On trade-ins, the gain or loss on the disposal of the old asset is measured as the difference between the carrying value of the old asset and the trade-in allowance assigned to it in the exchange transaction.
            i. Losses are recognized, gains are not; the new asset's carrying value is increased by the amount of any cash given in the exchange.

IV. Natural resources are nonrenewable assets such as coal deposits and oil rights.
    A. Cost of the initial investment follows the same general guidelines used for assigning costs to plant assets.
    B. Depletion—allocation of the cost of natural resources as expense over the periods they benefit.
        1. Generally calculated using the units-of-production method.
        2. Recorded depletion is not immediately expensed.
        3. Depletion is added to the cost of the company's inventory of natural resources.
            a. When the natural resource is sold, depletion is included as a component of cost of goods sold.

V. Intangible assets convey legal rights or benefits to their owner.
    A. Patent—legal right to the commercial benefits of a specified product or process.
        1. Legal life is 20 years; useful economic life may be much shorter.
        2. Cost includes purchase price and legal fees.
            a. Research and development costs cannot be included in the cost of internally created patents.
    B. Copyright—exclusive right to the reproduction and sale of a literary or artistic work.
        1. Legal life is the life of the creator plus 70 years; economic useful life is often much shorter.
        2. In many cases, only purchased copyrights are capitalized as assets.
    C. Trademark—identifies a particular company or product.
        1. Right to use remains with the originator for as long as the trademark continues to be used.
        2. Registered with indefinite renewals for intervals of 20 years.
        3. Cost includes legal and development costs.
        4. Expensed over a period not to exceed 40 years.

D. Franchise—exclusive right to operate or sell a brand name product or service in a specified territory.

E. Leasehold—conveyed by a lease to use equipment, land, and/or buildings for a specified period of time.

F. Goodwill—represents the value assigned to a purchased company's ability to generate an above average return on invested capital.
   1. Companies record goodwill only when they pay for it as part of the purchase price to acquire another company.
   2. Goodwill is the excess of the total price paid to purchase the company over the fair value of the purchased company's underlying net assets.
   3. Internally generated goodwill is not recorded.
   4. Goodwill is not amortized.

G. Amortization—the process of allocating the cost of intangible assets to expense over the periods they benefit.
   1. Use the straight-line method.
   2. Amortize the full cost of the asset; no salvage value is used.

VI. Issues related to the reporting of operational investments.
   A. Financial statements disclose information to external users.
      1. Balance sheet reports the carrying value of operational assets and discloses the methods of depreciation.
      2. Income statement reports the depreciation expense and the gains/losses from the disposal of operational assets.
      3. The statement of cash flows reports the amount of cash used and provided by the acquisition and disposal of operational investments.

Problem I

Indicate whether the following statements are either true (T) or false (F).

_____1. Annual repairs will be considered capital expenditures.
_____2. Installation costs of equipment will be capitalized.
_____3. Research and development costs are capitalized and included as assets on the balance sheet.
_____4. Depreciation represents the decline in value of the asset during the year.
_____5. Goodwill is only recorded when another company is acquired.
_____6. An extraordinary repair may be expensed in the year paid.
_____7. A sale of a plant asset at an amount that is greater than its book value will result in the recognition of a gain.
_____8. Both gains and losses are recognized on the exchange of dissimilar assets.
_____9. The economic life of a patent may be less than 17 years.
_____10. A franchise is considered an intangible asset.

Problem II

Indicate the correct answer by circling the appropriate letter.

1. Maxex Corporation purchased a building and land for $180,000. The land had been appraised for $40,000 and the building for $160,000. What amount will Maxex use in calculating its annual depreciation on the building?
   a. $160,000
   b. $180,000
   c. $144,000
   d. $120,000

Use the following information for the next two questions:
X Corporation purchased a machine for $55,000. The machine has a useful life of 5 years and an expected salvage value of $5,000.

2. What will depreciation expense be for year three under the straight-line method?
   a. $8,000
   b. $10,000
   c. $11,000
   d. $15,000

3. What will depreciation expense be for year one under the double-declining balance method?
   a. $10,000
   b. $12,000
   c. $20,000
   d. $22,000

4. Company Y purchased equipment for $21,000. The equipment was expected to produce 4,000 units over its life and have a salvage value of $1,000. Two hundred units were produced in year one. What amount of depreciation expense will be reported if the units-of-production method is used?
   a. $200
   b. $1,000
   c. $3,000
   d. $4,000

5. Z Corporation sold equipment for $26,000. The equipment originally cost $40,000 and $15,000 of depreciation had been recorded up to the date of the sale. Which of the following is true?
   a. The equipment account will be reduced by $40,000.
   b. Z Corporation will report a $1,000 gain on the sale.
   c. Accumulated depreciation will be reduced by $15,000.
   d. All of the above are true.

6. Z Corporation purchased a machine for $100,000. The machine has a useful life of 10 years and an expected salvage value of $15,000. What will depreciation expense be for year two under the double declining balance method?
   a. $20,000
   b. $16,000
   c. $14,000
   d. $17,000

7. Ktar Corporation purchased a patent for $320,000 on July 1, 1999. The patent has a remaining legal life of 12 years but management expects its useful life to only be 8 years. What amount will Ktar report as amortization expense for 1999?
   a. $40,000
   b. $26,667
   c. $20,000
   d. $13,333

Study Guide: An Introduction to Accounting, An Integrated Approach

8. LL Corporation purchased equipment for $40,000 on April 1, 1999. The equipment has a useful life of 4 years and an expected salvage value of $4,000. Assuming that LL Corporation uses the mid-year convention, what will depreciation expense be for 1999 under the straight-line method?
   a. $9,000
   b. $6,750
   c. $5,000
   d. $4,500

9. Which of the following would not be considered an intangible asset?
   a. goodwill
   b. franchises
   c. leasehold improvements
   d. all of the above are intangible assets

10. The purchase of equipment will be shown in the _____ section of the cash flow statement.
   a. operating
   b. investing
   c. financing
   d. non-cash activities

Problem III

Following is a list of important ideas and key concepts from the chapter. To test your knowledge of these terms, match the term with the definition by placing the number in the space provided.

_____ accelerated depreciation   _____ leasehold
_____ amortization   _____ leasehold improvement
_____ capital expenditure   _____ materiality
_____ capitalize   _____ midyear convention
_____ copyright   _____ natural resources
_____ depreciable cost   _____ patent
_____ depletion   _____ plant assets
_____ extraordinary repairs and betterments   _____ revenue expenditure
_____ franchise   _____ salvage value
_____ goodwill   _____ trademark

1. An intangible asset giving its owner the exclusive legal right to the commercial benefits of a specified product or process.

2. An intangible asset that identifies a particular company or product

3. An intangible asset representing the value assigned to a purchased company's ability to generate an above average return on invested capital.

4. An accounting concept that relates to whether an item's dollar amount or its inherent nature is significant enough to influence a financial statement user.

5. An intangible asset that gives its owner the exclusive legal right for the reproduction and sale of a literary or artistic work.

6. Tangible assets acquired primarily for use in a business over a time span covering more than one accounting period.

7. The convention that reflects depreciation expense for each asset as if it were purchased or disposed of exactly halfway through the company's fiscal year.

8. A method of depreciation that recognizes relatively greater expense in early years of asset use and progressively less expense as time passes.

9. An intangible asset representing the amounts paid by a lessee to make physical improvements that are an integral part of leased property.

10. The process of allocating the cost of natural resources to an expense over the periods they benefit.

11. To add an expenditure to the cost of an asset, rather than expensing it immediately.

12. Nonrenewable assets such as coal mines or oil rights.

13. The expected fair market value of a plant asset at the end of its useful life. Also referred to as residual value.

14. An intangible asset representing the exclusive right to operate or sell a brand name product in a specified territory.

15. The process of allocating the cost of intangible assets to an expense over the periods they benefit.

Study Guide: An Introduction to Accounting, An Integrated Approach

16. An intangible asset conveyed by a lease to use equipment, land, and/or buildings for a specified period of time.

17. An expenditure that creates the expectation of future benefits that apply beyond the current accounting period.

18. An expenditure that provides benefits exclusively during the current accounting period.

19. Expenditures that extend the remaining useful life of an operational investment and/or improve performance capabilities.

20. The portion of a plant asset's total cost that will be depreciated over its useful life.

Problem IV

Complete the following sentences by filling in the correct response.

1. A capital expenditure creates the expectation of a _____ benefit.

2. The expected value of a plant asset at the end of its useful life is referred to as the _____ value.

3. A plant asset's _____ less its _____ _____ equals the depreciable cost.

4. _____ repairs extend the useful life of an asset and _____ represent capital expenditures that improve the asset's performance capabilities.

5. The accounting concept of _____ causes _____ but not _____ to be recognized on the exchange of similar assets.

6. Intangibles are amortized using the _____ method over their _____ _____ but not to exceed _____ years.

Problem V

Prepare the necessary journal entries for the following selected property transactions:

a) A patent with an estimated useful life of 10 years is purchased for $160,000.

b) Equipment originally costing $45,000 with $38,000 of accumulated depreciation is discarded as worthless.

c) Machinery originally costing $100,000 with $65,000 of accumulated depreciation is sold for $41,000.

d) The company traded a delivery truck that originally cost $22,000 (accumulated depreciation of $16,000) for a new delivery truck. The new truck cost $26,000. The company was given a trade-in allowance on the old truck of $9,000 and paid $17,000 in cash.

e) The patent acquired in (a) above was used for 3 months during the year.

Study Guide: An Introduction to Accounting, An Integrated Approach

Problem V (continued)

General Journal

Date	Account Title	Debit	Credit

Solutions for Chapter 16

Problem I

1. F
2. T
3. F
4. F
5. T
6. F
7. T
8. T
9. T
10. T

Problem II

1. c
2. b
3. d
4. b
5. d
6. b
7. c
8. d
9. d
10. b

Problem III

8	accelerated depreciation	16	leasehold
15	amortization	9	leasehold improvement
17	capital expenditure	4	materiality
11	capitalize	7	midyear convention
5	copyright	12	natural resources
20	depreciable cost	1	patent
10	depletion	6	plant assets
19	extraordinary repairs and betterments	18	revenue expenditure
14	franchise	13	salvage value
3	goodwill	2	trademark

Problem IV

1. future
2. salvage or residual
3. cost, salvage value
4. Extraordinary, betterments
5. conservatism, losses, gains
6. straight-line, useful lives, 40

Problem V

	General Journal		
Date	Account Title	Debit	Credit
a)	Patent	160,000	
	Cash		160,000
b)	Loss on disposal	7,000	
	Accumulated depreciation	38,000	
	Equipment		45,000
c)	Cash	41,000	
	Accumulated depreciation	65,000	
	Machinery		100,000
	Gain on sale		6,000
d)	Truck (new)	23,000	
	Accumulated depreciation	16,000	
	Truck (old)		22,000
	Cash		17,000
e)	Amortization expense - Patent	4,000	
	Patent		4,000
	($160,000/10 = 16,000 per year) X 3/12		

Chapter 17
Company Performance: Profitability

Chapter Overview

The preceding chapters presented the planning and performing phases for the operating, financing, and investing processes. Chapter 17 is the first chapter related to evaluation. This chapter examines firm performance through the lens of profitability. The income statement is an important tool for communicating performance to both external and internal users. Components of income are discussed, and the limitations of the income statement are presented. The chapter also describes the differences among the absorption, variable, and throughput costing methods. The chapter concludes with a discussion of return on investment.

In this chapter, you will need to become familiar with the components of income and learn to interpret what this information may reveal about the firm's past and future performance. Go to several well-known companies' web sites and examine their most recent income statements. You will discover variations in terminology, but see if you can identify the components of income discussed in the chapter. You will discover that not all components of income will appear on every company's income statement; only those components directly related to the company's performance appear on its income statement.

Read and Recall Questions

Learning Objective:
LO. 1 Discuss the importance of income from continuing operations and net income.

Explain the purpose of the income statement and discuss how it helps to fulfill the FASB's three objectives of financial reporting.

Identify the elements of comprehensive income.

Distinguish between earnings and net income.

Briefly discuss comprehensive income.

What are discontinued operations? Why are they presented separately on the income statement?

When a segment of a business is discontinued, what two items are reported? Are these items reported before tax or net of tax?

Describe extraordinary items. Give two examples of extraordinary items.

Are extraordinary items reported before tax or net of tax?

Study Guide: Introduction to Accounting, An Integrated Approach

Explain cumulative accounting adjustments. Why are these presented on the income statement? Are they reported before tax or net of tax?

Describe earnings per share. Will the earnings per share be distributed to stockholders as dividends? Explain.

How are earnings per share calculated?

Briefly discuss diluted earnings per share. Why is this earnings number reported on the income statement?

Why do companies disclose the per share effect of extraordinary items and accounting changes?

Which items must be disclosed for identifiable segments of a company?

Learning Objective:
LO. 3 Explain the purpose of, and calculate, income using variable, absorption, and throughput costing for internal reporting purposes.

Which accounting principle leads to the inconsistent application of the historical cost principle when reporting items on the income statement?

How do cost allocations affect reported income?

What is full-absorption costing? What distortions can full-absorption costing introduce into income?

Using absorption costing, how might a manager increase reported earnings?

Study Guide: Introduction to Accounting, An Integrated Approach

Identify and distinguish among the four types of responsibility centers.

Briefly describe the variable costing method of reporting income internally.

Briefly discuss the throughput costing method of reporting income internally.

Why do variable and throughput costing methods discourage managers from overproducing inventory?

Why does the throughput costing method produce lower income than absorption or variable costing methods?

Describe product-line (divisional) income reports.

Why do companies use product-line (divisional) income reports?

Define the following terms:

- Product margin

- Segment margin

What is return on investment (ROI)? How is ROI calculated?

When is return on investment used to evaluate performance?

Describe the Du Pont method of return on investment. How is it calculated?

What is the purpose of the asset turnover ratio?

Outline of Key Concepts

I.   Purpose of the income statement is to reflect the earnings generated by the company during the accounting period.

    A. Income statement helps to fulfill the FASB's three objectives of financial reporting.

        1. Provides information useful for making investment and credit decisions.

        2. Provides information useful for assessing cash flow prospects.

        3. Provides information relevant to evaluating resources, claims to those resources, and changes in those resources.

    B. Comprehensive income—reflects all changes in owners' equity during the period except those resulting from investments by or distributions to owners and those resulting from the corrections of errors made in previous periods.

        1. The elements of comprehensive income include:

                + Revenues

                -   Expenses

                + Gains

                -   Losses

                = Earnings (income from continuing operations)

                +/- Discontinued operations (net of tax)

                +/- Extraordinary items (net of tax)

                +/- Cumulative accounting adjustments (net of tax)

                =   Net Income

                +/- Other comprehensive income items (net of tax)

                = Comprehensive income

    C. Earnings include revenues minus expenses plus gain and minus losses.

        1. Earnings result from business activities that are assumed to be recurring.

339

D. Discontinue operations are the result of a company selling or disposing of a segment of its business.
   1. A business segment is either a separate major line of business or a separate class of customers.
   2. Two items are reported about discontinued operations.
      a. Income or loss generated based on the operations of the segment from the beginning of the accounting period through the disposal date (net of tax).
      b. Gain or loss resulting from the disposal of the segment's net assets (net of tax).
E. Extraordinary items are events that occurred during the accounting period that are both unusual and infrequent.
   1. Reported net of tax.
F. Cumulative accounting adjustments are modifications made to the accounting records that result from changes in accounting principles.
   1. Occur when a company switches from one generally accepted accounting principle to another one.
   2. The switch results in a lack of consistency between statements for consecutive reporting periods.
      a. The reason for the inconsistency must be disclosed.
      b. The cumulative effect of the change is shown because it is not feasible to restate all previous years' financial statements to make them comparable to the current period's statement.
   3. Reported net of tax.

II. Earnings per share (EPS)—a common-size measure of a company's earnings performance that allows the comparison of the operating performance of large and small corporations on a per share basis.
   A. EPS is a required disclosure on the face of the income statement.
      1. Is not the amount each shareholder will receive as dividends.
   B. The basic form of earnings per share is (Net income – Preferred stock dividends) / (Weighted-average number of common shares outstanding)
      1. Subtract preferred dividends from net income because preferred stockholders have a first claim on the firm's earnings if any dividends are paid.
      2. Weighted-average number of shares reflects adjustments made for issuances and repurchases of shares during the period.
   C. Diluted earnings per share—reported when a company has issued stock options or securities that may be converted to common stock.
      1. Shows the decreased earnings per share that would occur as a result of conversions and the exercise of stock options.
   D. Companies must also report the per share effect of extraordinary items and accounting changes.

Study Guide: Introduction to Accounting, An Integrated Approach

III. Several reporting issues affect the income statement.
   A. Most income statement items are reported at historical cost.
      1. Conservatism leads a company to anticipate losses but defer gains that results in inventory being reported at lower-of-cost-or-market.
         a. The inventory will be reported on the balance sheet at it market value, and the unrealized loss will be reported.
   B. Cost allocations do not measure the economic deterioration of assets.
      1. Allocates the cost of the asset over its expected useful life.
      2. Cost allocation methods are disclosed in the notes to the financial statements.
   C. Full-absorption costing—required for external reporting on the income statement.
      1. Assigns all production costs such as direct materials, direct labor, and unit-related, batch-related, product-sustaining, and facility-sustaining manufacturing overhead to the units produced during the period.
      2. Distortions in income result when overhead costs are treated as though they vary with the level of production.
      3. Companies can increase income by increasing the number of units produced during the period, even if the number of units sold remains the same.

IV. Managers need more than the income statement to evaluate financial performance.
   A. Portions of the business are often evaluated as responsibility centers.
      1. Cost center—responsible for controlling costs and providing a good or service in an efficient manner.
         a. Evaluated on costs only.
      2. Revenue center—responsible for generating revenues and promoting the company's products and services effectively.
         a. Evaluated on revenues only.
      3. Profit center—responsible for making a profit; it must effectively generate revenues and efficiently control costs.
         a. Evaluated on profits.
      4. Investment center—responsible for using assets in an effective and efficient manner to generate profits.
         a. Evaluated on profits and return on investment.
   B. Variable costing method—a way of reporting income internally where only costs that vary with production are included in the cost of goods sold.
      1. Facility-sustaining costs are expensed in the period incurred.
      2. A contribution format income statement is often used.
   C. Throughput costing method—a way of reporting income internally where only direct materials are included in the cost of goods sold.
      1. All other production costs are expensed in total in the period incurred.
      2. Will produce lower income than either absorption or variable costing methods.

a. Assigns the fewest costs to inventory and expenses the greatest amount of costs.

D. Product line (divisional) income reports—specific-purpose reports designed to provide more detailed information than general-purpose disclosures of the results of operations for a product line or company division.

1. Product line or divisional managers often evaluated and rewarded as profit or investment centers.

    a. Reward based on those items for which a manager has control.

2. These reports eliminate costs assigned to the product or division that the manager cannot control and to overcome problems associated with absorption costing.

E. Return on investment for the division—a common measure of divisional performance that reflects not only profits but also the amounts that are invested in the division's operations.

1. (Profit of the division) / (Assets of the division)

F. Du Pont method of return on investment—a measure to assess profitability that is a combination of the return on sales ratio and the asset turnover ratio.

1. Asset turnover ratio—activity ratio that measures profitability because it relates a company's ability to generate sales to the amount of assets that the company uses.

    a. (Net sales) / (Average total assets)

2. Sales return ratio x Asset turnover ratio

Problem I

Indicate whether the following statements are either true (T) or false (F).

_____1. Comprehensive income only includes those items that are recurring by nature.
_____2. Income from discontinued operations will be shown separately on the income statement net of any income tax expense.
_____3. Earnings per share is the amount each stockholder received in dividends during the year.
_____4. In calculating earnings per share, preferred stock dividends must be subtracted from net income.
_____5. An investment center is responsible for generating revenues and promoting the company's products and services effectively.
_____6. Full absorption costing may cause distortions in the income statement due to fixed manufacturing costs that are allocated based on the number of units produced.
_____7. Product line income reports are generally less detailed than external income statements.
_____8. The purpose of the income statement is to reflect earnings generated by the company during the accounting period.
_____9. A change in accounting principle is considered a non-recurring item and would be shown separately on the income statement.
_____10. All comprehensive income items are closed to retained earnings.

Problem II

Indicate the correct answer by circling the appropriate letter.

1. During the year, X Corporation had 20,000 shares of $10 par value common stock and 1,000 shares of $100 par value, 10% preferred stock outstanding. X Corporation reported net income of $50,000 for the year. The earnings per share for the year is _____.
   a. $2.00
   b. $2.50
   c. $3.00
   d. $3.50

2. Which of the following would not be included in the computation of earnings (income from continuing operations)?
    a. Revenues
    b. Gains
    c. Losses
    d. Cumulative accounting adjustments

3. Which of the following is not shown net of tax on the income statement?
    a. Extraordinary losses
    b. Cumulative effect of accounting changes
    c. Income from discontinued operations
    d. Gain on sale of equipment

4. Zectar Corporation reported net income of $100,000 for the calendar year 19X4. At the beginning of the year, Zectar had 40,000 shares outstanding. On June 30, 19X4, the company issued 4,000 additional shares of stock. What will the company report as earnings per share for 19X4?
    a. $2.00
    b. $2.50
    c. $2.27
    d. $2.38

5. Which of the following would not have to be disclosed for any identifiable segment of a company?
    a. revenues from external customers
    b. depreciation expense of the segment
    c. segment profit or loss
    d. research and development costs of the segment

6. Which of the following would not be included in the statement of changes in retained earnings?
    a. net income or loss
    b. cash or stock dividends declared
    c. prior period adjustments
    d. all of the above are included

7. A _____ center is responsible for both effectively generating revenues and efficiently controlling costs.
    a. cost
    b. revenue
    c. profit
    d. target

Study Guide: Introduction to Accounting, An Integrated Approach

8. Which of the following costs will be included in cost of goods sold if the unit-variable accounting method is used?
   a. direct labor cost
   b. batch-related costs
   c. product-sustaining costs
   d. facility-sustaining costs

9. When the throughput accounting method is used, only _____ costs are included in cost of goods sold.
   a. direct labor
   b. direct materials
   c. product-sustaining
   d. facility-sustaining

Problem III

Following is a list of important ideas and key concepts from the chapter. To test your knowledge of these terms, match the term with the definition by placing the number in the space provided.

_____ comprehensive income   _____ extraordinary items
_____ cost center   _____ investment center
_____ cumulative accounting adjustments   _____ product line (divisional) income report
_____ diluted earnings per share   _____ profit center
_____ discontinued operations   _____ revenue center
_____ earnings   _____ throughput costing method
_____ earnings per share   _____ variable costing method

1. Earnings per share that reflect the amount of decrease in earnings per share that would occur as a result of activities like conversions and the exercise of stock options

2. A center that is responsible for using assets in an effective and efficient manner to generate profits

3. Modifications made to the accounting records that result from changes in accounting principles which occur when a company switches from one generally accepted method of accounting to another or when a company adopts a new accounting principle

4. A center that is responsible for making a profit; it must effectively generate revenues and efficiently control costs

5. A center that is responsible for controlling costs and providing a good or service in an efficient manner

6. Specific purpose internal reports designed to provide more detailed information than general purpose income statements regarding the results of operations for a product line or company division

7. A method of determining profits in which only costs that vary with the number of units produced are included in cost of goods sold and facility-sustaining overhead costs are expensed as incurred

8. Income that reflects all changes in owners' equity during the period except those resulting from investments by, or distributions to, owners and those resulting from errors made in previous periods

9. A common-size measure of a company's earnings performance; the reported net income of the company less preferred dividends for the period divided by the weighted-average number of common shares outstanding

10. Income from continuing operations; consisting of revenues minus expenses and also gains minus losses

11. A method of determining profits in which only direct materials are included in cost of goods sold and all other production costs are expensed as incurred

12. Events that occurred during the accounting period that are both unusual and infrequent

13. A center that is responsible for generating revenues and promoting the company's products and services effectively

14. The result of a company selling or disposing of a segment of its business

Study Guide: Introduction to Accounting, An Integrated Approach

Problem IV

The following account balances were reported by Ace Company for the accounting year:

Cost of goods sold	$240,000	Income from discontinued operations	$60,000
Interest income	5,000	Gain on sale of equipment	8,000
Flood loss	100,000	Net sales	800,000
Selling expenses	75,000	Interest expense	12,000
General and administrative expense	213,000		

The flood loss is considered both unusual and infrequent. Ace Company's effective tax rate is 40 percent.

1. Prepare a multi-step income statement for the accounting period.

_____
_____
_____
_____
_____
_____
_____
_____
_____
_____
_____
_____
_____
_____
_____
_____
_____
_____
_____
_____
_____
_____
_____
_____
_____

Problem V

Complete the following sentences by filling in the correct response.

1. The purpose of the income statement is to reflect the _____ generated by the company during the _____ period.

2. Earnings include those items that are _____ by nature.

3. Extraordinary items are events that are both _____ and _____.

4. Earnings per share is the _____ _____ available to _____ shareholders, divided by the _____ number of shares outstanding.

5. The _____ statement is the most widely quoted of the financial statements

Study Guide: Introduction to Accounting, An Integrated Approach

Solutions for Chapter 17

Problem I

1. F
2. T
3. F
4. T
5. F
6. T
7. F
8. T
9. T
10. F

Problem II

1. a
2. d
3. d
4. d
5. d
6. d
7. c
8. a
9. b

Problem III

8	comprehensive income	12	extraordinary items
5	cost center	2	investment center
3	cumulative accounting adjustments	6	product line (divisional) income report
1	diluted earnings per share	4	profit center
14	discontinued operations	13	revenue center
10	earnings	11	throughput costing method
9	earnings per share	7	variable costing method

Problem IV

1.

Ace Company
Income Statement

Net sales		$800,000
Less cost of goods sold		240,000
Gross margin		$560,000
Operating expenses:		
Selling expenses	$ 75,000	
General and administrative expenses	213,000	288,000
Income from operations		$272,000
Other revenues/\<expenses\>:		
Interest expense	<12,000>	
Interest income	5,000	
Gain on sale of equipment	8,000	1,000
Income from continuing operations before taxes		$273,000
Income tax expense		109,200
Income from continuing operations		$163,800
Discontinued operations:		
Income from discontinued division, net of taxes		36,000
Income before extraordinary items		$199,800
Extraordinary loss from flood, net of taxes		60,000
Net Income		$139,800

Problem V

1. earnings, accounting
2. recurring
3. unusual, infrequent
4. net income, common, weighted-average
5. income

Chapter 18
Company Performance: Owners' Equity and Financial Position

Chapter Overview

Chapter 18 continues the examination of the evaluation phase. It discusses the statement of owners' equity and the statement of financial position, more commonly known as the balance sheet. The balance sheet presents a company's assets and claims to those assets by owners and creditors. The classification of assets, liabilities, and owners' equity allows users of the balance sheet to assess the significance of each category, evaluate future profit and cash flow potential, and evaluate the liquidity and solvency of a firm.

By examining a company's financial position, a user has another perspective for evaluating the results of a firm's operations. It is important that you learn to classify asset, liability, and owners' equity accounts correctly. As in the previous chapter, you may want to go to the websites of well-known companies and examine their balance sheets and statements of owners' equity. This exercise will help you see which types of information appear on the face of the statements and which information is reported in the notes to the financial statements.

Read and Recall Questions

Learning Objective:
LO. 1 Discuss the importance of the statement of owners' equity.

Identify the three primary components of the statement of owners' equity.

SFAS No. 130 requires companies to report comprehensive income in addition to net income. Identify the items included in comprehensive income.

What are available-for-sale securities?

How are unrealized gains and losses from available-for-sale securities reported?

Identify the sources of changes to the Retained Earnings account.

Define a prior period adjustment.

How is a prior period adjustment recorded and reported?

What information about stock equity accounts is typically reported in the statement of owners' equity?

Study Guide: An Introduction to Accounting, An Integrated Approach

What is the purpose of the statement of financial position?

What are the three characteristics of a company that a balance sheet describes?

Explain the concept of financial position.

How does financial position reveal future profit potential?

Distinguish between liquidity and solvency.

Define current assets.

Define current liabilities.

How would the reclassification of a liability from current to long term affect how investors and creditors perceive liquidity and solvency?

Companies classify assets according to their purpose and/or useful life. Identify the five most common asset classifications.

In what order are assets listed on the balance sheet.

Identify the assets that typically are classified as current assets.

What is a compensating balance? How should it be classified on the balance sheet?

What items are included in marketable securities?

At what amount are accounts receivable reported on the balance sheet?

At what amount should inventories be reported on the balance sheet?

Why are prepaid expenses classified as current assets?

Describe the composition of the investments section of the balance sheet.

What types of items are reported in the property, plant, and equipment section of the balance sheet?

How are natural resources reported on the balance sheet?

At what amount are intangible assets, other than goodwill, reported on the balance sheet?

What types of items are reported as other assets on the balance sheet?

Identify the four events that result in the creation of a current liability.

Define long-term liabilities. Is it possible for a liability that will be paid in the coming fiscal period to be classified as long term? Explain.

How do bonds payable differ from notes payable?

Study Guide: An Introduction to Accounting, An Integrated Approach

What types of information about a bond issue may be presented in the notes to the financial statements?

What types of obligations would be classified as other liabilities?

Define contingent liabilities.

What is off-balance sheet financing? How might off-balance sheet financing affect an investor's or creditor's perception of a company's financial position?

Why is stockholders' equity divided into contributed capital and retained earnings?

Which items appear on the balance as contributed capital?

Why may companies restrict retained earnings?

Briefly describe accumulated other comprehensive income items.

How is treasury stock reported on the balance sheet?

Learning Objective:
LO. 3 Explain why internal balance sheet information may be different from external balance sheet information.

Describe current replacement cost valuation of assets.

Why may current cost valuations be used for internal reporting?

Study Guide: An Introduction to Accounting, An Integrated Approach

Outline of Key Concepts

I.   Statement of owners' equity has three primary components.

     A. Comprehensive income includes four items.

          1. Foreign currency translation adjustments.

          2. Maximum pension liability adjustments.

          3. Derivative-related adjustments.

          4. Unrealized gains and losses from certain debt and equity transactions.

               a. Available-for-sale securities—securities that management does not intend to sell in the next year so the fluctuations in their market value is reported as part of stockholders' equity.

     B. Retained earnings are changed by three events.

          1. Net income or loss.

          2. Cash or stock dividends declared.

          3. Prior period adjustments—correction of a previously undetected material error that affected the net income of a previous accounting period.

               a. The correction is made to the beginning retained earnings balance, net of tax.

     C. Other disclosures typically relate to capital stock.

          1. Report changes in dollar amount as well as number of shares.

II.   Financial position conveys information about the nature of the company's resources and obligations, its ability to meet its obligations, and its prospects for future profitability.

     A. Balance sheet (statement of financial position)—reports the amounts and types of assets the firm controls and the claims the owners and creditors have on those assets on the last day of the reporting period.

     B. Classifying assets and liabilities as current or noncurrent helps creditors and others assess the company's short-term liquidity and solvency.

          1. Liquidity—time required for a firm to convert its assets to cash.

          2. Solvency—ability to meet obligations when they are due.

          3. Decision to classify assets and liabilities as short term or long term is often subjective.

          4. Management realizes that reporting more assets as current and classifying liabilities as long term enhances the appearance of a firm's liquidity.

III.   Asset classifications on the balance sheet are listed in order of their liquidity, which is how quickly the firm will convert them to cash or consume them as part of operations.

     A. Current assets are also listed in order of liquidity.

          1. Cash is reported at its stated value.

               a. Does not include compensating balances—minimum cash balance that the depositor must maintain to either continue to earn interest on the amount deposited in the bank account or to avoid certain fees from the bank.

    2. Marketable securities are temporary investments that a company intends to convert to cash when needed.

        a. Reported at their market value.

    3. Accounts receivable are reported at their net realizable value.

        a. Notes to the balance sheet may disclose the amount of the allowance for doubtful accounts.

    4. Inventory—must disclose the inventory method and whether the inventory amount is reported at the lower of its cost or market value at the end of the period.

    5. Prepaid expenses—support the operating activities of the firm and are usually consumed during the operating cycle.

B. Investment classification—describes the type and extent of the company's long-term, nonoperational investments.

    1. Notes provide detailed description of a company's investments.

C. Property, plant, and equipment reports the tangible operational investments that support the infrastructure of the firm.

    1. Depreciable assets are shown at their book or carrying value.

    2. Includes capital leases and natural resources.

D. Intangible assets, which have no physical substance but generate future economic benefits, are reported at their original cost less amortization taken to date.

E. Other assets are items that do not fit in other asset classifications.

    1. Includes items like noncurrent receivables, special funds, and deferred charges.

        a. Deferred charges—long-term prepayments that a company amortizes over the period management believes the firm will benefit from the expenditures.

IV.   Liabilities are debts and other obligations to creditors and other outside parties.

A. Current liabilities are listed first and result from:

    1. The receipt of loan proceeds by the company.

    2. The receipt of goods and services when using credit as a means of payment.

    3. The receipt of prepayments for goods and services promised to be provided in subsequent periods by the company.

    4. Includes the reclassification of the portion of long-term debt that comes due within the coming fiscal year.

        a. Liability remains long-term if the debt will be repaid with long-term assets or will be refinanced.

B. Long-term liabilities are not expected to come due within one year or the operating cycle, whichever is longer.

    1. Terms and features of the long-term debt agreements are disclosed in the notes to the financial statements.

    2. Bonds are reported at their carrying value.

C. Other long-term liabilities include items such as pension obligations and deferred income tax liabilities.
   1. Deferred income tax liabilities (or assets) arise from the differences between computing income using generally accepted accounting principles and computing taxable income using tax law.
D. Contingent liabilities—represent events that could create negative financial results for a company at some future point.
E. Off-balance sheet financing—borrowing money in ways that would avoid having to record such borrowings on the balance sheet.

V. Dividing stockholders' equity into contributed capital and retained earnings reflects the resources provided by the owners and the claims generated by retaining the corporation's profits.
A. Contributed capital reflects the amounts invested in the company by the stockholders.
   1. Preferred and common stocks are reported separately.
   2. Notes to the financial statements disclose information about number of shares outstanding, stock splits or dividends, preferred stock liquidation values, and treasury stock transactions.
B. Retained earnings reflect the reinvested earnings of the corporation.
   1. Restrictions of retained earnings limit the dividend paying ability of the corporation.
C. Accumulated other comprehensive income items—the balance is increased by increases in comprehensive income items and is decreased by comprehensive loss items.
   1. It is a permanent part of stockholders' equity and is not closed to retained earnings.
D. Treasury stock is a temporary reduction in the total amount of stockholders' equity.

VI. Balance sheets prepared for internal users may use current replacement cost valuation rather than historical cost.
A. Current cost valuation has two problems.
   1. Obtaining current cost values may be costly.
   2. Current cost valuations may be subjective.

361

Problem I

Indicate whether the following statements are either true (T) or false (F).

_____1. Management's classification of current and noncurrent assets and liabilities may be subjective.

_____2. Financial position is used to communicate the future profit potential of a company.

_____3. Restricting retained earnings will limit the dividend-paying ability of a company.

_____4. Internal management reports must follow GAAP reporting requirements.

_____5. Classifying assets and liabilities into current and noncurrent helps in the assessment of a company's short-term liquidity.

_____6. The beginning retained earnings balance is adjusted for corrections of previously undetected errors.

_____7. A liability that is due in six months and that will be refinanced with a twenty-year bond, will be classified as a current liability.

_____8. Bonds are always carried on the balance sheet at their face value.

_____9. Deferred tax liabilities (assets) are generated due to differences between the computation of financial reporting income and taxable income.

_____10. Treasury stock is added to other contributed capital in the stockholders' equity section of the balance sheet.

Problem II

1. Classifying assets and liabilities as current and noncurrent helps to answer questions about a company's _____.
   a. short-term liquidity
   b. asset utilization
   c. short-term profitability
   d. long-term profitability

2. An asset will generally be classified as current if it will be converted to cash or used in operations within _____ of the balance sheet date.
   a. 6 months
   b. one year
   c. 18 months
   d. 2 years

3. Which of the following would not be considered a current liability?
    a. accounts payable due in 60 days
    b. note payable due in 9 months
    c. interest payable due in 3 months
    d. bond payable maturing in 2 months that will be refinanced with a twenty-year bond

4. Inventory will be carried on the balance sheet at _____.
    a. cost
    b. market value
    c. lower of cost or market
    d. its sales price

5. Buildings will be carried on the balance sheet at _____.
    a. cost
    b. market value
    c. replacement value
    d. book value

6. Which of the following would not be considered an asset of a company?
    a. cash
    b. patent
    c. lease obligation
    d. copyright

7. Which of the following would not be shown in the stockholders' equity section of the balance sheet?
    a. retained earnings
    b. donated capital
    c. treasury stock
    d. marketable securities

8. A contingent liability must be reported on the balance sheet if the following condition(s) is/are met.
    a. the event is considered probable
    b. the company can estimate the monetary effect
    c. it is possible the company will have to pay
    d. both (a) and (b) must be met

9. Which of the following would not be considered a current asset.
    a. inventory
    b. accounts receivable
    c. equipment
    d. prepaid rent

363

10. Late in 20X1 it was discovered that Y Corporation failed to accrue $100,000 of vacation pay in 20X0. If Y Corporation's effective tax rate for 20X0 was 40 percent, what adjustment would be made to the beginning retained earnings balance to correct the error?
    a. Increase by $40,000.
    b. Decrease by $60,000.
    c. Decrease by $100,000.
    d. No adjustment is made to retained earnings.

Problem III

Following is a list of important ideas and key concepts from the chapter. To test your knowledge of these terms, match the term with the definition by placing the number in the space provided.

_____ compensating balance   _____ off-balance sheet financing
_____ contingent liabilities   _____ prior period adjustment
_____ deferred charges

1. A minimum cash balance that the depositor (company) must maintain either to continue to earn interest on the amount deposited in the bank account or to avoid certain fees, such as service charges.

2. Long-term prepayments frequently found in the "other assets" classification that companies amortize over various lengths of time, depending on how long the company will benefit from the expenditures.

3. A correction of previously undetected material error that affected the net income or loss of a previous accounting period.

4. Borrowing money in ways that would avoid having to record the obligation on the balance sheet.

5. Events that could create negative financial results for a company; required to be recorded when the event is probable and estimable in terms of its monetary effects.

Problem IV

Complete the following sentences by filling in the correct response.

1. The _____ _____ reports the amount and type of assets the firm controls
   and the _____ the owners and creditors have on those assets.

2. Segments can by identified on _____ region or _____ line basis.

3. Financial position is measured at a _____ in time whereas net income is
   measured for a _____ of time.

4. Intangible assets have no _____ substance, but are expected to generate some
   future _____ benefit.

5. Contingent liabilities must be recorded in the financial statements if the event is considered
   _____ and the amount can be reasonably _____.

Problem V

The following account balances are available for the Sunflex Company as of December 31, 20X1.

Sales	900,000	Accounts receivable	89,000
Bonds payable	600,000	Capital stock	500,000
Cost of goods sold	500,000	Inventory	165,000
Equipment	700,000	Accumulated depreciation	145,000
Patents	75,000	Selling expenses	85,000
Short-term notes payable	40,000	Interest expense	70,000
Premium on bonds payable	143,000	Land	245,000
General and admin. expenses	210,000	Accounts payable	61,000
Treasury stock	19,000	Retained earnings (beginning of year)	184,000
Cash	62,000	Allow. for uncollectible accounts	6,000
Prepaid insurance	8,000	Marketable securities (trading)	23,000
Salaries payable	17,000	Investment in stock - X Company	345,000

Required: Prepare a classified balance sheet.

Problem VI

Using the following legend, indicate the proper balance sheet classification for each account:

CA	Current assets	NL	Noncurrent liabilities
PPE	Property, plant, and equipment	CC	Contributed capital
INT	Intangibles	RE	Retained earnings
ONA	Other noncurrent assets	OOE	Other owners' equity
CL	Current liabilities		

_____1. Cash
_____2. Salaries payable
_____3. Prepaid rent
_____4. Mortgage payable
_____5. Preferred stock
_____6. Land
_____7. Retained earnings
_____8. Equipment
_____9. Common stock
_____10. Unearned service revenue
_____11. Accounts receivable
_____12. Goodwill
_____13. Accounts payable
_____14. Copyrights
_____15. Bonds payable
_____16. Notes payable (due in 6 months)
_____17. Treasury stock
_____18. Paid-in-capital common stock
_____19. Inventory
_____20. Supplies

Solutions for Chapter 18

Problem I

1. T
2. T
3. T
4. F
5. T
6. T
7. F
8. F
9. T
10. F

Problem II

1. a
2. b
3. d
4. c
5. d
6. c
7. d
8. d
9. c
10. b

Problem III

1 compensating balance
5 contingent liabilities
2 deferred charges

4 off-balance sheet financing
3 prior period adjustment

Problem IV

1. balance sheet, claims
2. geographical, product
3. point, period
4. physical, economic
5. probable, estimated

Problem V

Current Assets:

Cash		$ 62,000
Marketable securities		23,000
Accounts receivable	89,000	
Less: Allowance for uncollectible accounts	6,000	83,000
Inventory		165,000
Prepaid insurance		8,000
Total current assets		341,000

Property, Plant and Equipment:

Land		245,000
Equipment	700,000	
Less: Accumulated depreciation	145,000	555,000
Total property, plant and equipment		800,000

Intangible Assets - Patents		75,000
Other Assets - Investment in stock - X Company		345,000
Total Assets		$1,561,000

Liabilities and Stockholders' Equity
Current Liabilities:

Accounts payable		$ 61,000
Notes payable		40,000
Salaries payable		17,000
Total current liabilities		118,000

Non-current Liabilities:

Bonds payable	600,000	
Add: Premium on bonds payable	143,000	743,000

Stockholders' Equity:

Capital stock		500,000
Retained earnings		219,000
		719,000
Less: Treasury stock		19,000
Total stockholders' equity		700,000
Total Liabilities and Stockholders' Equity		$1,561,000

Problem VI

1. CA
2. CL
3. CA
4. NL
5. CC
6. PPE
7. RE
8. PPE
9. CC
10. CL
11. CA
12. INT
13. CL
14. INT
15. NL
16. CL
17. OOE
18. CC
19. CA
20. CA

Chapter 19
Company Performance: Cash Flows

Chapter Overview

Chapter 19 examines the statement of cash flows. The chapter presents both the direct and indirect methods for preparing the statement. The purpose of the statement of cash flows is to report the cash flows arising from the operating, investing, and financing activities of a firm. The chapter discusses how external and internal users can use the cash flow information to assess a company's ability to generate positive future cash flows and to meet its obligations.

The FASB recommends that the direct method be used to present the statement of cash flows and that a reconciliation of net income and operating cash flows be provided as supplemental information. This reconciliation takes the form of an indirect method of calculating operating cash flows. As a result, many companies present only statements of cash flows using the indirect method. Again, go to the websites of well-known companies and check out their statements of cash flows. Determine whether each company is presenting operating cash flows using a direct method or indirect method format. Your instructor may ask you to learn both methods for preparing the statement of cash flows, or he/she may prefer that you focus your attention on only one method.

Read and Recall Questions

> **Learning Objective:**
> LO. 1 Discuss the purpose of and prepare the operating section of the statement of cash flows using the direct method.

Identify the four primary purposes of the statement of cash flows.

Why is the statement of cash flows divided into three sections?

What types of cash flows are included in the operating activities section of the statement of cash flows?

Briefly distinguish between the direct and indirect formats for the statement of cash flows.

Using the direct format, briefly explain how to determine the cash flows for a particular operating item from the income statement.

Why do a company's revenues reported on the income statement differ from its cash inflows from operations?

How is the amount of cash collections from accounts receivable customers calculated?

How is the amount of cash received from prepaid customers calculated?

Study Guide: An Introduction to Accounting, An Integrated Approach

Why do a company's expenses differ from the amounts of cash paid for expense items?

How is the amount of cash paid for prepaid expenses calculated?

How is the amount of cash paid for accrued expenses calculated?

How is the amount of cash paid for inventory determined?

Learning Objective:
LO. 2 Explain the purpose of and prepare the operating section of the statement of cash flows using the indirect method.

Identify the four adjustments that must be made to convert net income to cash from operations.

Explain how noncash income statement items must be adjusted to convert net income to cash from operations? What are two common noncash adjustments?

Why must net income be adjusted for gains and losses when converting it to cash flows from operations?

What are noncash current operating assets? What does an increase in a noncash current asset indicate?

Would a decrease in a noncash current operating asset related to revenues be added to or subtracted from net income to determine cash flows from operations? Explain.

Would a decrease in a noncash current operating asset related to expenses be added to or subtracted from net income to determine cash flows from operations? Explain.

What are current operating liabilities? What does an increase in a current operating liability indicate?

Study Guide: An Introduction to Accounting, An Integrated Approach

When a current operating liability related to revenues increases, would the increase be added to or subtracted from net income to determine cash flows from operations? Explain.

When a current operating liability related to expenses increases, would the increase be added to or subtracted from net income to determine cash flows from operations? Explain.

When a company uses the indirect format, what two additional disclosures must be made either on the statement of cash flows itself or in the accompanying notes?

Learning Objective:
LO. 3 Identify the purpose of and prepare the investing section of the statement of cash flows.

What do the cash flows from the investing activities section reflect?

How are the cash flows associated with trading securities determined?

How are the cash flows associated with buildings determined?

How are the cash flows associated with equipment determined?

| **Learning Objective:** |
| LO. 4 Explain the purpose of and prepare the financing section of the statement of cash flows. |

With which types of accounts are the cash flows from financing activities associated?

How are the cash flows associated with notes payable determined?

How are the cash flows associated with treasury stock determined?

How are the cash flows associated with dividends determined?

Study Guide: An Introduction to Accounting, An Integrated Approach

Why are significant noncash investing and financing events reported either on the statement of cash flows itself or in the notes to the financial statements?

Briefly explain the cash flow per share ratio. How is this ratio calculated?

Outline of Key Concepts

I.   Statement of cash flows provides a link between the accrual-based income statement and the balance sheet.
A.   FASB identified four primary purposes of the statement of cash flows.
1.   Assess the entity's ability to generate positive future cash flows.
2.   Assess the entity's ability to meet its obligations and pay dividends, and its need for external financing.
3.   Assess the reasons for differences between income and associated cash receipts and payments.
4.   Assess both the cash and noncash aspects of the entity's investing and financing transactions during the period.
B.   The statement is divided into three major sections.
1.   Operating activities involve transactions that result from the earning process of the company.
a.   Cash inflows come primarily from customers, interest and dividends received by the company.
b.   Cash outflows result from the payments made for operating expenses, including the purchase of inventory.

2. Investing activities involve acquiring and disposing of property, plant, and equipment; other long-term investments; and short-term or temporary investments that are not cash equivalents.

3. Financing activities involve borrowing from and repaying creditors, raising funds from owners, and distributing funds to owners that are either a return on or a return of investment.

II. The direct format of the statement of cash flows shows the actual cash inflows and outflows from operating activities.

    A. FASB requires a reconciliation of accrual-based net income to the amount of cash flows from operating activities (essentially the same as the indirect format).

    B. To determine the cash flows for a particular item, companies use the beginning and ending balances of a given balance sheet account, along with the related revenue or expense amount from the income statement.

        1. Revenues differ from cash inflows for two reasons.

            a. The revenue is earned before the cash is collected; for example,

                Beginning balance of Accounts Receivable, net

                + Net sales on account during the period

                = Maximum amount of cash owed by customers

                - Uncollectible accounts expense

                - **Cash collections from customers during the period**

                = Ending balance of Accounts Receivable, net

            b. The cash is collected before the revenue is earned; for example,

                Beginning balance of revenue collected in advance

                + **Cash received from customers during the period**

                = Maximum goods or services owed to customers

                - Revenues earned during the period

                = Ending balance of revenue collected in advance

        2. Expenses may not equal cash paid for two reasons.

            a. The expenses are incurred before the cash is paid; for example,

                Beginning balance of prepaid expense

                + **Cash paid for prepaid expense**

                = Maximum prepaid expenses available

                - Expense for the period

                = Ending balance of prepaid asset

            b. The expenses are incurred after the cash is paid; for example,

                Beginning balance of accrued liability

                + Expense for the period

                = Maximum amount of cash owed

                - **Cash paid during the period**

                = Ending balance of accrued liability

            c. To determine cash flows for interest, must examine the interest payable account as well as the premium or discount accounts associated with long-term debt.

3. Determining the amount of cash paid for inventory.

     Beginning balance of inventory
+ **Net purchases during the period**
= Maximum amount of inventory available for sale
- Cost of goods sold
= Ending balance of inventory

then

     Beginning balance of Accounts Payable
+ Net purchases during the period
= Maximum amount of cash owed for inventory
- **Cash paid for inventory during the period**
= Ending balance of Accounts Payable

C. When a company received revenue at the same time it is recognized as earned and when an expense is paid at the same time it is incurred, the amount of the revenue or expense is equal to the cash inflow or outflow.

III.   Indirect format for the statement of cash flows presents the amount of cash generated from operations by adjusting net income for items that cause cash from operations to differ from accrual-based net income.

A. Four adjustments are made to net income to determine cash flows from operations.

    1. Adjustments for noncash income statement items.

       a. Noncash income statement items increase or decrease net income but do not affect operating cash flows.

       b. Depreciation, depletion, and amortization are added back to net income.

       c. Interest expense adjustments due to the amortization of premiums or discounts are deducted from or added to net income.

       d. Interest income adjustments due to the amortization of premiums or discounts are added to or deducted from net income.

    2. Adjustments for gains or losses from either investing or financing activities.

       a. Gains must be subtracted from net income.

       b. Losses must be added to net income.

    3. Noncash current operating assets—represent operating activities.

       a. Not all current accounts fall into this category; for example, trading securities which are investing activities.

       b. The increase in a noncash current operating asset must be deducted from net income.

       c. The decrease in a noncash current operating asset must be added to net income.

    4. Current operating liabilities—represent operating obligations.

       a. Nontrade notes payable, bank loans payable, and dividends payable are excluded because they are financing activities.

b. The increase in a current operating liability must be added to net income.
c. The decrease in a current operating liability must be deducted from net income.

B. FASB requires two additional disclosures when the indirect method format is used.
1. The amount of cash paid for interest.
2. The amount of cash paid for taxes.

C. The amount of net cash flows from operating activities is the same regardless of whether the direct or indirect method is used.
1. Direct format shows the amounts of cash received and paid for various items.
   a. It is a good tool for analyzing specific changes in operating cash flows (internal use).
2. Indirect format shows the reconciliation of net income to cash flows from operations.

IV. Cash flows from the investing activities reflect the amount of cash received from sales of long-term and current nonoperating assets and the amount of cash paid to purchase these assets.
A. Each long-term and current nonoperating asset account and any related accounts must be analyzed for changes to determine cash received or cash paid.
B. Users evaluate investing cash flows to determine if a company is making adequate investments in long-term assets and other investments.

V. Cash flows from financing activities are associated with long-term liabilities; current nonoperating liabilities, such as nontrade notes payable and dividends payable; and the owners' equity of the company.
A. Includes the issuance and repayment of notes and bonds, the sale and repurchase of stock, and the distribution of the company's earnings.
1. Does not include the changes in owners' equity caused by the company's net income.
B. Each long-term and current nonoperating liability account must be analyzed for changes to determine cash received or paid.
C. Users evaluate financing cash flows to determine if the company is obtaining adequate amounts of cash to enable it to invest in long-term assets.

VI. Noncash investing and financing activities that are important to the financial statement users are reported either on the statement itself or in the notes to the financial statements.
A. Typical noncash events reported include:
1. Acquisition of assets by issuing debt or equity securities.
2. Exchanges of assets.
3. Conversion of debt or preferred stock to common stock.
4. Issuance of common or preferred stock to retire debt.
B. These events are important because of their future cash flow implications.

Study Guide: An Introduction to Accounting, An Integrated Approach

VII. Internal users have additional information about cash flows that are not available to external users.
   A. Internal users have information about the timing of cash receipts and payments.
   B. Internal users know the expected or budgeted cash flows at the beginning of the period and can compare the flows to actual results.
   C. Cash flow per share ratio—indicates the cash generated by operating activities on a per share basis.
      1. (Cash flows from operating activities – Preferred dividends) / Weighted average common shares outstanding.

Problem I

Indicate whether the following statements are either true (T) or false (F).

_____1. Net cash flows from operating activities will be the same under both the direct and indirect format.

_____2. The sale of equipment will be shown in the financing activities section of the cash flow statement.

_____3. The issuance of common stock will be shown in the investing activities section of the cash flow statement.

_____4. A company's revenues on the income statement will generally equal its cash receipts from operations.

_____5. Interest expense paid on a bond payable will be shown in the operating activities section of the cash flow statement.

_____6. The payment of a cash dividend will be shown in the financing activities section of the cash flow statement.

_____7. The cash flow statement is used to assess both the cash and noncash aspects of the entity's investing and financing transactions during the period.

_____8. Most companies use the direct method to report cash flows from operating activities.

_____9. The issuance of a bond payable will be shown in the investing activities section of the cash flow statement.

_____10. Cash collected from customers will be shown in the operating activities section of the cash flow statement.

Problem II

Indicate the correct answer by circling the appropriate letter.

1. During the year X Corporation reported salary expense of $235,000 in its income statement. Salaries payable had a beginning balance of $28,000 and an ending balance of $21,000. Cash paid for wages during the year was _____.
   - a. $235,000
   - b. $242,000
   - c. $228,000
   - d. $258,000

2. Z Corporation reported interest income of $32,000 for the year. The interest receivable account had a beginning balance of $14,000 and an ending balance of $2,000. What was the cash received from interest for the year?
   - a. $34,000
   - b. $32,000
   - c. $44,000
   - d. $20,000

3. Y Corporation reported insurance expense of $12,000 for the most recent accounting period. At the beginning of the period the prepaid insurance account had a $2,400 balance and at the end of the period it had a balance of $1,200. Cash paid for insurance for the accounting period was

   _____.
   - a. $12,000
   - b. $13,200
   - c. $10,800
   - d. $14,400

4. The following selected information is available for the year:

Net income	$500,000
Depreciation expense	34,000
Loss on early retirement of bonds	5,000
Decrease in inventory	12,000
Increase in supplies	2,000
Amortization expense-patent	9,000

What is the company's net cash flow from operations?
   - a. $516,000
   - b. $456,000
   - c. $504,000
   - d. $558,000

Study Guide: An Introduction to Accounting, An Integrated Approach

Use the following information for the next three questions:

Following are selected account balances for the Suntime Company:

Sales (all on credit)	$450,000
Cost of goods sold	245,000
Supplies expense	9,000

	Beginning balance	Ending balance
Accounts receivable	$85,000	$73,000
Inventory	68,000	93,000
Supplies	1,200	1,500
Accounts payable (inventory purchases)	38,000	25,000

5. Cash collections from customers for the year were _____.
   a. $450,000
   b. $462,000
   c. $438,000
   d. $365,000

6. Cash payments for inventory during the year was_____.
   a. $207,000
   b. $283,000
   c. $243,000
   d. $233,000

7. Cash paid for supplies during the year was _____.
   a. $9,000
   b. $9,300
   c. $8,700
   d. $10,500

8. Which of the following is a purpose of the cash flow statement?
   a. Assess the entity's ability to generate positive future cash flows.
   b. Assess the entity's ability to meet obligations and pay dividends.
   c. Assess the reasons for differences between income and associated cash receipts and payments.
   d. All of the above are purposes of the cash flow statement.

9. The following selected information is available for the year:

Net income	$400,000
Depreciation expense	67,000
Gain on sale of equipment	9,000
Interest expense	12,000
Increase in accounts receivable	20,000
Increase in accounts payable	1,000
Decrease in interest payable	3,000

What is the company's net cash flow from operations?
   a. $436,000
   b. $400,000
   c. $367,000
   d. $496,000

10. During the year Z Corporation reported interest expense of $65,000 from a bank loan on its income statement. Interest payable had a beginning balance of $2,000 and an ending balance of $7,000. Cash paid for interest during the year was _____.
   a. $65,000
   b. $72,000
   c. $60,000
   d. $70,000

Problem III

Following is a list of important ideas and key concepts from the chapter. To test your knowledge of these terms, match the term with the definition by placing the number in the space provided.

_____ current operating liabilities
_____ direct format
_____ indirect format
_____ noncash current operating asset

1. Shows the differences between accrual-based net income and cash flows from operations.

2. Noncash accounts that represent operating activities.

3. Shows the actual cash inflows and outflows from each operating activity reported on the income statement.

4. Accounts representing operating obligations.

384 _____

Problem IV

The financial statements of Jax Corporation are present below:

Jax Corporation
Balance Sheet
As of December 31, 19X7 and 19X8

		19X8		19X7
Current Assets				
Cash		$ 37,000		$ 3,000
Accounts receivable		85,000		25,000
Marketable equity securities		9,000		16,000
Total current assets		$131,000		$ 44,000
Property, plant and equipment				
Buildings, furniture and equipment	$245,000		$260,000	
Less: Accumulated depreciation	85,000	160,000	55,000	205,000
Goodwill		235,000		240,000
Total Assets		$526,000		$489,000
Current Liabilities				
Accounts payable		$ 55,000		$105,000
Interest payable		13,000		11,000
Total current liabilities		$ 68,000		$116,000
Noncurrent Liabilities:				
Mortgage payable		200,000		160,000
Stockholders' Equity:				
Common stock		145,000		130,000
Paid-in-capital common stock		23,000		18,000
Retained earnings		90,000		65,000
		258,000		213,000
Total Liabilities and Stockholders' Equity		$526,000		$489,000

Problem IV (continued)

Jax Corporation
Income Statement
For the Year Ended December 31, 19X8

Revenues:

Service revenue	$650,000	
Gain on sale of equipment	7,000	$657,000

Expenses:

Selling, general and administrative expenses	540,000	
Depreciation expense	40,000	
Loss on sale of marketable securities	2,000	
Interest expense	10,000	
Goodwill amortization	5,000	597,000
Net Income		$ 60,000

Additional information:

1. Jax paid a $35,000 cash dividend to shareholders.
2. Equipment originally costing $15,000 (accumulated depreciation of $10,000) was sold for $12,000.
3. Marketable equity securities originally costing $7,000 were sold for $5,000.

Required: Prepare a statement of cash flows using the indirect method.

Problem V

Use the following legend to indicate in which section of the cash flow statement each accounting event would be reported:

O Operating Activities   I   Investing Activities
F Financing Activities   NC Noncash Activities

_____1. Payment of a cash dividend to stockholders.
_____2. Sale of inventory to a customer.
_____3. Purchase of equipment to be used in production.
_____4. Borrowing money from a local bank.
_____5. Purchase of operating supplies.
_____6. Payment of salespersons' salaries.
_____7. Receipt of interest income from an investment in U.S. Treasury Bills.
_____8. Repayment of a short-term note payable.
_____9. Issuance of 1,000 shares of common stock.
_____10. Purchase of land by issuing a 20-year note payable.
_____11. Purchase of a two-year casualty insurance policy.
_____12. Purchase of thirty percent of the outstanding stock of X Corporation.

Solutions for Chapter 19

Problem I

1. T
2. F
3. F
4. F
5. T
6. T
7. T
8. F
9. F
10. T

Problem II

1. b
2. c
3. c
4. d
5. b
6. b
7. b
8. d
9. a
10. c

Problem III

4   current operating liabilities
3   direct format
1   indirect format
2   noncash current operating asset

Problem IV

Jax Corporation
Statement of Cash Flows
For the Year Ended December 31, 19X8

Net Cash Flows from Operating Activities	
Net income	$60,000
Adjustments to Reconcile Net Income to the	
Net Cash Flows from Operations:	
Depreciation expense	40,000
Gain on sale of equipment	< 7,000>
Loss on sale of marketable securities	2,000
Amortization of goodwill	5,000
Deduct increase in accounts receivable	<60,000>
Deduct decrease in accounts payable	<50,000>
Add increase in interest payable	2,000
Cash used by operations	<$8,000>
Net Cash Flows from Investing Activities:	
Sale of equipment	$12,000
Sale of marketable equity securities	5,000
Cash provided by investing activities	$17,000
Net Cash Flows from Financing Activities:	
Borrowing through mortgage payable	40,000
Payment of cash dividends	<35,000>
Issuance of stock	20,000
Cash provided by financing activities	$25,000
Net Change in Cash during 19X8	$34,000
Add: Beginning Balance in Cash	3,000
Ending Balance in Cash	$37,000

Problem V

1. F
2. O
3. I
4. F
5. O
6. O
7. O
8. F
9. F
10. NC
11. O
12. I

Study Guide: An Introduction to Accounting, An Integrated Approach

Chapter 20
Company Performance: Comprehensive Evaluation

Chapter Overview

Chapter 20 concludes the text and the evaluation phase by examining how external users perform comprehensive financial analysis. The chapter explores the role of capital and information markets and identifies external sources of financial statement comparison information. In addition, the chapter discusses and illustrates how vertical analysis, horizontal analysis, and ratio analysis can be used to evaluate the performance of a company. The chapter concludes by examining the independent auditor's report.

As you study this chapter, it will become apparent that you need a thorough understanding of the financial statements and financial statement classifications to perform in-depth financial analysis. Although it is usually not necessary to memorize all the ratios, you must be able to correctly identify the elements of each ratio. More importantly, you should focus on the interpretation of each ratio. You will discover that financial analysis requires you to look at results over time and to compare results with industry standards. The numbers alone tell you little about a company's performance.

Read and Recall Questions

Learning Objective
LO. 4 Explain the various roles of the participants in the capital market.

Briefly discuss the capital market.

Explain how the investment perspectives of creditors and investors differ.

Briefly describe a free market economy.

Discuss the relationship between the product market and the capital market.

In the capital market, identify the returns that creditors seek.

In the capital market, identify the returns that investors seek.

Why is there a need for a financial information market?

Briefly discuss the two problems associated with the need for financial information.

Study Guide: Introduction to Accounting, An Integrated Approach

Explain the role of the independent auditor in the financial information market.

Learning Objective:
LO. 1 Perform a vertical analysis to analyze a company.

Identify the three primary methods of financial analysis.

What are the benefits of studying comparative financial statements?

Why are external standards important for performing financial statement analysis?

Identify at least four sources of external standards.

Briefly describe vertical analysis.

Why do analysts, creditors, and investors compare the results of the vertical analysis of a particular company with the results of competitors and external industry standards?

Learning Objective:
LO. 2 Demonstrate horizontal analysis to analyze a company.

Briefly describe horizontal analysis.

What is the purpose of horizontal analysis? What time frame is typically used for horizontal analysis?

Learning Objective:
LO. 3 Perform a ratio analysis to analyze a company.

What is the broad purpose of ratio analysis?

Identify the types of relationship that may be compared through ratio analysis.

What is the purpose of activity ratios in general?

What is the purpose of the accounts receivable turnover ratio? How is it calculated?

Identify two computational issues that should signal caution when using and interpreting the accounts receivable turnover ratio.

What relationship does the inventory turnover ratio measure? Identify three factors that should impact the interpretation of this ratio.

What is the purpose of the accounts payable turnover ratio? How is it calculated?

Why is it important to assess a company's liquidity and solvency?

Distinguish between the current ratio and the quick ratio. How are each of these ratios calculated?

Why do analysts calculate cash flow per share?

Identify the two ratios commonly used by creditors to evaluate creditworthiness.

What is the purpose of the times interest earned ratio?

Study Guide: Introduction to Accounting, An Integrated Approach

Explain what a high debt-to-equity ratio indicates about a company.

What is profitability, and why is it important?

What is the purpose of the gross margin ratio?

Explain how return on sales differs from the gross margin ratio.

Explain what the return on assets ratio represents.

Discuss the difference between the return on owners' equity and return on common equity.

Define earnings per share.

What does the dividend payout ratio reveal about a company?

Discuss the purpose(s) of the organized stock markets.

What factors influence the price of stocks?

Describe the purpose of the price-earnings (PE) ratio. What does a high PE ratio suggest?

Define dividend yield. How is it calculated?

Study Guide: Introduction to Accounting, An Integrated Approach

What types of information may be contained in management's letter to stockholders?

Discuss the purpose of the auditor's report.

Briefly describe the four kinds of auditor's reports that may be issued.

Outline of Key Concepts

I.   Capital market—the entire group of creditors and investors who provide capital to businesses to finance their investments.
    A. Investment decisions are based on the perception of the risk and potential return for each business.
        1. Financial statements are the principal source of information.
    B. There are significant differences between creditors and investors.
        1. Creditors lend a fixed amount of money over a limited term and generally have legal documents that give them legal recourse in recovering their investment from the businesses to which they lend.
        2. Investors have no limited or fixed terms. They commit funds until the business ceases to operate or until they sell their stock to another investor.
           a. They have few guarantees for the money they invest.
    C. Free market economy—do not rely on government dictates. It creates a product market where consumers determine the types of goods and services they need and want.

399

1. In turn, creates opportunities for providers of goods and services to meet consumers' demands.

II. There is a relationship among product markets, capital markets, and the information markets.
   A. The capital market is the link between those who produce goods and services and the creditors and investors who own the capital.
      1. The owners of capital want the highest possible return possible, at an acceptable level of risk.
         a. For creditors, the return is the interest charged to the borrower plus the amount of change in the market value of debt not held to maturity.
         b. For investors, return consists of the dividends received plus the increase in the value of the stocks held.
      2. External investors and creditors cannot observe business activities, and they do not have ready access to much information about these activities. This creates a market for information.
         a. Producers provide financial information that conforms to GAAP, such as the annual report.
         b. Once information is published anyone can use it.
         c. Investors and creditors may have difficulty determining whether the information fairly presents the financial condition of the company. The independent auditor plays an important role as an objective reviewer of the information.
         d. Industry trade publications and government statistics can reveal broader economic factors.

III. Financial statement aids external users to make investment and credit decisions.
   A. Comparative financial statements report two or more years' financial statements side by side in a columnar format.
      1. Studying comparative financial statements helps the reader to become familiar with the company's reporting practices, the accounts and classifications it uses, and the general range of amounts it reflects.
      2. An evaluation of the changes in reported financial data over time helps determine the general trend of operations and assists in deciding whether the company is better off or worse off than in previous periods.
         a. See trends as they develop.
         b. Should use caution in projecting historical trends into the future.
   B. External standards provide an average and a range of quantitative values for rations of firms in the same or similar industries.
      1. Provides a comparison among investment alternatives.
      2. *RMA Annual Statement Studies* summarizes financial information by industry using SIC codes.
      3. *Moody's Handbook of NASDAQ Stocks* and *Moody's Handbook of Common Stocks* provides one-page summaries of the history and principal products as

well as detailed financial tables for many of the companies whose stock is traded in the United States.

 C. Vertical analysis—shows the relationship of all other items on the financial statement to the base item.

  1. On the income statement, the base is total sales.

  2. On the balance sheet, the base is total assets.

  3. Reveals the relative importance of various financial statement items to the base.

  4. May compare a company's relationships against industry averages.

 D. Horizontal analysis—shows a comparison of each item on a financial statement with that same item on statements from previous periods.

  1. Compares one item to itself over time on a percentage basis to indicate the changes over time.

  2. Helpful for discovering short-term trends.

  3. Typically done for three to five-year periods.

IV. Ratio analysis makes it easy to compare relationships for firms over time, different firms, and with standards such as industry standards.

 A. Activity ratios—financial ratios that help in judging a firm's efficiency in using its current assets and liabilities.

  1. Accounts Receivable Turnover—measures how many times the company collected the average accounts receivable balance in the period.

   a. Net credit sales / Average net accounts receivable

  2. Inventory Turnover—measures how many times the company sold the average amount of inventory in the period.

   a. Cost of goods sold / Average inventory

   b. When evaluating, must note inventory methods used and seasonality of the company.

  3. Accounts Payable Turnover—measures how many times the company paid for the average amount of accounts payable during the period.

   a. Cost of goods sold / Average accounts payable

   b. Assumes that accounts payable represents primarily purchases of inventory on account.

 B. Liquidity and solvency analysis—concerned with cash flows and the adequacy of current assets to meet current liabilities.

  1. Current Ratio—measures the relationship between the current assets and current liabilities of the company.

   a. Current assets / Current liabilities

  2. Quick Ratio—provides a stricter test of the adequacy of current assets to meet current liabilities because it excludes current assets that are not readily convertible to cash.

   a. (Cash + temporary investments + receivables) / Current liabilities

  3. Cash Flow per Share

a. (Cash flow from operations – Preferred dividends) / Weighted average number of shares of common stock

C. Debt paying ability ratios—used by creditors to evaluate a company's creditworthiness.

    1. Times Interest Earned—compares earnings before deducting interest and taxes to the amount of interest charges.
        a. Net income before interest and taxes / Interest expense
        b. A company whose income before interest is barely sufficient to cover its interest expense is riskier from a creditor's point of view than one with a high times interest earned ratio.

    2. Debt-to-Equity Ratio—measures a company's risk as an investment by the extent to which it relies on debt rather than ownership financing.
        a. Total liabilities / Total shareholders' equity
        b. Also provides a picture of financial flexibility.

D. Profitability ratios—measures the return on funds invested by the owners and achieved by the efforts of management.

    1. Gross Margin Ratio—measures whether there is sufficient gross margin to cover operating expenses.
        a. Gross margin / Net sales

    2. Return on Sales—measures the net income generated per dollar of sales.
        a. Income from continuing operations / Net sales

    3. Return on Assets—measures profitability by including both earnings and investment.
        a. Net income before interest and taxes / Average total assets
        b. Measures the effectiveness of management in utilizing the resources at its command.

    4. Return on Owners' Equity—measures the return earned relative to the portion of the company that belongs to the owners.
        a. Net income / Average total stockholders' equity

    5. Earnings per Share—measures the net income of the company on a common-size basis.
        a. (Net income – Preferred dividends) / Weighted average number of shares of common stock

E. Market-based ratios—use the market price of the stock as part of the calculation.

    1. Price-Earnings (PE) Ratio—reflects the relationship between the current market price of the company's common stock and the earnings of the company.
        a. An overall approximation of the market's assessment of a company's prospective earnings performance.
        b. Current market price per common share / Earnings per share

    2. Dividend Yield—measures the return that an investor would receive on a company's stock at the current price, if dividends paid in the recent past continue into the foreseeable future.
        a. Dividends paid per share of stock / Market price per share of stock

Study Guide: Introduction to Accounting, An Integrated Approach

    b. Does not measure the return from the appreciation of the stock price.

V. The annual report is the principal way that mangers communicate their assessment and perception of the company.
 A. Management's letter to stockholders—gives an overview of the items in the report other than the financial statements and highlights important aspects of financial performance.
   1. Addresses strengths and weaknesses of the company.
   2. Highlights key operating data and discusses operating results.
 B. Segment and quarterly data—stakeholders can assess major parts of the company and can compare performance across quarters.
 C. Auditor's report—provides the CPA's opinion about the fairness of the financial statements using GAAP as the criteria.
   1. Unqualified opinion—means the financial statements are representations of the business's financial position, cash flows, and reported income, and that GAAP has been applied appropriately.
   2. Qualified opinion—indicates that either the auditor found part of the company's financial statements not in accordance with GAAP or the auditor's ability to examine the underlying records used to develop the financial statements was limited.
   3. Adverse opinion—indicates the external auditor believes that the financial statements are not fair representations of the company's financial position or income.
   4. Disclaimer of opinion—the auditor was not able to gather sufficient evidence to support an opinion or that the auditor was not sufficiently independent of the company to issue an opinion.
   5. Audit report does not guarantee that the company is a good investment nor does it guarantee that the company will not declare bankruptcy.

403

Problem I

Indicate whether the following statements are either true (T) or false (F).

_____1. In a free market economy, consumer demand determines the nature of businesses that exists and how much of a given product or service is available.

_____2. The debt-to-equity ratio measures the extent that a company relies on debt rather than equity to finance operations.

_____3. Free market economies rely on government to dictate the type of businesses and the amount of a product or service to provide.

_____4. Most potential investments offer the same risk and return.

_____5. Financial statements are difficult to interpret without an external standard against which they can be compared.

_____6. One means of assessing a business's liquidity is through the use of activity ratios.

_____7. The dividend yield does not take into account the return from appreciation in the stock price.

_____8. The earnings per share ratio is an approximation of the market's assessment of a company's prospective earnings performance.

_____9. In vertical analysis, each balance sheet item is divided by total assets.

_____10. The quick ratio provides a more conservative measure of short-term liquidity than the current ratio.

Problem II

Indicate the correct answer by circling the appropriate letter.

1. Which of the following is not considered a liquidity ratio?
    a. Current ratio.
    b. Payables turnover ratio.
    c. Quick ratio.
    d. Cash flow per share ratio.

2. Ratio analysis makes it easy to compare relationships _____.
    a. for a company over time
    b. of different companies
    c. with standards such as industry averages
    d. All of the above are correct.

Study Guide: Introduction to Accounting, An Integrated Approach

Use the following information for the next four questions:
Selected information for the Y Corporation is presented below:

Net sales	$100,000
Net income before interest and taxes	$ 30,000
Net income	$ 20,000
Average total assets	$400,000
Earnings per share	$1.2
Current market price per share	$10
Average stockholders' equity	$160,000

3. The price-earnings ratio is _____.
   a. 8.333
   b. 12.1
   c. 6.7
   d. .12

4. Y Corporation has no preferred stock outstanding. During the year, the company paid $2,000 in dividends to common shareholders. The dividend payout ratio is _____.
   a. 5%
   b. 20%
   c. 32%
   d. 10%

5. The return on sales is _____.
   a. 10%
   b. 15%
   c. 20%
   d. 25%

6. The return on total assets is _____.
   a. 7.5%
   b. 5%
   c. 9.2%
   d. 1%

7. Which of the following is not considered an activity ratio?
   a. Accounts receivable turnover ratio.
   b. Inventory turnover ratio.
   c. Average collection period ratio.
   d. Current ratio.

8. Z Corporation's accounts receivable turnover ratio was 12.1 for the year. The average collection period would be _____.
   a. 30.16 days
   b. 25.78 days
   c. 12.1 days
   d. 62.7 days

9. Which of the following ratios is not used to assess a firm's profitability?
   a. Return on assets ratio.
   b. Return on owners' equity ratio.
   c. Gross margin ratio.
   d. All of the above are used assess profitability.

10. Z Corporation has 10,000 shares of $5 par value common stock and 1,000 shares of $100 par, 10% cumulative preferred stock outstanding. Net income for the year was $140,000 and total stockholders' equity is $600,000. The liquidation value of the preferred stock is its par value. Return on common equity for the year is _____.
   a. 12%
   b. 18%
   c. 22%
   d. 26%

Problem III

Complete the following sentences by filling in the correct response.

1. The group of creditors and investors who provide capital to businesses make up what is referred to as the _____ _____.

2. Investors invest money in companies expecting return in the form of _____ and/or _____ _____ for the stock they hold.

3. Financial statements provide information that is used to assess a company's _____, longer-term debt-paying ability, and _____.

4. _____ ratios are helpful in judging a company's efficiency in using its _____ assets and liabilities.

5. The inventory turnover ratio is calculated by taking _____ and dividing it by average _____.

Study Guide: Introduction to Accounting, An Integrated Approach

6. The payables turnover is calculated by taking _____ and dividing by average _____ except for _____.

7. The quick ratio is calculated by taking the _____ plus _____ plus _____ and dividing the amount by the total _____.

8. The _____, _____ and _____ ratios are used to assess a company's long-term debt-paying ability.

9. The debt-to-equity ratio is calculated by dividing _____ by _____.

10. The return on common equity is calculated by dividing _____ less any _____ by _____ minus the _____ value of preferred stock.

11. The price-earnings ratio is calculated by taking the current _____ and dividing by the _____.

Problem IV

The financial statements of Zectar Corporation are present below:

Zectar Corporation
Balance Sheet
As of December 31, 20X1 and 20X2

Current Assets		20X2		20X1
Cash		$ 37,000		$ 3,000
Accounts receivable		85,000		25,000
Inventory		120,000		90,000
Marketable equity securities		9,000		16,000
Total current assets		$251,000		$134,000
Property, plant and equipment				
Buildings, furniture and equipment	$245,000		$260,000	
Less: Accumulated depreciation	85,000	160,000	55,000	205,000
Other Assets				
Goodwill		235,000		240,000
Total Assets		$646,000		$579,000
Current Liabilities				
Accounts payable		$175,000		$195,000
Interest payable		13,000		11,000
Total current liabilities		$188,000		$206,000
Noncurrent Liabilities:				
Bonds payable		200,000		160,000
Stockholders' Equity:				
Common stock		145,000		130,000
Paid-in-capital common stock		23,000		18,000
Retained earnings		90,000		65,000
Total		258,000		213,000
Total Liabilities and Stockholders' Equity		$646,000		$579,000

Study Guide: Introduction to Accounting, An Integrated Approach

Problem IV (continued)

Zectar Corporation
Income Statement
For the Year Ended December 31, 20X2

Revenues:

Net Sales (all on credit)		$700,000
Expenses:		
Cost of goods sold	340,000	
Selling, general and administrative expenses	235,000	
Depreciation expense	40,000	
Interest expense	10,000	625,000
Net Income		$ 75,000

Required: Calculate the following ratios for Zectar Corporation for 20X2.

1. Current ratio.

2. Accounts receivable turnover ratio.

3. Inventory turnover ratio.

4. Quick ratio.

5. Debt-to-equity ratio.

6. Gross margin ratio.

7. Return on owners' equity ratio.

Study Guide: Introduction to Accounting, An Integrated Approach

Solutions for Chapter 20

Problem I

1. T
2. T
3. F
4. F
5. T
6. F
7. T
8. F
9. T
10. T

Problem II

1. b
2. d
3. a
4. d
5. c
6. a
7. d
8. a
9. d
10. d

Problem III

1. capital market
2. dividends, higher prices
3. liquidity, profitability
4. Activity, current
5. cost of goods sold, inventory
6. total cash expenses, current liabilities, bank loans
7. cash, temporary investments, accounts receivable, current liabilities
8. times interest earned, debt-to-equity, long-term debt-to-equity
9. total liabilities, total shareholders' equity
10. net income, preferred stock dividends, stockholders' equity, liquidating
11. market price, earnings per share

Problem IV

1. Current ratio $= \dfrac{\$251,000}{\$188,000} = 1.34$

2. Accounts receivable turnover $= \dfrac{\$700,000}{(\$85,000 + \$25,000)/2} = 12.73$

3. Inventory turnover $= \dfrac{\$340,000}{(\$120,000 + \$90,000)/2} = 3.24$

4. Quick ratio $= \dfrac{\$37,000 + \$85,000 + \$9,000}{\$188,000} = .697$

5. Debt-to-equity ratio $= \dfrac{\$388,000}{\$258,000} = 1.5$

6. Gross margin ratio $= \dfrac{\$700,000 - \$340,000}{\$700,000} = 51.4\%$

7. Return on owners' equity ratio $= \dfrac{\$75,000}{(\$258,000 + \$213,000)/2} = 31.9\%$

Study Guide: Introduction to Accounting, An Integrated Approach